Social Dynamics

Economic Learning and Social Evolution
General Editor
Ken Binmore, Director of the Economic Learning and Social
Evolution Centre, University College London.

Social Dynamics

Edited by
Steven N. Durlauf and
H. Peyton Young

Brookings Institution Press
Washington, D.C.

The MIT Press
Cambridge, Massachusetts
London, England

This book was set in Palatino by Best-set Typesetter Ltd., Hong Kong.

Printed and bound in the United States of America.

Library of Congress Cataloging-in-Publication Data
Social dynamics / edited by Steven N. Durlauf and H. Peyton Young.
    p. cm. — (Economic learning and social evolution)
   Includes bibliographical references and index.
   ISBN 0-262-04186-3 (alk. paper)
   1. Social interaction.   2. Social interaction—Economic aspects.
  3. Economics—Sociological aspects.   I. Durlauf, Steven N.   II. Young, H. Peyton,
  1945–   III. MIT Press series on economic learning and social evolution.
  HM1111 .S55 2001

                              00-064586

This book was made possible by grants from the Alex C. Walker Educational and Charitable Foundation and the John D. and Catherine T. MacArthur Foundation.

Contents

Series Foreword

The MIT Press series on Economic Learning and Social Evolution reflects the widespread renewal of interest in the dynamics of human interaction. This issue has provided a broad community of economists, psychologists, philosophers, biologists, anthropologists, and others with a sense of common purpose so strong that traditional interdisciplinary boundaries have begun to melt away.

Some of the books in the series will be works of theory. Others will be philosophical or conceptual in scope. Some will have an experimental or empirical focus. Some will be collections of papers with a common theme and a linking commentary. Others will have an expository character. Yet others will be monographs in which new ideas meet the light of day for the first time. But all will have two unifying features. The first will be a rejection of the outmoded notion that what happens away from equilibrium can safely be ignored. The second will be a recognition that it is no longer enough to speak in vague terms of bounded rationality and spontaneous order. As in all movements, the time comes to put the beef on the table—and the time for us is now.

Authors who share this ethos and would like to be part of the series are cordially invited to submit outlines of their proposed books for consideration. Within our frame of reference, we hope that a thousand flowers will bloom.

Ken Binmore
Director
Economic Learning and Social Evolution Centre
University College London
Gower Street
London WC1E 6BT, England

Preface

A striking feature of the social sciences over the last decade has been a breaking down of traditional barriers between disciplines. More often than not, this has entailed the transference of economic methodology to other social sciences. One example is the emergence of rational choice models in political science, in which methodological individualism has been applied to phenomena ranging from elections to the behavior of juries. Similarly, empirical sociology has adopted formal approaches that have traditionally been found in econometrics.

At the same time, however, striking changes are at work within economics itself. Many economists have become persuaded that the traditional model of *homo economicus* needs to be invested with greater social and psychological realism. There are several reasons for this development. First, public policy has begun to focus on questions where social and psychological explanations of behavior seem essential in supplementing conventional economic explanations. In understanding persistent poverty, for example, any analysis that ignores role models, peer groups, and family environment in favor of facile conceptions of human capital formation would appear to be handicapped from the start.

Second, methodological advances in economic theory have permitted the incorporation of richer conceptions of human behavior into the formalism with which economics is conducted. One component of these methodological advances falls under the rubric of interactions-based models, which employ techniques from statistical mechanics and complex systems theory. Both components facilitate the modeling of heterogeneous populations of socioeconomic actors in ways that account for heterogeneity across individuals as well as direct as opposed to market-mediated interdependencies.

When this body of work is assessed as a whole, we do not think it is an exaggeration to say that a new social economics paradigm has begun to emerge. The chapters in this book are intended to give an overview of this development, and to show how this methodology can be brought to bear on substantive social science problems. At the same time, the chapters suggest the present limitations of our knowledge, and areas where further theoretical and empirical work are needed to complete the picture.

1   The New Social Economics

Steven N. Durlauf and
H. Peyton Young

This volume surveys recent efforts to study an old problem: the inter-relationship between group and individual behavior. A distinguishing feature of this new research is that it melds together ideas that have traditionally been pursued separately in economics and sociology. Sociology brings to this endeavor a rich conceptualization of the role of social influences on individual preferences and cognition. Economics provides methods that allow one to model aggregate behavior formally as the outcome of individual decisions when these decisions are made interactively. Hence we do not regard it as an exaggeration to say that this volume represents a survey of an emerging social economics. This new social economics, we believe, holds the promise of providing new insights into social and economic dynamics through the explicit study of the interactions that link individual behavior and group outcomes.

The starting point for analyses in social economics is the assumption that individuals are influenced by the choices of others. Because people typically make choices sequentially, a feedback loop exists from past choices of some people to future choices by others. The resulting dynamical system is the object of study. To make this program concrete, we need to address several methodological questions. First, we need to articulate what aggregate properties of this system we are interested in studying. Second, we need to maintain the individuality of the subjects at all times, so that the behavioral rules apply to individuals rather than to representative agents, averages, and the like. Third, we need to know how people respond to their beliefs concerning the characteristics and behaviors of others. Fourth, we need to specify how these beliefs are formed. This depends, in turn, on the ability of individuals to learn, reason, and process information. Fifth, we need to allow for random perturbations that may arise from variations in the environment, errors in the transmission of information, and hetero-geneity in individual responses.

The combination of these elements yields a stochastic dynamical system whose aggregate properties we wish to study. Typically such a system will exhibit very complicated behavior that is often far from a steady state; in this sense alone, social dynamic models have a different "look and feel" than more standard modeling approaches in economics. But the dissimilarities do not end here. Since we insist on maintaining the individuality and heterogeneity of agents in the description of the system, the dimensionality of the state space that describes the system can be gigantic. This limits our ability to fully characterize the behavior of the process. Instead, the objective of analysis is the identification of aggregate or long-run properties that can be tracked in spite of the system's unwieldy size. A variety of analytical methods exists for accomplishing aspects of this, drawn from statistical mechanics and the theory of stochastic processes with large deviations. Computer simulations complement the analy-tical approaches by allowing the study of intermediate-term behavior of large-dimensional systems, as illustrated in Axtell, Epstein, and Young (chapter 7).

As an example of how these elements fit together, consider the dynamics of residential segregation, a problem first studied by Thomas Schelling (1971). Schelling's model was designed to elucidate the con-ditions under which individual decisions about where to live will inter-act to produce neighborhoods that are segregated by race. His model shows that this can occur even though individuals do not act in a coor-dinated fashion to bring about these segregated outcomes. Notice that in posing the question in this way, we have already identified the macroscopic property—the degree of segregation—that we propose to study. The object of the analysis is to explore how (and whether) this property can result from the uncoordinated, self-interested decisions of many individuals. Schelling proposed a prototype model in which individual agents are of two types, say red and blue, and are placed randomly on the squares of a checkerboard. The *neighborhood* of an agent is defined to be the eight squares adjoining his location. Each agent has preferences over the composition of his neighborhood, defined as the proportion of reds and blues. In each period, the most dissatisfied agent moves to an empty square provided a square is avail-able that he prefers to his current location. The process continues until no one wants to move.

This is one of the earliest examples of a social dynamics model in the sense described above. First, the object of the exercise is to determine what patterns of integration or segregation emerge from decentralized decision making. Second, individual agents are modeled as making decisions about where to move given their preferences over neighborhood composition and their beliefs about neighborhood characteristics. The individuality of agents is maintained throughout—each has a particular location and set of preferences. Third, agents care about the actions of others, namely, where others choose to live. Fourth, information is transmitted via a neighborhood structure, that is, through an exogenously determined geography. Fifth, each agent is myopically rational. He does not optimize given his beliefs about the future course of the process; rather, he simply chooses among the best available alternatives in the current period. Finally, the order in which agents make decisions is random.

Schelling did not analyze this model rigorously but simulated its behavior through repeated trials from different initial conditions. Young (chapter 5) shows how to analyze the asymptotic behavior of a variant of the model using the concept of a stochastic potential function. Moreover, this analytical approach shows that Schelling's intuitions and simulation results can be rigorously justified: with high probability, the system will reside in a state such that agents are almost completely segregated by type. Furthermore, this is true even if *all* agents would prefer to live in integrated neighborhoods. In other words, this is a system in which the pursuit of self-interest leads to outcomes that are socially suboptimal, due to the externalities created by the individual location decisions.

This example illustrates the distinctive features of social dynamics as we have defined them. To see how these insights can be embedded in a formal model, let us proceed as follows. Assume that I agents are situated in a social or geographic space that determines lines of communication and degrees of social influence. In particular, we suppose that each agent is situated at the vertex of a directed graph, and that each directed edge (i, j) is weighted by its importance, say $d_{i,j}$, which we take as nonnegative. Each agent has a finite repertoire of X possible actions or behaviors, which are observable by others. A state of the system is a collection of actions by each agent, $\underline{\omega}_t = (\omega_{1,t}, \ldots, \omega_{I,t})$, where $\omega_{i,t}$ is agent i's action at t. Each agent i is affected by the actions of others, so it is useful to define $\underline{\omega}_{-i,t} = (\omega_{1,t}, \ldots, \omega_{i-1,t}, \omega_{i+1,t}, \ldots, \omega_{I,t})$. Over time, possibly randomly, agents reconsider what they are doing in the light of current circumstances and have the opportunity to alter their actions. Agent i's choice of actions is governed by i's personal preferences concerning actions, independent of what others are doing, plus the actions of others, weighted by their importance to i.

Formally, we may represent this situation as follows. Let Θ_i denote a vector of characteristics of i that influence his payoff from each possible action. In choosing an action $\omega \in X$, agent i receives a private payoff $v(\omega_{i,t}, \Theta_i)$ plus a social payoff $\sum_{j \neq i} d_{i,j} s(\omega_{i,t}, \omega_{j,t}, \Theta_i)$. Hence each actor makes a choice in order to maximize

$$U_i(\omega_{i,t}, \omega_{-i,t}, \Theta_i) = v(\omega_{i,t}, \Theta_i) + \sum_{j \neq i} d_{i,j} s(\omega_{i,t}, \omega_{j,t}, \Theta_i).$$

We could assume that each individual's choice is perfectly predicted from this maximization problem, but this would require perfect knowledge of the determinants of each actor's behavior. It seems more reasonable to model behavior as a random variable reflecting unobserved heterogeneity in the ways that people respond to their environments. A standard and analytically convenient representation is to assume that the logarithm of the probability that agent i chooses a particular action is a positive linear function of the action's expected utility, that is,

$$\log(\text{Prob}(\omega_{i,t} | \omega_{-i,t}, \Theta_i)) = \beta U_i(\omega_{i,t}, \omega_{-i,t}, \Theta_i).$$

Here β is a sensitivity parameter: the larger β is, the less uncertainty there is in the agent's response. These are known in the literature as log linear response models (Blume 1993, 1995; McFadden 1981).

By varying the interaction weights $d_{i,j}$ one can analyze a rich variety of socioeconomic contexts. When people care only about the behavior of their near neighbors, then $d_{i,j} = 0$ except when i and j are "close" according to some notion of social distance (as in Schelling's model of preferences over neighborhood racial composition). In other settings, agents may be influenced by near neighbors as well as social aggregates. One such example is smoking, where the behavior of an agent's friends, ethnic group, and national age peer group may all influence individual choice.

One version of this framework is the Brock-Durlauf model, which deals with the case of binary choices. Agents choose either $\omega_i = -1$ or 1 based on maximizing

$$V_i(\omega_i, \omega_{-i}, \Theta_i) = \upsilon(\omega_i, \Theta_i) + E_i\left(\sum_{j \neq i} d_{i,j} s(\omega_i, \omega_j, \Theta_i)\right) + \varepsilon_i(\omega_i),$$

where $E_i(\cdot)$ is a function that represents agent i's calculation of expected values and

$$\text{Prob}(\varepsilon_i(-1) - \varepsilon_i(1) \leq z) = \frac{1}{1 + exp(-\beta_i z)}; \qquad \beta_i \geq 0.$$

This assumption about the random utility term $\varepsilon_i(\omega_i)$ in the individual decision problem yields the log linear probability structure we have described. Notice that in this model, agents are not assumed to know the actual behaviors of others. Rather, they form expectations about them and act accordingly. This seems particularly natural when the population is large. In chapter 2 Blume and Durlauf discuss this and related models and show how these models often have multiple equilibria that depend on the relative strength of the individual and social components of the payoffs.

Suppose that agents are now allowed to update their choices at random times whose occurrences are governed by independent Poisson processes. One then obtains a *social dynamic* whose properties can be studied using a combination of stochastic dynamical systems theory and simulation techniques. In particular, one obtains a theory of social norms and customs (Young 1993, 1998).

What Phenomena Are We Trying to Explain?

The new social economics has been used in studies of a wide range of phenomena. One area falls under the general rubric of social pathologies such as crime (Case and Katz 1991; Glaeser, Sacerdote, and Scheinkman 1996; Glaeser and Scheinkman, chapter 4), teenage pregnancy and high school dropout rates (Crane 1991), and cigarette smoking (Jones 1994; Krosnick and Judd 1982), among others. The contribution of the new social economics to the understanding of these phenomena is its explicit analysis of the role of group-level influences in determining these behaviors.

Group-level influences imply far different properties for populationwide behavior than found in more conventional models. As illustrated by Durlauf (1997) and Brock and Durlauf (2000a), for example, peer group influences can induce multiple equilibria in average community behavior. Hence the interdependences induced by the desire to conform to one's peers can lead to very different aggregate behaviors for communities of apparently identical individuals. Alternatively, as described by Glaeser and Scheinkman (chapter 4), intragroup interactions can induce intergroup heterogeneity. Such interactions can have powerful effects on individuals. For example, interactions in education may lead to persistent inequality, when economic segregation of neighborhoods means that different students experience different role model and peer influences (Bénabou 1993, 1996; Durlauf 1996a, b).

To give a sense of how these models have the potential to provide explanatory power for empirical phenomena, consider the case of teenage smoking. As exhaustively documented in a U.S. Department of Health and Human Services (1998) report, substantial differences exist in smoking rates among teenagers of different ethnic groups and genders. It is difficult to see how an explanation of smoking behavior that relies solely on individual and family background measures, or even on regional smoking differences (which might well be due to interactions) can explain differences along both of these dimensions simultaneously. For example, gender differences cannot be readily attributed to differences in family income or educational levels. Some evidence of social interactions as an explanation of racial differences is found in Krauth (1999), although a full investigation of the role of interactions in demography of smoking patterns has yet to be accomplished.

Social pathologies are an example of a broader class of socioeconomic phenomena in which the distribution of individual characteristics of a population fail to uniquely specify its aggregate behavioral characteristics. Intuitively, when individual decisions depend on the decisions of others, there is indeterminacy in what the population as a whole actually does. Interdependence implies only that whatever the members of the population do, they behave relatively similarly. In turn, this indeterminacy introduces a role for history, conventions, and social norms in understanding both short-run and long-run socioeconomic phenomena—a role that is typically absent in neoclassical economic models.

One context where social influences seem likely to be important is demography. As described in Mason (1997), while the pattern of fertility transitions across countries is arguably the most important phenomenon in understanding world demography, no single theory has proven particularly successful in explaining the heterogeneity in national demographic experiences. Mason goes on to argue that an understanding of demographic transitions is emerging only through the combination of economic and cultural explanations. While Mason interprets this understanding as requiring the abandonment of a single theory, such a combination is precisely what can be achieved in models with interactions, a claim made in Dasgupta (1995) and Durlauf and Walker (1998). In the context of the basic model we have described, private economic incentives manifest themselves in the private utility term whereas cultural influences can be conceptualized in the context of the social utility term. Empirical evidence in support of this claim has been found by Kohler (1997), Montgomery and Casterline (1996), and Munshi and Myaux (1998).

While systematic work has yet to be done, there are many other areas where we would speculate that interaction effects are important. One area, discussed by Blume and Durlauf (chapter 2) is dialect use. Sociolinguistics has demonstrated, for example, that the use of nonstandard syntax and pronunciation is partially predictable from the socioeconomic background of a speaker (Chambers 1995). Similarly, ethnic and regional dialects in the United States have proven to be remarkably resistant to convergence even in the presence of homogenization of language in radio and television (McWhorter 1998). These facts are strongly indicative of the importance of language in expressing identity, with ramifications for how an individual's peer group is determined and what social norms he regards as salient. By implication, the evolution of dialect variation can be formalized through the modeling of an interacting, heterogeneous population.

Another area of possible application is democracy. As seems clear in cases ranging from ancient Athens to the United States to postcommunist Russia, the success or failure of democratic institutions can only be understood if, in addition to formal procedures, one understands the political norms that condition individual behavior. In the case of Athens, it is remarkable that democratic institutions were so stable during the Peloponnesian War in the face of plague, military catastrophe in Sicily, and eventual defeat and occupation by Sparta (Finley 1983; Ober 1991, 1996). For the United States it has been argued that the supremacy of democratic values was not produced instantaneously by the American Revolution, but rather evolved through the general broadening of the conception of what rights adhered to all citizens (Wiebe 1995). (It is often forgotten that the universal franchise in the United States was not enshrined by the adoption of the Constitution but rather emerged during the 1800s, with adoption in all states associated with the "age of Jackson" (Williamson 1960). Conversely, a number of commentators have attributed the failings of nascent democracy in Russia to the absence of democratic values and norms of behavior (Hough 1998; McDaniel 1996; Steele 1994). Such a perspective is consistent with Putnam's (1993) work on civic institutions in Italy, which has provided strong evidence of the role of culture in determining the success or failure of democratic institutions. Indeed, a critical feature of the design of formal democratic procedures is how they lead to the reinforcement of those norms necessary for democratic efficacy and stability.

As far as we know, there has yet to be any formal modeling of the evolutionary dynamics of democratic norms and institutions in which democracy is valued as an intrinsic good,[1] although there is of course a rich qualitative literature on these issues. The other side of this question is the identification of those conditions under which a social contract may break down. Binmore (chapter 8) presents a framework for studying the relative stability of various social contracts when these contracts are viewed as equilibria in which individual behaviors adhere to some cooperative norm. Bowles (chapter 6) complements this type of analysis by describing how preferences can evolve that undergird cooperative behavior, drawing on group selection arguments from evolutionary biology. We believe that the arguments in Binmore's and Bowles's chapters, and more generally the methods discussed throughout this book, could provide a basis for the development of formal models of democracy that may even be amenable to statistical analysis.

Empirical Evidence

Although there are a number of statistical analyses that have produced evidence of group-level influences on individual behavior (see Brooks-Gunn et al. 1993; Corcoran et al. 1992; and Crane 1991 for well-known examples and Moffitt, chapter 3 for discussion), the question of empirical evidence on interactions is currently quite controversial (Brock and Durlauf 2000b and Manski 1993).

One reason for controversy concerns data quality. It is relatively rare that a researcher knows a priori which groups influence an individual, or (if these groups consist of a small network as opposed to a large community) what the characteristics of the relevant groups are. Second, there is the related question of how to distinguish group influences from unobserved individual effects. Consider the possibility that growing up in a ghetto reduces one's life prospects, conditional on one's parents' characteristics. The problem is that residence in a ghetto is at least partially determined by one's parents characteristics. Unless these characteristics are fully controlled for, a statistical correlation between individual outcomes and ghetto membership may occur if there are parental characteristics that are unobservable to the researcher.

One approach to overcoming the issues of group measurements and unobserved individual characteristics is the use of "natural experiments" to identify group effects. In a natural experiment, a researcher identifies two populations of individuals with initially similar characteristics, one of which has been subjected to an exogenous change of neighborhood. Differences in the outcomes for the two populations thus become a measure of group effects.

The best known of these experiments is the Gautreaux program, which has moved a number of disadvantaged families out of inner-city Chicago to adjacent suburban communities. As documented by Rosenbaum and Popkin (1991) and Rosenbaum (1995), movement to suburbs had strong positive effects on high school dropout rates and post–high school wages. Some aspects of these studies have been questioned, in particular the extent to which individuals who experience changes of groups are randomly selected. Nevertheless, this literature adds to the overall evidence that interactions matter. Further, the Moving to Opportunity Demonstration, currently being conducted by the Department of Housing and Urban Development (see Goering 1996 for details), will replicate a Gautreaux-type experiment with stricter attention to randomization of the neighborhood changes and so might resolve some of these concerns. Preliminary evidence on Moving to Opportunity may be found in Katz, Kling, and Liebman (1997) and Ludwig, Duncan, and Hirschfield (1998).

Additionally, evidence supportive of interactions has been accumulated in detailed studies that have gathered data on individuals and their circles of peers. Steinberg (1996) does this through the use of detailed time diaries for high school students. The importance of peer group influences is clear in their data. In a very different example, Moskos and Sibley (1997) have argued that the U.S. Army provides a unique environment for African Americans. What makes this environment unique is the very stringent set of penalties for discriminatory behavior by soldiers or officers and the relative large leadership role of blacks in the army when compared to civilian society. As an illustration of the effects of participation in army life, Moskos and Sibley (1997) look at attitudes towards O. J. Simpson's guilt—a question where differences of opinion have been widely treated as evidence of an unbridgeable racial gulf in the United States. In a July 1994 Gallup poll, 68 percent of all whites thought Simpson definitely or probably guilty, whereas only 24 percent of all blacks did, while 15 percent of all whites thought him definitely or probably innocent whereas 60 percent of all blacks believed this. Moskos and Sibley found, on the other hand, that among black soldiers, 48 percent considered Simpson likely guilty and only 29 percent considered him likely innocent. Moskos and Sibley demonstrate that such differences in attitudes between black soldiers and the black population as a whole are reflected across a wide range of attitudes toward society. While membership in the military is of course not randomly determined, these authors make a compelling case that the military environment is causally responsible for these attitudinal differences.

Even in those cases where the data are of sufficiently high quality to overcome these problems, there are issues of identification. As discussed in Manski (1993), ideally one would like to distinguish between three effects in understanding why members of a group behave similarly: correlation of individual characteristics, influences of group characteristics on individuals, and feedbacks of group behavior onto individual behavior. Distinguishing these effects may be problematic because of the dependence of a group's behavior on a group's characteristics. Moffitt (chapter 3) illustrates this difficulty using a simple simultaneous equations model in economics. Excessive pessimism concerning the possibility of identification of social determinants of individual behavior is not, however, warranted. Brock and Durlauf (2000b) provide a relatively general framework for understanding when identification of interaction effects can and cannot be achieved. Interestingly, the endogeneity of groups may well facilitate identification of social determinants, as it introduces nonlinearities and instrumental variables that facilitate estimation of the behavioral process. Young (chapter 5) shows how endogenous selection and conformity, while distinct processes, can both be modeled using stochastic process techniques that are amenable to empirical analysis. Continued work in this area is a high priority.

Finally, there is the question of how to relate various types of social economics models to data. The econometric approaches we have been discussing may be interpreted as estimating the parameters of various specific structural models of interactions (Brock and Durlauf 2000b). These models are relatively simple in terms of the degree of heterogeneity they permit with respect to individual actors as well as the way in which agents are interconnected. Glaeser and Scheinkman (chapter 4) provide alternative ways of uncovering interactions through the use of cross-group variability. The idea here is that conformity effects can lead to differing behaviors across otherwise identical groups.

An alternative to analytical modeling is the use of computer simulations to study various socioeconomic environments. A key advantage of the simulation approach is the richness of the environments which may be modeled—see Axtell, Epstein, and Young (chapter 7) and Epstein and Axtell (1996) for examples. An outstanding question is how to relate these models to data.

Concluding Comments

The chapters in this volume illustrate some of the insights offered by the new social economics. The hallmarks of this approach are, first, to explicitly model a socioeconomic system as a collection of heterogeneous individuals. Second, individuals interact directly as well as through prices generated by markets. Peer groups, social networks, role models, and the like have a prominent place when it comes to determining individual behavior. Third, individual preferences, beliefs, and opportunities are themselves influenced by the interactions that characterize the system. Fourth, the analysis of such processes draws from methods in stochastic dynamical systems theory, supplemented by large-scale simulation techniques.

As a nascent field, it is unsurprising that there is a great deal left to accomplish. A particular challenge is the fuller integration of theoretical and empirical work. While there have been steps in this direction, many of which are reported in this volume, much remains to be done. What we hope is that this book brings a richer view of human behavior and human interactions to the analysis of economic phenomena.

Note

1. In contrast, there is a recent literature that studies the emergence of democracy in the context of conflicts over resource allocation. In models of this type, political power is sought by various groups in order to determine the distribution of economic resources through mechanisms such as taxes. An elite that monopolizes power may voluntarily democratize in order to avoid the cost of revolutionary conflict. See Acemoglu and Robinson (1998) for an example.

References

Acemoglu, D., and J. Robinson. 1998. "Why Did the West Extend the Franchise? Democracy, Inequality, and Growth in Historical Perspective." Mimeo. MIT.

Bénabou, R. 1993. "Workings of a City: Location, Education, and Production." *Quarterly Journal of Economics* 108: 619–652.

———. 1996. "Equity and Efficiency in Human Capital Investment: The Local Connection." *Review of Economic Studies* 62: 237–264.

Blume, L. 1993. "The Statistical Mechanics of Strategic Interaction." *Games and Economic Behavior* 5: 387–424.

———. 1995. "The Statistical Mechanics of Best-Response Strategy Revision." *Games and Economic Behavior* 11: 111–145.

Brock, W., and S. Durlauf. 2000a. "Discrete Choice with Social Interactions." Mimeo. University of Wisconsin and forthcoming, *Review of Economic Studies*.

———. 2000b. "Interactions-Based Models." Mimeo. University of Wisconsin and forthcoming, *Handbook of Econometrics*, vol. 5, James Heckman and Edward Leamer, eds., Amsterdam: North Holland.

Brooks-Gunn, J., G. Duncan, P. Klebanov, and N. Sealand. 1993. "Do Neighborhoods Affect Child and Adolescent Development?" *American Journal of Sociology* 99: 353–395.

Case, A., and L. Katz. 1991. "The Company You Keep: The Effects of Family and Neighborhood on Disadvantaged Families." National Bureau of Economic Research Working Paper no. 3705.

Chambers, J. K. 1995. *Sociolinguistic Theory*. Oxford: Blackwell Publishers.

Corcoran, M., R. Gordon, D. Laren, and G. Solon. 1992. "The Association Between Men's Economic Status and Their Family and Community Origins." *Journal of Human Resources* 27: 575–601.

Crane, J. 1991. "The Epidemic Theory of Ghettos and Neighborhood Effects on Dropping Out and Teenage Childbearing." *American Journal of Sociology* 96: 1226–1259.

Dasgupta, P. 1995. "The Population Problem: Theory and Evidence." *Journal of Economic Literature* 33: 1879–1982.

Durlauf, S. 1996a. "A Theory of Persistent Income Inequality." *Journal of Economic Growth* 1: 75–93.

————. 1996b. "Neighborhood Feedbacks, Endogenous Stratification, and Income Inequality." In *Dynamic Disequilibrium Modelling: Proceedings of the Ninth International Symposium on Economic Theory and Econometrics*, ed. W. Barnett, G. Gandolfo, and C. Hillinger. New York: Cambridge University Press.

Durlauf, S. 1997. "Statistical Mechanics Approaches to Socioeconomic Behavior." In *The Economy as a Complex Evolving System II*, ed. W. B. Arthur, S. Durlauf, and D. Lane. Redwood City, CA: Addison-Wesley.

Durlauf, S., and J. Walker. 1998. "Social Interactions and Fertility Transitions." Mimeo. University of Wisconsin at Madison.

Epstein, J., and R. Axtell. 1996. *Growing Artificial Societies: Social Science from the Bottom Up*. Cambridge, MA: The MIT Press.

Finley, M. 1983. *Politics in the Ancient World*. Cambridge: Cambridge University Press.

Glaeser, E., B. Sacerdote, and J. Scheinkman. 1996. "Crime and Social Interactions." *Quarterly Journal of Economics* 111: 507–548.

Goering, J. 1996. "Expanding Housing Choices for HUD-Assisted Families: First Biennial Report on The Moving to Opportunity for Fair Housing Demonstration." Department of Housing and Urban Development, Office of Policy Development and Research.

Hough, J. 1998. "The Failure of Party Formation and the Future of Russian Democracy." In *Growing Pains: Russian Democracy and the Election of 1993*, ed. T. Colton and J. Hough. Washington, DC: Brookings Institution Press.

Jones, A. 1994. "Health, Addiction, Social Interaction, and the Decision to Quit Smoking." *Journal of Health Economics* 13: 93–110.

Katz, L., J. Kling, and J. Liebman. 1997. "Moving to Opportunity in Boston: Early Impacts of a Housing Mobility Program." Mimeo. Harvard University.

Kohler, H.-P. 1997. "Fertility and Social Interaction: An Economic Approach." Ph.D. diss. Department of Economics, University of California, Berkeley.

Krauth, B. 1999. "Social Interactions and Aggregate Neighborhood Outcomes." Ph.D. diss. Department of Economics, University of Wisconsin.

Krosnick, J., and C. Judd. 1982. "Transitions in Social Influence in Adolescence: Who Induces Cigarette Smoking." *Developmental Psychology* 81: 359–368.

Ludwig, J., G. Duncan, and P. Hirschfield. 1998. "Urban Poverty and Juvenile Crime: Evidence from a Randomized Housing-Mobility Experiment." Mimeo. Georgetown Public Policy Institute.

McDaniel, T. 1996. *The Agony of the Russian Idea*. Princeton: Princeton University Press.

McFadden D. 1981. "Econometric Models of Discrete Choice." In *Structural Analysis of Discrete Data with Econometric Applications*, ed. C. Manski and D. McFadden. Cambridge, MA: The MIT Press.

McWhorter, J. 1998. *The Word on the Street: Fact and Fable About American English*. New York: Plenum Press.

Manski, C. 1993. "Identification of Endogenous Social Effects: The Reflection Problem." *Review of Economic Studies* 60 (July): 531–542.

Mason, K. 1997. "Explaining Fertility Transitions." *Demography* 34: 443–454.

Montgomery, M., and J. Casterline. 1996. "Social Learning, Social Influence and New Models of Fertility." *Population and Development Review Supplement to Volume* 22: 151–175.

Moskos, C., and J. B. Sibley. 1997. *All That We Can Be: Black Leadership and Racial Integration the Army Way*. New York: Basic Books.

Munshi, K., and J. Myaux. 1998. "Social Effects in the Demographic Transition: Evidence from Matlab, Bangladesh." Mimeo. Boston University.

Ober, J. 1991. *Mass and Elite in Democratic Athens: Rhetoric, Ideology, and the Power of the People*. Princeton: Princeton University Press.

———. 1996. *The Athenian Revolution*. Princeton: Princeton University Press.

Putnam, R. 1993. *Making Democracy Work: Civic Traditions in Modern Italy*. Princeton: Princeton University Press.

Rosenbaum, J. 1995. "Changing the Geography of Opportunity by Expanding Residential Choice: Lessons from the Gautreaux Program." *Housing Policy Debate* 6: 231–269.

Rosenbaum, J., and S. Popkin. 1991. "Employment and Earnings of Low-Income Blacks Who Move to Middle Class Suburbs." In *The Urban Underclass*, ed. C. Jencks and P. Peterson. Washington, DC: Brookings Institution Press.

Schelling, T. 1971. "Dynamic Models of Segregation." *Journal of Mathematical Sociology* 1: 143–186.

Steele, J. 1994. *Eternal Russia: Yeltsin, Gorbachev, and the Mirage of Democracy*. Cambridge: Harvard University Press.

Steinberg, L., with B. Brown and S. Dornbusch. 1996. *Beyond the Classroom*. New York: Simon and Schuster.

U.S. Department of Health and Human Services. 1998. "Tobacco Use Among U.S. Racial/Ethnic Minority Groups—African Americans, American Indians, and Alaska Natives, Asian Americans and Pacific Islanders, and Hispanics: A Report of the Surgeon General." Atlanta: U.S. Department of Health and Human Services, Centers for Disease Control and Prevention, National Center for Chronic Disease Prevention, Office on Smoking and Health.

Wiebe, R. 1995. *Self Rule: A Cultural History of American Democracy*. Chicago: University of Chicago Press.

Williamson, C. 1960. *American Suffrage*. Princeton: Princeton University Press.

Young, H. P. 1993. "The Evolution of Conventions." *Econometrica* 61: 57–84.

———. 1998. *Individual Strategy and Social Structure*. Princeton: Princeton University Press.

2 The Interactions-Based Approach to Socioeconomic Behavior

Lawrence E. Blume and
Steven N. Durlauf

2.1 Introduction

The last decade has seen the emergence of a growing body of research using interactions-based methods in economics.[1] This work has developed both in terms of abstract theory (Blume 1993, 1995, 1997; Brock 1993; Brock and Durlauf 2000a, b; Durlauf 1997b; Morris 1996; Young 1993, 1998) and in terms of substantive applications.[2] Despite these advances, the use of interactions-based methods in economic analysis is still in its infancy. Further, considerable skepticism exists in many quarters as to the utility of these methods. The purpose of this essay is to provide a perspective on why interactions-based models represent a natural and powerful language for studying economic and related phenomena. Our intended audience in this discussion consists of both fellow economists as well as the broader community of social scientists.

Any argument that economists should concern themselves with a particular modeling approach runs the danger of looking for economic problems to rationalize the use of the tools. This danger is real, as is illustrated by the now-irrelevant work applying catastrophe theory to economics. Recognizing this danger, we nevertheless feel that interactions-based methods embody an extremely broad perspective on economics, one that finds ready application across many specific questions. Further, these approaches are, we will argue, a methodology that can expand the social and psychological richness of formal economic modeling.

Our interest in interactions-based modeling stems from the belief that a common general structure underlies such apparently different problems as the level of out-of-wedlock births, the agglomeration of firms in particular regions and the diffusion of technologies. In each case, the basic phenomenon of interest is the collective behavior of a group of interacting, heterogeneous agents. Our claim is that interactions-based approaches provide a powerful way of understanding these phenomena.

In terms of substantive departures from other types of economic modeling, the interactions-based approach focuses on direct interdependences between economic actors rather than those indirect interdependences that arise through the joint participation of economic actors in a set of markets. Indeed, the various types of interactions that have been the primary object of study in this literature have generally been ones that are not mediated by market structures. Standard examples include peer group and role models effects or interdependent preferences. The sorts of insights found in Clark's (1982) classic work on the ghetto, which relate direct group effects to individual outcomes, are precisely those that the interactions-based approach attempts to formally model.

We emphasize the role of these models in studying heterogeneous populations for three reasons. First, many of the questions we wish to examine concern the distributions of types of behaviors across populations. The ability of these models to formally characterize feedbacks between individuals within a population as well as characterize the aggregate implications of these feedbacks thus make them a natural way of addressing such questions. A key substantive idea of the interactions-based approach is that a precise mathematical characterization can be made that maps various interaction structures to associated populationwide distributions. Second, many economic environments of interest embody imperfections (relative to the baseline environment of general equilibrium theory) such as incomplete markets or asymmetric information that most sensibly occur in the presence of heterogeneity. Interactions models, which are driven by complementarities and spillovers between agents, thus allow for the analysis of these market imperfections in heterogeneous agent contexts. Third, models with heterogeneous agents often have very different properties from their homogeneous agent counterparts. This is trivially obvious in some cases; for example, incompleteness of markets in an exchange economy may not matter if agents possess identical endowments. A deeper example is found in the work of Grandmont (1989) and Hildenbrand (1994), who give some sufficient conditions on individual heterogeneity that produce an aggregate law of demand (roughly speaking, a negative relationship between price and aggregate demand).

One interesting feature of interactions-based models, which we shall only focus on indirectly, is that they incorporate many of the cases in which complexity theory has been applied to economics. As the literature on socioeconomic interactions becomes better developed, we believe that mathematics of complexity, with its emphasis on phenomena such as self-similarity and scaling laws, will prove to be of substantial value to social scientists.

In making a case for the importance of interactions-based analysis in economics, we proceed as follows. Section 2.2 describes a framework that illustrates how an interactions-based approach can facilitate different types of economic modeling. This framework is designed to illustrate how interactions-based approaches can complement conventional modeling strategies. Section 2.3 describes two senses in which interactions models can facilitate the development of substantive social science insights. Section 2.4 discusses how the interactions-based approach complements general equilibrium theory. General equilibrium theory, embodied by the Arrow-Debreu model and its many extensions, constitutes the bedrock of much economic analysis. It is therefore important to understand in what sense the analysis of interactions facilitates either extensions of or alternatives to the general equilibrium paradigm. Section 2.5 discusses what implications interactions-based modeling holds for methodological individualism and reductionism in economics. Section 2.6 suggests some areas where interactions-based modeling may be of value. Section 2.7 provides summary and conclusions.

2.2   The Basic Structure of Interactions-Based Models

2.2.1   Interdependent Decision Making

The underlying logic of interactions models is straightforward. The object of a typical exercise using these models is to understand the behavior of a population of economic actors rather than that of a single agent. The focus of the analysis is on the role of externalities across actors in determining the populationwide behavior. These externalities are in turn the source of interactions. These interactions are taken to be direct. The decision problem of any one actor takes as parameters the decisions of other actors. In examining the collective behavior, the interactions approach treats aggregate socioeconomic behavior as a statistical regularity of the collection of individual decisions as they are determined through the interactions and idiosyncratic characteristics of the agents. In treating aggregate behavior as a statistical regularity, it turns out that individual behavior need not be as tightly modeled as it is in traditional economic models. Individual choice is guided by payoffs, but has a random component. For this example, the randomness can be attributed to individual-specific variables not observed by the modeler, or to some form of bounded rationality; none of our substantive conclusions will depend on the interpretation.

Random choice models have been of long-standing importance in both theoretical and empirical economics, and the analysis of externalities is certainly not new. However, the combination of the two along with an analytical focus on population behavior gives rise to new and interesting phenomena. These systems are highly nonlinear and have multiple steady states, so that the individual decision rules do not, by themselves, uniquely characterize the population as a whole. A system's response to shocks can further be quite complex.

Interactions models typically specify an explicit probability measure characterizing individual behavior conditional on exogenous (to the individual) characteristics that can be either common to all members of the population or individual-specific, and an interaction structure that specifies who affects whom. The microeconomic structure of the environment under consideration determines these individual-level conditional probabilities. The goal of the analysis is to characterize a joint probability measure over all agents in the population that is compatible with these conditional probability measures. This sort of question is standard in the mathematics of random fields and complexity.

To fix ideas, consider first a population of actors facing identical choices, denoted as ω_i, in which no externalities are present. Conditional on a set of exogenous individual-specific characteristics X_i, the contemporaneous behavior of each agent is independent of the behavior of the rest of the population. Thus the joint probability measure characterizing population choices may be factored, so that

$$\text{Prob}(\omega_1, \dots, \omega_I | X_1, \dots, X_I) = \prod_{i=1}^{I} \text{Prob}(\omega_i | X_i). \tag{1}$$

Conditional independence is sufficient to allow one to characterize aggregate behavior of the population through one of the many laws of large numbers. Under very weak conditions, one has

$$I^{-1}\sum_{i=1}^{I}\omega_i \approx I^{-1}\sum_{i=1}^{I}E(\omega_i|X_i) \tag{2}$$

for large I (when these expectations exist).

When individual decisions are contemporaneously interdependent, however, the factorization in equation (1) may fail to exist. Further, the presence of cross-agent externalities introduces a potential strategic element into decision making that needs to be incorporated into the specification of the model. One modeling strategy that preserves the factorization is to introduce a set of variables Z into the model that are endogenously determined by the system, yet preserve the conditional independence of the individual choices. This means that we can model each decision as obeying

$$\text{Prob}(\omega_i|X_i,Z) \tag{3}$$

and model the joint conditional probability measure of all decisions as

$$\text{Prob}(\omega_1,\dots,\omega_I|X_1,\dots,X_I,Z) = \prod_{i=1}^{I}\text{Prob}(\omega_i|X_i,Z). \tag{4}$$

In order to solve for the behavior of the population as a whole, it is of course necessary to specify how Z is determined; and such a specification can only be justified by the particular environment under study. For instance, Z may represent the expected value of the average choice in the population. Such an assumption is relatively appealing when one is working with a large population, as occurs when one is asking a question such as how the average smoking behavior of all teenagers influences individual smoking decisions.

From the perspective of analyzing aggregate behavior, what is important is that for any common belief about this average choice, one can compute the mathematical expectation of the average choice. By requiring that the common belief about the average choice in the population equal this mathematical expectation, one can arrive at a model of choice based on the self-consistency condition that

$$Z = I^{-1}\sum_{i=1}^{I}E_i(\omega_i).$$

This type of argument, which was originally developed to solve rational expectations models, will be used to solve some examples below.

Operationally, interactions-based approaches are most useful when the underlying properties of a socioeconomic environment depend critically on direct connections between agents. Interactions play an essential role in models that describe interdependent binary decisions such as dropping out of school or committing a crime (Glaeser, Sacerdote, and Scheinkman 1996; Brock and Durlauf 2000a), imitation effects in consumption (Bell 1995), bilateral trade and economic specialization (Kelly 1997), and local technological complementarities and economic development (Durlauf 1993). While the particular substantive models differ, the dependencies among agents can be conceptualized and analyzed using formulations like those described by equations (1)–(3).

Again, modeling interdependent decisions in economics is not new per se. Modeling interrelationships that are direct rather than determined via markets is standard in game theory. What is important about interactions-based approaches is that the reasoning from probabilistic descriptions of individual behavior to populationwide aggregates provides a way to explicitly understand the emergence of collective properties in an economy.

2.2.2 A Baseline Model with Interdependences

To see how interactions-based methods can provide concrete insights, we provide some examples based on ideas in Brock (1993), Blume (1993, 1997), Brock and Durlauf (2000a, b) and Durlauf (1997), each of which studies binary choice decisions in the presence of social interactions. These examples illustrate how a choice-based model with standard economic assumptions can naturally produce an interactive environment. The general framework introduced below has been used (e.g., Brock and Durlauf 2000a) to interpret phenomena such as out-of-wedlock births and high school dropout rates, cases where individual decisions are likely to reflect the desire to conform to the behavior of a reference group.

Formally, consider a population of I individuals. Suppose that each individual chooses one of two actions, labeled -1 and 1. Suppose that each individual's utility is quadratic in his action and in the actions of others; what this means is that an individual experiences a payoff to his own choice that is influenced by the choice of each of the other agents in the population and that this effect depends on the square of the differences between the choices. Finally, we assume that each individual experiences a pair of stochastic shocks $\varepsilon_i(1)$ and $\varepsilon_i(-1)$ that influence the payoffs associated with the respective choices.

At the time of the choice, each individual is assumed to possess expectations E_i, which apply to the choices of the others in the population. We will assume that these expectations are fixed at the time when agents make choices, so as to avoid any feedback from the stochastic components of the economy into beliefs. Hence, one can regard the model as one where agents form beliefs about others, experience stochastic shocks that are only observable to themselves, and make decisions accordingly. As discussed above, this assumption will allow the joint probability measure to factor so that the relationship between the individual choice probabilities (which are conditional only on X_i) and aggregate behavior is easy to analyze. The model generates interesting collective behavior because individuals are linked by the determinants of these expectations, which will depend on past realized behavior.

When the various elements of a decision problem of this type are additive, it turns out that without loss of generality (see Brock and Durlauf 2000a for details) an individual's utility can be written (after normalization) as

$$V(\omega_i, X_i) = h(X_i)\omega_i - \frac{1}{2}E_i\left(\sum_{j \neq i} J(X_i, X_j)(\omega_i - \omega_j)^2\right) + \varepsilon_i(\omega_i). \tag{5}$$

This specification can be decomposed into an individual-specific component $h(X_i)\omega_i + \varepsilon_i(\omega_i)$ and an interaction-based component

$$-\frac{1}{2}E_i\left(\sum_{j \neq i} J(X_i, X_j)(\omega_i - \omega_j)^2\right).$$

We will refer to these two components as private and social utility, respectively. Private utility can be further decomposed (without loss of generality) into its mean $h(X_i)\omega_i$ and a stochastic deviation $\varepsilon_i(\omega_i)$. The terms $J(X_i, X_j)$ are measures of the strength of the disutility of nonconformity. This term can vary with the characteristics and identities of each of the agents. Most important, when the $J(X_i, X_j)$'s are all positive, there are collective incentives to conform that may lead to multiple equilibria and interesting dynamics.

In order to close the model, we place an assumption on the distribution of the random terms; this allows one to characterize the probabilities of different configurations of choices among the population of agents. We assume that the random terms are independent and extreme-value distributed, which in turn means that the difference between $\varepsilon_i(1)$ and $\varepsilon_i(-1)$ is logistically distributed with parameter $\beta(X_i)$

$$\text{Prob}(\varepsilon_i(-1) - \varepsilon_i(1) \leq \gamma) = \frac{1}{1 + \exp(-\beta(X_i)\gamma)}, \qquad \beta(\cdot) \geq 0. \tag{6}$$

Under this assumption,[3] the model reduces to a particular instance of the standard binary choice framework when there are no interaction effects, namely, $J(X_i, X_j) = 0 \; \forall \; i,j$. One advantage of this equivalence is that our theoretical model is written in a form that means it can be directly taken to data, for structural econometric estimation, as discussed in Brock and Durlauf (2000b).

From this distribution the individual choice probabilities can be computed.

$$\text{Prob}(\omega_i | X_1, \ldots, X_I, Z) \sim$$

$$\exp\left(h(X_i)\omega_i + E_i\left(\sum_{j \neq i} (\beta(X_i)J(X_i, X_j)\omega_i\omega_j) \right) \right). \tag{7}$$

The conditional probability measures can be multiplied to construct the joint probability measure of the vector of choices $\underset{\sim}{\omega} = (\omega_1, \ldots, \omega_I)$. This joint measure is of the form

$$\text{Prob}(\underset{\sim}{\omega} | X_1, \ldots, X_I, Z) \sim$$

$$\exp\left(\sum_i h(X_i)\omega_i + \left(\sum_i \sum_{j \neq i} E_i(\beta(X_i)J(X_i, X_j)\omega_i\omega_j) \right) \right). \tag{8}$$

Once we have included a set of rules for expectation formation, the model is complete. Our model can be solved directly for several different specifications of the underlying parameters h, J, and β, which together characterize the private valuations, conformity effects, and distributions of individual-specific randomness in the population.

The model we have described falls into a well-studied class of probabilistic systems. It is an example of a *random field*.[4] Random fields describe the joint distribution of large sets of random variables. In such systems, the probabilities describing one random variable conditional on the realizations of others are taken as given. The object of the study is to demonstrate the existence of a joint probability measure consis-

tent with these conditional probabilities and to characterize the resul-
tant aggregate properties of the system. The joint probability measures
are sometimes known as Gibbs measures due to their importance and
historical origins in statistical mechanics.

2.2.3   Global Interactions

One class of models that falls into this framework has been studied in
Brock and Durlauf (2000a). Suppose that all agents are homogeneous,
so that there are no differences across individuals in the parameters
used to characterized private utility; specifically, assume each individual is characterized by a common h and β. Suppose too that each
agent interacts with every other agent symmetrically, in the sense that

$$J(X_i, X_j) = \frac{J}{I-1} \ \forall \ j \neq i. \tag{10}$$

It is clear that under this specification,[5] to the extent that agents wish
to conform to the behavior of others, they wish to match the average
behavior in the population, which we denote m. Hence we may take
each individual as solving

$$\max_{\omega_i} h\omega_i + \varepsilon_i(\omega_i) + J\omega_i E_i(m). \tag{11}$$

Expressed this way, each choice is conditionally independent of the
others, and so the set of decisions is an example of the mathematical
structure described by equation (1). Since all agents are identical,
self-consistency of beliefs requires that

$$m = E_i(m), \tag{12}$$

which in this case means that the expected value of the choice level in
the population is any m that solves

$$m = \tanh(\beta h + \beta J m). \tag{13}$$

Equation (13)[6] is well known in the world of statistical physics as
the mean field approximation of the Curie-Weiss model of magnetism.
The following theorem characterizes the solutions to this equation.

THEOREM: Multiple versus unique steady states

i.   If $\beta J < 1$ and $h = 0$, $m = 0$ is the unique solution to equation (13).

ii.   If $\beta J < 1$ and $h \neq 0$, there is a unique solution to equation (13) whose
sign is the same as h.

iii. If $\beta J > 1$ and $h = 0$, there exist three solutions to equation (13): $m = 0$, and $\pm m^*(\beta J)$. Furthermore, $m^*(\beta J) > 0$ and $\lim_{\beta J \to \infty} m^*(\beta J) = 1$.

iv. If $h \neq 0$ and for fixed β and J there exists a threshold $H(h) > 0$ such that

    a. if $|h| < H$, there exist three solutions to equation (13), one of which has the same sign as h, and the others possessing opposite sign.

    b. for $|h| > H$, there exists a unique solution to equation (13) with the same sign as h.

This theorem illustrates both the nonlinearities and multiple steady states which are the hallmarks of interacting systems. Multiple equilibria exist in the sense that individual choices can, so long as βJ is large enough relative to βh, exhibit one of several distinct expected values, each of which renders those choices individually rational. This occurs in two senses. First, for a given βh, there will exist a threshold value such that if βJ exceeds this value, then there will exist three equilibria; otherwise, there will exist one equilibrium. Alternatively, for a given βJ greater than one, there will exist a threshold such that if βh is below it, there exist three equilibria; otherwise the equilibrium is unique. What this means is that aggregate behavior of the population is determined by a complicated interplay between the strength of the social interactions effect, measured by J, the strength of common private incentives to make one choice or another, h, and the degree of unobserved heterogeneity across individuals, as measured by the parameter β, which indexes the likelihood of large absolute values of the difference in the stochastic components, namely, $\varepsilon_i(1) - \varepsilon_i(-1)$.

The model is nonlinear with respect to the effect of a change in h on m. Hence, changes in private incentives will have very different effects on aggregate behavior depending on the level of the incentives and the strength of the social interaction effects. Indeed, the effect of a change in h will partially depend on whether it changes the number of equilibria, which will exceed one when the strength of the interactions effects are great enough.

What does such an abstract model say about a concrete social issue such as the rate of nonmarital fertility in poor communities? In our view, the model illustrates how peer-group effects and socially reinforced behavior produce nontrivial aggregate consequences and therefore speaks to such a problem. In particular, the model makes clear how the interplay of private incentives embodied in h and $\varepsilon_i(\omega_i)$ interact with social influences embodied in J to create the possibility of widespread social pathologies that are collectively undesirable although produced by individually rational behavior.

To give one example of how this framework provides policy-relevant insights, the model indicates how attempts (which we feel frequently occur in public policy discussions) to blame inner-city social pathologies on either the culture of poverty or lack of economic opportunities are each incomplete. It is only when economic incentives associated with one or another type of behavior are weak (i.e., the magnitude of h is small) that strong social interactions (measured by J) can produce socially undesirable but individually rational behavior. In this sense, the model illustrates how common explanations of inner-city pathologies are in fact complementary, despite the fact that they are usually portrayed as alternatives.

2.2.4 Local Interactions

A class of alternatives to the global interaction models is that of models with spatial structure. Agents have a location and are affected only by the behavior of their (suitably defined) neighbors. Schelling (1971) explored racial clustering of neighborhoods in a model of this type. Specifically, he analyzed the consequences for residential segregation when individual families possess a mild preference for neighbors like themselves. The consequence of individuals caring only about the identity of their immediate neighbors proved to be a global pattern of residential racial segregation. More recently, local interaction models have achieved some popularity in evolutionary game theory in the work of Blume (1993, 1995), Ellison (1993), and Binmore, Samuelson, and Vaughn (1995), among others. In addition, Glaeser, Sacerdote, and Scheinkman (1996) have taken local interactions models to data and found evidence consistent with a role of social interactions in determining cross-community crime rates.

Local interactions can be introduced into the baseline model by locating the agents on the vertices of a graph such that any one pair of individuals are said to be neighbors if their respective vertices are connected by an edge. Formally, this has typically been done by setting $J(X_i, X_j) = 0$ if i and j are not neighbors, although alternative weighting schemes are certainly possible.

In the particular case of uniform local interactions, each individual is associated with a neighborhood n_i; $\#(n_i)$ denotes the neighborhood's population size. Each member of the neighborhood receives an equal conformity weight, so that $J_{i,j} = J/\#(n_i)$. A self-consistent equilibrium for this system is any set of solutions $m_1 \ldots m_I$ to the set of I equations

$$m_i = \tanh\left(\beta h + \frac{\beta J}{n_i} \sum_{j \in n_i} m_j \right). \tag{14}$$

This mapping must possess at least one fixed point, and hence at least one self-consistent equilibrium exists.[7]

This system must exhibit at least one symmetric equilibrium, namely, $m_i = m_j \; \forall \; i, j$, since at a common solution m the model reduces to the global interactions case. However, this framework allows for the possibility of multiple asymmetric equilibria as well; see Young (1999) for further discussion. While such cases can be technically complicated, they do point to the possibility of rich cross-group behavioral differences and thus provide a set of complementary approaches to capturing the phenomena that motivate Glaeser, Sacerdote, and Scheinkman (1996).[8] In a very different strand of work, Topa (1997) has used spatial correlation methods as a way of uncovering interactions and finds spatial correlations in Chicago neighborhood unemployment rates that is consistent with an interactions-based model based on information flows.

2.2.5 Dynamics

Our discussion of multiple equilibria has thus far been static. In dynamic contexts, it is natural to ask whether and how a system of interactions of the type we described cycles between the steady state equilibria. Blume and Durlauf (1999) analyze this question and show that over long horizons, the average population choice at a given point in time will tend to be close to the "best" (in an average welfare sense) equilibrium.[9] Intuitively, randomness means that a population will periodically switch across basins of attraction; the fact that one equilibrium produces higher average payoffs means that switches away from this equilibrium will be relatively less frequent than others. This result is compatible with a situation where the waiting times between switches are arbitrarily large for different equilibria. Hence, for population groups with different initial conditions, the multiple equilibria that emerge in the static case can represent arbitrarily persistent differences between groups over time. See Kandori, Mailath, and Rob (1993) for similar types of findings.

2.3   How Do Interactions-Based Models Contribute to the Understanding of Social Science Phenomena?

2.3.1   Substantive Phenomena

By providing a framework for studying heterogeneous populations of agents, interactions-based models represent a natural environment for interpreting a number of interesting microeconomic specifications. Much of the exciting recent work in economic theory focuses on the aggregate implications of various deviations from the Arrow-Debreu model. Such deviations include incomplete markets, increasing returns to scale in production, and incomplete information. Further, substantial attention has now been given to studying the implications of different rationality assumptions. In our view, microeconomic assumptions such as imperfect communication between agents, which leads to market incompleteness, or lack of a priori knowledge of the structure of the aggregate economy, which leads to nontrivial learning, make most sense in the context of complex, heterogeneous environments. Put differently, an assumption such as rational expectations seems relatively natural in a representative or homogeneous agent environment. Heterogeneity of beliefs becomes relatively compelling as a behavioral assumption when the set of markets and agents becomes large.[10]

To be sure, topics ranging from monopoly behavior to learning have been productive and should continue to be explored in environments simpler than those that are best studied using interactions. Where interactions-based models seem uniquely useful is in the study of phenomena that are most naturally embedded in large heterogeneous populations.

2.3.2   Interactions-Based Models as a Language for Research

Interactions-based methods are also useful because they make the analysis of particular questions simpler than would be the case using alternative approaches. In this regard, we distinguish between methods that are uniquely able to permit certain types of analysis and methods that make the analysis relatively simpler to achieve. Socioeconomic systems admit many different levels and types of description (as do natural systems, of course). Different types of description, whether in terms of conditional probabilities characterizing agents, or an explicit extensive form game formulation of strategies, and so forth, may act to facilitate analysis. Hence, it is possible that the choice of a particular modeling structure has practical implications for the ability of researchers to make progress. Theoretical work has made clear that the mathematical structures by which one describes an interacting system are extremely conducive to the identification and analysis of emergent patterns in heterogeneous environments. While such patterns may otherwise be deducible using alternative descriptions, the exercise may be much more tedious and demanding. Hence, even if the insights obtainable from interactions models can be obtained through other modeling approaches, the interactions-based approach is still useful.[11]

More generally, we reject the idea that there exists a unique set of "natural kinds" through which one accurately represents a socioeconomic system. Rather, particular phenomena may be better understood using one language versus another even when these languages are perfectly translatable from one to another. By analogy, the typical Hilbert space can be generated from more than one basis, each of which can be used to analyze all properties of the space. Nevertheless, in particular contexts, one basis may facilitate analysis relative to others. For example, the complex exponentials are a particularly useful basis for the Hilbert space of L^2 functions; this fact is of course the basis for the importance of Fourier analysis in applied (as opposed to theoretical) mathematics. Similarly, a computer language can be relatively good for a particular programming need, even though the same need can be met with an alternative.

To see how this language argument works, observe that in a standard neoclassical general equilibrium environment, it is possible to describe each individual's behavior as a function of the decisions of other agents, so long as this function reflects market clearing conditions. However, it is far from clear how this would facilitate analysis. For example, such a redescription would, we believe, have made it far more difficult to establish the First Welfare Theorem, whose standard proof is based on budget sets and does not in fact really rely on market clearing, at least in terms of the actual structure of the proof; rather, the proof works with prices. Price variables would be substituted out if one were to write the model exclusively in terms of interactions.

Our argument on the value of interactions-based models as a language for conducting research is related to the one made in McIntyre (1996) that the identification of laws in the social sciences is a function of the type of description employed. We differ from McIntyre in that while he argues that the existence of laws may be description-specific, we argue that, as a practical matter, the ability of scientists to identify laws concerning the relationship may be description-specific.[12]

2.4   Interactions-Based Modeling and General Equilibrium Theory

General equilibrium theory is well equipped, under standard sets of assumptions concerning the completeness of markets, convexity of technology and preferences, and so forth, to characterize a number of features of economies with heterogeneous populations. These features include the existence and uniqueness of sets of equilibrium prices as well as welfare theorems concerning the optimality of the resulting allocations. However, the Sonnenschein-Mantel-Debreu theorem (Sonnenschein 1973; Mantel 1974; Debreu 1974) indicates that under a set of the standard assumptions under which general equilibrium theory has been developed, there exist essentially no restrictions on the behavior of data aggregates, either within a cross-section or intertemporally. By implication, there are essentially no restrictions placed by the theory on aggregated data.[13] This absence of empirical restrictions on aggregate data in no way challenges the importance of general equilibrium theory as an overarching organizing framework for economics. Rather, the absence of aggregate empirical restrictions in general equilibrium theory suggests that the theory, at least as classically conceived, is incomplete as a way of understanding economic phenomena.

This incompleteness is evident when one tries to account for the presence of common types of aggregate behavior that emerge across different economic environments. A list of such common aggregate behaviors (and associated interactions-based explanations would include the following: (1) Zipf's law, which states that within a country, the natural logarithm of a city's population is proportional to its population ranking (Krugman 1996), (2) large cross-community differences in socioeconomic outcomes despite similar microeconomic characteristics (Glaeser, Sacerdote, and Scheinkman 1996; Brock and Durlauf 2000a), (3) stratification of communities by income and ethnicity (Bénabou 1993, 1996; Durlauf 1996a, b), and (4) spatial agglomeration of economic activity (Arthur 1987).

What makes these aggregate features interesting is their presence in many different contexts despite the presence of substantial heterogeneity across or within the groupings in which they occur. This heterogeneity suggests that a number of features of economic behavior exist whose aggregate properties are robust with respect to at least some features of the microeconomic specifications of individual actors. In other words, a number of phenomena such as racial segregation, the ratios of population among the largest cities of a country, and substantial persistence in business cycles characterize a range of very different socioeconomic environments. Interactions-based systems embody the mathematics of such robust properties, and in this regard commend themselves as tools in economic modeling.

Of course, recognizing that general equilibrium theory (as opposed to particular general equilibrium models) fails to generate aggregate data restrictions, any of the common features that one might identify are perfectly compatible with the theory. The relevant point is that this compatibility does not mean that general equilibrium theory provides an understanding of these features.[14]

To see why compatibility is not equivalent to understanding, consider the relation between the neo-Darwinian synthesis and speciation. Modern evolutionary theory provides a framework in which to study patterns of speciation. However, without a successful theory of developmental biology to explain how genetic information expresses itself in phenotypes, evolutionary theory is not capable of explaining why some speciation patterns emerge and not others. By analogy, we are interested in asking how the application of interactions modeling to economics can provide a deeper understanding of common aggregate features beyond the formal compatibility of these features with general equilibrium theory.

The interactions approach can contribute to the development of such an understanding by identifying how certain aggregate behaviors emerge from particular classes of individual characteristics and particular specifications of how individuals interact. One does not, however, get something for nothing by employing this approach in order to generate aggregate dynamics. Particular emergent phenomena depend upon particular sets of individual-level specifications; these methods can only be valuable to the extent that these individual specifications are plausible descriptions of actual economic environments. In the absence of any restrictions on the distribution of individual characteristics, the Sonnenschein-Mantel-Debreu theorem implies that general equilibrium theory imposes only extremely limited restrictions on aggregate data. What interactions methods bring is the possibility that common types of aggregate behavior emerge for widely varying collections of individual characteristics.

The strategy of identifying classes of individual interactions that produce common data implications is paralleled by some recent work on aggregation in economics. Grandmont (1989), Caplin and Leahy (1991), Hildenbrand (1994), and Caballero and Engel (1995) have studied economic environments in which restrictions on the distribution of initial conditions and/or individual characteristics allow inferences about aggregate behavior. However, they have not emphasized the collective and emergent features of aggregate behavior that are the hallmark of the interactions approach.

Finally, we would note that for many of the aggregate phenomena in which we are interested, externalities or other types of market failures typically exist. Such features do not, in general, fall under the purview of general equilibrium theory. (General equilibrium theory with incomplete markets—see Magill and Quinzii (1996)—is an important exception to this.) In this sense, interactions-based models again complement general equilibrium theory, this time by characterizing alternative microeconomic foundations.

2.5   Interactions-Based Models and Reductionism in Economics

The application of interactions-based analysis to economics illustrates a context in which economic analysis is and ought to be nonreductionist. We argue this in two senses.

First, in many economic environments, a unique mapping does not exist between specific microeconomic characteristics to aggregate properties, at least when these characteristics are restricted to individual preferences and technologies. As discussed in Blume (1997), this indeterminacy can be attributed to the absence of an explicit characterization of the interaction structure between individual actors. The mathematics of interactions provide tools that can resolve the problem of multiple equilibria (in the sense of explaining how a particular equilibrium is selected), which is necessary to bridge microeconomic structures and macroeconomic outcomes.

Second, the linkage between classes of interaction structures and aggregate outcomes is necessary if the goal of economic modeling is to understand aggregate behavior. While knowledge of the characteristics of each economic agent can, in principle, allow one to characterize a particular aggregate environment, in such environments this knowledge does not provide much insight as to why the environment emerges. As Anderson (1972) puts it, such environments are not "constructivist" in that it is impossible to reason from the properties of the individual objects by themselves to the property of aggregates. It is the nature of collective interactions that is critical in understanding aggregate economic behavior.

Here, some standard examples taken from science are helpful. The statement that a group of water molecules have formed into ice is not reducible in an explanatory sense to information about each water molecule in isolation. Similarly, knowledge of the DNA structure of all species would not lead to an understanding of the collective properties of the biosphere, a point emphasized by Lewontin, Kamin, and Rose (1985). The property of ice or biosphere diversity is emergent in the sense that it occurs at a more aggregated level of measurement than the level at which the individual elements of the system are described. Crutchfield (1994) defines an emergent property in essentially this way.[15]

To see how this applies to economics, again consider our model of binary choice with social interactions under the assumptions of global interactions and rational expectations. When $\beta J > 1$ and $h = 0$, all individuals are identically specified and each has an ex ante 50 percent chance of using either 1 or -1, yet their behavior is compatible with two average choice levels with nonzero mean. This asymmetric outcome from a symmetric underlying structure, referred to in physics as broken symmetry, is a canonical example of an emergent phenomenon (Anderson and Stein 1984).

Notice that this example is not consistent with Crutchfield's definition, since each agent in the global case reacts to the expected average choice, while the realization of the average choice is the object under analysis. However, similar properties hold for the local interactions case. For example, if $h = 0$, and agents are arrayed on a two-dimensional lattice, then there exists a critical J_c such that if $J > J_c$, the model exhibits multiple average choice levels in the large economy limit, whereas if $J < J_c$ then the average will always converge to zero in the limit.

In our view, socioeconomic phenomena such as patterns of out-of-wedlock births, racial residential segregation, and technology diffusion have a similar interpretation. This claim is at least partially justified by the success of theoretical models of these phenomena in demonstrating how they can emerge from the combination of well-specified individual decision rules and relatively simple interaction structures. In short, while we accept the central role of microfoundations in macroeconomics as articulated by the modern Chicago school of macroeconomics, we also believe that macroeconomics is a distinct discipline from microeconomics (and by implication neoclassical general equilibrium theory) due to the presence of these emergent properties. This argument in favor of a nonreductive explanation of socioeconomic phenomena appeared earlier when we discussed the relationship between interactions models and general equilibrium theory.

While we emphasize the nonreductionist aspect of interacting economic models, one should recognize that neoclassical economic analysis often focuses on emergent properties.[16] Perhaps the clearest case is the First Welfare Theorem of Economics, which states that (under a well-specified set of conditions) every competitive equilibrium is Pareto efficient—namely, it is impossible to make anyone better off without making someone else worse off. This aggregate-level efficiency is an emergent property of a system in which individual agents are pursuing their own ends. Other types of emergent properties abound within the context of specific economic environments. Becker (1962) provides a set of cases in which aggregate implications of neoclassical economics survive as emergent properties in environments that deviate from neoclassical assumptions. Thus, we regard our emphasis on the nonreductionist aspects of interactions-driven economic environments to be consistent with the spirit of much existing analysis.

At the same time, interactions-based models are fully consistent with methodological individualism, which we define as the requirement that the individual agents within an economic system follow well-defined decision rules and that the analysis of the system proceed from the specification of these rules. This requirement simply means that any higher-order properties of the system emerge either directly or indirectly from the rules that determine the behavior of individuals. These higher-order properties would occur, for example, if one were to find scaling laws in residential segregation patterns, in which the scaling laws exist with reference to communities, whose compositions are endogenously determined by individual decisions.

While the general ideas of methodological individualism are fully compatible with interactions, this approach is important in extending methodological individualism to richer environments than those that are conventionally studied in economics. As discussed in Blume (1997) a powerful critique of the particular instantiation of methodological individualism found in most modern economic theory may be based on the failure of many theories to account for the relationships between individual decision making and different levels of aggregation of the environment in which they interact. This failure lies at the heart of some of the most severe criticism made by social scientists who are not economists as well as by some heterodox economists; Granovetter (1985) summarizes this position well: "Classical and neoclassical economics operates, in contrast, with an atomized and *under*socialized conception of human action . . . The theoretical arguments disallow by hypothesis any impact of social structure and social relations on production, distribution, or consumption" (55). It is precisely this ability to provide socially mediated connections between individual behavior and larger socioeconomic aggregates that makes the interactions approach useful in breaking what we regard as obviously artificial disciplinary barriers between economics and sociology when studying complicated problems such as social pathologies.

2.6   New Applications of Interactions-Based Modeling

As should be clear from this discussion, nothing about conventional economic problems makes interactions-based modeling especially appropriate. Indeed, our view is that there are a wide range of social and political phenomena where interactions-based approaches can be fruitful.

2.6.1   Language

Sociolinguistic studies have made clear that there exists a deep relationship between socioeconomic status and language use. For example, it is well documented that the use of nonstandard grammar or pronunciation by a given individual is more probable when someone is poor and male, controlling for other factors—see Chambers (1995 chap. 2) and Wardhaugh (1995 chap. 7), for surveys of evidence on this. What the sociolinguistics and psychology literatures makes clear is that language is closely tied to individual identity and that both are in turn influenced by one's reference groups; see Akerlof and Kranton (1999) for a provocative discussion of how identity shapes socioeconomic outcomes; their discussion places sociolinguistics findings in a broad context. Further, there is some recognition that dialectic choice, defined in terms of adherence of standard grammar or pronunciation, can have important economic consequences. For example, Jupp, Roberts, and Cook-Gumperz (1982) and Akinasou and Ajirotutu (1982) argue that ethnic minorities are at a relative disadvantage in job interviews due to differences in language structure and style.

While sociolinguistic studies seem to have made clear that linguistic behavior is determined by one's economic and social status, there has been little formal modeling of the processes by which language and socioeconomic communities evolve jointly across time.[17] This would appear to be an ideal case for understanding the interplay of private and social incentives. The use of Black English, for example, is a choice that is conditioned both by social interactions (the language choices of one's social network) as well as the incentives set by the economy as a whole.[18] In turn, use of Black English influences socioeconomic opportunities. Formal modeling using interactions could both make rigorous many standard ideas in sociolinguistic theory as well as provide a nice test case for the assessment of statistical tools designed to uncover interactions.

Beyond the issue of dialect choice, one can also imagine using interactions-based models to study regional patterns in pronunciation.[19] Labov (1996) is a recent example of empirical work on this issue, documenting the evolution and persistence (despite homogenizing factors such as mass media) of such differences. These spatial patterns would intuitively seem to be a prime candidate for a social interactions explanation, since it hard to imagine any purely private incentives for such choices. Put differently, since pronunciation does nothing more than facilitate communication with others, the choices of others are naturally the object that determines these choices; pronunciation choices may even be thought of as examples of network externalities of the type that apply to choice of computer operating systems.

2.6.2   Security Issues

Interactions models have had little application in security issues.[20] However, it is clear that many of the ideas and metaphors that motivate socioeconomic contexts are also relevant in this case. One possible question is the probability of a nuclear weapons accident. As made clear in Sagan (1993), understanding the probability of an accidental launch requires understanding the behavioral outcomes of an organization (military, of course) comprised of many decentralized yet highly interdependent decision makers. Indeed, a major argument in defense of so-called normal accidents theory (so dubbed by Sagan), at least as developed by Perrow (1984), is that there exist sufficiently many nonlinear interactions between elements of large organizations that mistakes will invariably arise that cannot be accommodated by safety features that can only accommodate foreseeable contingencies. Rochlin (1997) has further argued that the extremely high degree of computerization of defense capabilities has produced an extremely high degree of interdependence within various defense organizations, so this general concern about organizations seems especially applicable to defense.

Could interactions-based methods help clarify the probability of a nuclear weapons-related accident? It is certainly plausible to believe that the answer is yes. Formal modeling of command and control systems could be achieved with a great deal of accurate detail about microstructures. We are willing to conjecture two features of such an exercise. First, it will be possible to produce scenarios under which accidents occur at unacceptably high frequencies. One message of interactions-based studies of stock price movements generated by interdependent traders (Arthur et al. 1997) or the distribution of rates of social pathologies (Glaeser, Sacerdote, and Scheinkman 1996) is that extreme outcomes in the sense of highly correlated behavior in a population have a nontrivial probability of occurring due to positive feedback effects; hence, a similar result in the context of nuclear accidents seems reasonable. Second, it may nevertheless be possible to design redundancies and safety mechanisms within the system to render this probability negligible. Why? Because the same interdependence that may make accidents seem relatively likely can also mean that small but common influences on individual decisions can have large aggregate effects. By making each actor in the system slightly more cautious, the feedback effects may render the system as a whole much more cautious. How this can be done naturally requires expertise in the details of the organization of interest (and indicates why interactions models complement rather than substitute for institutional knowledge), but the capacity for large heterogeneous systems to experience collective order due to positive interactions suggests that this goal can in principle be accomplished.

One might argue that normal accidents theories are based on the claims that certain contingencies cannot be foreseen rather than on claims about the complexity of organizations per se. However, if the concern about interactive environments is that there are contingencies whose nature we cannot characterize, let alone whose probabilities we cannot evaluate, then it is incoherent to talk about the probability of accidents being high or low. Moreover, the issue for system performance is not the identifiability of the range of possible shocks to the system, but rather the identification of the range of responses and interconnections. If the argument that complex interdependent organizations are likely to produce errors is to make sense, it is presumably a statement about how the interactions in such systems evolve, which is why interactions-based modeling seems a natural approach.

2.7 Conclusions

Interactions-based models provide a powerful set of structures that are conducive to studying a wide range of socioeconomic environments. These models are capable of incorporating individual heterogeneity and cross-individual dependencies that have proven difficult to analyze in the past and are able to do so in ways with interesting empirical implications, in particular with respect to aggregate patterns.

  Although we are confident that interactions-based analysis has much to offer economics, we recognize that our views are still fairly speculative. While this approach has provided numerous theoretical insights, a decisive empirical demonstration has yet to be made either of the interactions that underlie the microstructure of the approach or of the presence of the sorts of emergent phenomena that are the hallmark of aggregate implications of these theories. Even Zipf's Law, which is often taken as the most evident scaling law in economics, has yet (at least in our opinion) to be subjected to sufficiently rigorous econometric examination. Further, as made clear in Manski (1993, 1997) and Brock and Durlauf (2000b), the econometric identification of interaction effects is complicated, with identifiability depending sensitively on details of the modeling context.

  At this same time, it should be recognized that there have been a number of interesting developments on the empirics of interactions. One problem in the empirical analysis of interactions is that one is interested in inferences about these effects for heterogeneous populations in just the same way as one wishes to theorize in the presence of heterogeneity. Such populations are, for cases such as neighborhoods and schools, endogenously sorted into relevant groups. Manski (1995) provides many insights into how to obtain bounds on various effects in the presence of self-selection and heterogeneity; Brock and Durlauf (1999b) show how to adapt these ideas to identify interactions effects. Additionally, Brock and Durlauf (1999b) provide conditions under which self-selection, if properly modeled, can facilitate identification. Both these approaches seem very promising, although much remains to be done. Beyond the development of new econometric methods, it will likely be necessary to construct new data sets in order to accurately characterize the microstructure of particular types of interactions. See Rauch (1996) for an interesting exercise along these lines.

Despite these interesting developments, the long-run success of the interactions-based approach in economics depends on a clear demonstration of its empirical salience over a range of contexts. This of course will require that more empiricists and econometricians participate in the analysis in order to complement the economic theorists whose work launched the field. The interactions between these groups should themselves prove to be two-sided. Just as empirical research is needed to characterize the nature of interactions in actual socioeconomic phenomena, which should then inform the ways theories are constructed, theoretical research can help identify new ways of thinking about data.

Notes

The National Science Foundation, John D. and Catherine T. MacArthur Foundation and Santa Fe Institute have supported this work. We thank William Brock, Donald Hester, Andros Kourtellos, Jonathan Parker, Kenneth West, Christopher Wheeler, and Peyton Young for helpful comments.

1. Schelling (1971) and Föllmer (1974) are important forerunners of this recent literature.

2. These applications include the location and concentration of economic activity (Arthur 1987 and Krugman 1996), the adoption of new technologies (Arthur 1989), asset price behavior (Brock 1997), the emergence of communication and trading patterns (Ioannides 1990; Kirman 1983; Kelly 1997), income inequality (Durlauf 1996a, b), social pathologies such as out-of-wedlock births and crime (Brock and Durlauf 2000a; Glaeser, Sacerdote, and Scheinkman 1996), evolution of political parties (Kollman, Miller, and Page 1992), expectation formation (Brock and Hommes 1997), aggregate growth and business cycles (Bak et al. 1993; Blume 1994; and Durlauf 1993), among many others.

3. This functional form is standard in the discrete choice literature. See Anderson, de Palma, and Thisse (1992) for a justification.

4. Liggett (1985) and Durrett (1988) are standard references.

5. The normalization I in this expression makes the marginal substitution between private and social utility independent of population size.

6. $\tanh(x) = (\exp(x) - \exp(-x))/(\exp(x) + \exp(-x))$. Brock and Durlauf (2000a) derive this equilbrium condition from first principles.

7. These equations represent continuous mappings of elements of $[0,1]^I$ (the I = dimensional unit cube) into itself, which means that Brouwer's Fixed Point Theorem applies.

8. As formally discussed in Durlauf (1997), the local interactions model of Glaeser, Sacerdote, and Scheinkman (1996) is a special case of the general interactions model we have described.

9. To be precise, when $h \neq 0$, any equilibrium with an expected average choice level with the same sign as h produces higher average utility than one that does not. This permits one to make social welfare statements about equilibria in our model. However, in general it will not be the case of one equilibrium Pareto dominating another, since it is always possible that the realized distribution of random utility terms is such (with likelihood approaching 1 as the number of agents goes to infinity) that some agents make choices with different signs at each possible equilibrium, which means someone is always made worse off in moving from one equilibrium to another.

10. For particular cases of deviations from neoclassical modeling assumptions, one can of course be much more precise in articulating the relationship between an economic environment and the likelihood or plausibility of these deviations. For example, cognitive science has documented many circumstances in which human beings are most likely to deviate from strict definitions of rationality. See Piattelli-Palmarini (1994) for a survey of these issues. So far as we know, there has been no work using interactions-based methods in which the modeling has been based on a detailed empirically motivated approach to loosening standard neoclassical assumptions on rationality. Rather, the work has typically used an ad hoc form of myopic belief formation.

11. See Little (1991, 188) for an example of how a similar pragmatic argument can be made in defense of methodological individualism.

12. See Anderson (1972) for related discussion.

13. It is worth noting that the Sonnenschein-Mantel-Debreu theorem has not been extended to infinite horizon economies, where equilibrium existence proofs typically employ more restrictive assumptions than other cases. Moreover, Boldrin and Montruccio (1986) have found a similar result that says that a representative agent model can be constructed that replicates any set of aggregate time series on investment and consumption.

14. The meaning of "understanding" in the context of scientific theories is controversial among philosophers of science; see Little (1991) for a discussion. For our purposes, we say that a theory provides understanding of a phenomenon when it provides a causal explanation of how and why the phenomenon occurs in a way that permits a researcher to extrapolate to related contexts. We proceed on the basis that the argument in favor of theories that produce understanding is robust to whatever ambiguities exist at the borders of the concept.

15. It can be far from a simple matter to determine whether a system exhibits emergence. In one prominent case, philosophers and cognitive scientists are actively debating whether consciousness is an emergent property of the brain; see Searle (1993) and Churchland (1986) for expositions of opposing sides in this debate.

16. General invisible hand arguments of the type discussed by Nozick (1974, 18–22), implicitly rely on the existence of particular (and conjectured) emergent properties of social systems.

17. Among economists, a notable exception is Lazear (1995). Lang (1986) discusses the effects of language barriers on wages. Akerlof (1997) discusses the importance of understanding the interdependence of language and economic status.

18. Notice that this type of choice need not be conscious. What we mean is that the choice-based framework we employ can be used to understand how individuals take up behaviors, such as belief in God, tendency toward liberal versus conservative political views, and so forth, in which the private and social incentives are not employed in a conscious calculus, but rather simply represent factors that influence individual outcomes.

19. We thank William Brock for this suggestion.

20. This is not to say that security and defense issues have not been subject to formal modeling—see Epstein (1997) for a nice introduction to successful examples of the applications of mathematics to issues in this area.

References

Akerlof, G. 1997. "Social Distance and Social Decisions." *Econometrica* 65: 1005–1027.

Akerlof, G., and R. Kranton. 1999. "Economics and Identity." Mimeo. University of Maryland. Forthcoming in *Quarterly Journal of Economics*.

Akinasou, F. N., and C. S. Ajirotutu. 1982. "Performance and Ethnic Style in Job Interviews." In *Language and Social Identity*, ed. J. Gumperz. Cambridge: Cambridge University Press.

Anderson, P. 1972. "More is Different." *Science* 177: 393–396.

Anderson, P., and D. Stein. 1984. "Broken Symmetry, Emergent Properties, Dissipative Structures, Life: Are They All Related." In *Basic Notions of Condensed Matter Physics*, ed. P. Anderson. Menlo Park, CA: Addison-Wesley.

Anderson, S., A. de Palma, and J.-F. Thisse. 1992. *Discrete Choice Theory of Product Differentiation*. Cambridge, MA: The MIT Press.

Arthur, W. B. 1987. "Urban Systems and Historical Path Dependence." In *Urban Systems and Infrastructure*, ed. R. Herman and J. Ausubel. Washington, DC: National Academy of Sciences/National Academy of Engineering.

———. 1989. "Increasing Returns Competing Technologies and Lock-In by Historical Small Events: The Dynamics of Allocation under Increasing Returns to Scale." *Economic Journal* 99: 116–131.

Arthur, W. B., B. LeBaron, R. Palmer, and P. Tayler. 1997. "Asset Pricing Under Endogenous Expectations in an Artificial Stock Market." In *The Economy as a Complex Evolving System II*, ed. W. B. Arthur, S. Durlauf, and D. Lane. Menlo Park, CA: Addison-Wesley.

Bak, P., K. Chen, J. Scheinkman, and M. Woodford. 1993. "Aggregate Fluctuations from Independent Sectoral Shocks: Self-Organized Criticality in a Model of Production and Inventory Dynamics." *Ricerche Economiche* 47: 3–30.

Becker, G. 1962. "Irrational Behavior and Economic Theory." *Journal of Political Economy* 70: 1–13.

Bell, A. 1995. "Dynamically Interdependent Preferences in a General Equilibrium Environment." Mimeo. Department of Economics, Vanderbilt University.

Bénabou, R. 1993. "Workings of a City: Location Education and Production." *Quarterly Journal of Economics* 108: 619–652.

———. 1996. "Equity and Efficiency in Human Capital Investment: The Local Connection." *Review of Economic Studies* 62: 237–264.

Binmore, K., L. Samuelson, and R. Vaughn. 1995. "Musical Chairs: Modeling Noisy Evolution." *Games and Economic Behavior* 11: 1–35.

Blume, L. 1993. "The Statistical Mechanics of Strategic Interaction." *Games and Economic Behavior* 5: 387–424.

———. 1994. "An Evolutionary Analysis of Keynesian Coordination Failure." Mimeo. Cornell University.

———. 1995. "The Statistical Mechanics of Best-Response Strategy Revision." *Games and Economic Behavior* 11: 111–145.

———. 1997. "Population Games." In *The Economy as a Complex Evolving System II*, ed. W. B. Arthur, S. Durlauf, and D. Lane. Menlo Park, CA: Addison-Wesley.

Blume, L., and S. Durlauf. 1999. "Equilibrium Concepts for Models with Social Interactions." Mimeo. Cornell University.

Boldrin, M., and L. Montruccio. 1986. "On the Indeterminacy of Capital Accumulation Paths." *Journal of Economic Theory* 40: 26–39.

Brock, W. 1993. "Pathways to Randomness in the Economy: Emergent Nonlinearity and Chaos in Economics and Finance." *Estudios Economicos* 8 (1): 3–55; Social Systems Research Institute Reprint #410. Department of Economics University of Wisconsin at Madison.

———. 1997. "Asset Price Behavior in Complex Environments." In *The Economy as a Complex Evolving System II*, ed. W. B. Arthur, S. Durlauf, and D. Lane. Menlo Park, CA: Addison-Wesley.

Brock W., and S. Durlauf. 2000a. "Discrete Choice with Social Interactions." Mimeo. University of Wisconsin at Madison. Forthcoming in *Review of Economic Studies*.

———. 2000b. "Interactions-Based Models." Mimeo, University of Wisconsin at Madison. Forthcoming in *Handbook of Econometrics*, vol. V, ed. J. Heckman and E. Leamer. Amsterdam: North-Holland.

Brock W., and C. Hommes. 1997. "Rational Routes to Randomness." *Econometrica* 65: 1097–1128.

Caballero, R., and E. Engel. 1995. "Microeconomic Adjustment Hazards and Aggregate Dynamics." *Quarterly Journal of Economics* 108: 683–708.

Caplin, A., and J. Leahy. 1991. "State-Dependent Pricing and the Dynamics of Money and Output." *Quarterly Journal of Economics* 106: 683–708.

Chambers, J. K. 1995. *Sociolinguistic Theory.* Oxford: Blackwell Publishers.

Churchland, P. S. 1986. *Neurophilosophy*. Cambridge, MA: The MIT Press.

Clark, K. B. 1982. *Dark Ghetto*. Middletown, CT: Wesleyan University Press.

Crutchfield, J. 1994. "Is Anything Ever New? Considering Emergence." In *Complexity: Metaphors, Models, and Reality*, ed. G. Cowan, D. Pines, and D. Meltzer. Menlo Park, CA: Addison-Wesley.

Debreu, G. 1974. "Excess Demand Functions." *Journal of Mathematical Economics* 1: 15–21.

Durlauf, S. 1993. "Nonergodic Economic Growth." *Review of Economic Studies* 60: 349–366.

———. 1996a. "A Theory of Persistent Income Inequality." *Journal of Economic Growth* 1: 75–93.

———. 1996b. "Neighborhood Feedbacks, Endogenous Stratification, and Income Inequality." In *Dynamic Disequilibrium Modelling: Proceedings of the Ninth International Symposium on Economic Theory and Econometrics*, ed. W. Barnett, G. Gandolfo, and C. Hillinger. Cambridge: Cambridge University Press.

———. 1997. "Statistical Mechanics Approaches to Socioeconomic Behavior." In *The Economy as a Complex Evolving System II*, ed. W. B. Arthur, S. Durlauf, and D. Lane. Menlo Park, CA: Addison-Wesley.

Durrett, R. 1988. *Lecture Notes on Particle Systems and Percolation*. Belmont, CA: Wadsworth and Brooks/Cole.

Ellison, G. 1993. "Learning, Local Interaction, and Coordination." *Econometrica* 61: 1047–1072.

Epstein, J. 1997. *Nonlinear Dynamics, Mathematical Biology, and Social Science*. Menlo Park, CA: Addison-Wesley.

Föllmer, H. 1974. "Random Economies with Many Interacting Agents." *Journal of Mathematical Economics* 1: 51–62.

Georgii, H.-O. 1988. *Gibbs Measures and Phase Transitions*. New York: deGruyter.

Glaeser, E., B. Sacerdote, and J. Scheinkman. 1996. "Crime and Social Interactions." *Quarterly Journal of Economics* 111: 507–548.

Grandmont, J.-M. 1989. "Transformation of the Commodity Space, Behavioral Heterogeneity, and the Aggregation Problem." *Journal of Economic Theory* 57: 1–35.

Granovetter, M. 1985. "Economic Action and Social Structure: The Problem of Embeddedness." *American Journal of Sociology* 91: 481–510.

Hildenbrand, W. 1994. *Market Demand: Theory and Evidence*. Princeton: Princeton University Press.

Ioannides, Y. 1990. "Trading Uncertainty and Market Structure." *International Economic Review* 31: 619–638.

Jupp, T., C. Roberts, and J. Cook-Gumperz. 1982. "Language and Disadvantage: The Hidden Process." In *Language and Social Identity*, ed. J. Gumperz. Cambridge: Cambridge University Press.

Kandori, M., G. Mailath, and R. Rob. 1993. "Learning, Mutation, and Long Run Equilibrium in Games." *Econometrica* 61: 29–56.

Kelly, M. 1997. "The Dynamics of Smithian Growth." *Quarterly Journal of Economics* 112: 939–964.

Kirman, A. 1983. "Communication in Markets: A Suggested Approach." *Economic Letters* 12: 1–5.

Kollman, K., J. Miller, and S. Page. 1992. "Adaptive Parties in Spatial Elections." *American Political Science Review* 86: 929–937.

Krugman, P. 1996. *The Self-Organizing Economy*. Oxford: Basil Blackwell.

Labov, W. 1996. "The Organization of Dialect Diversity in North America." Mimeo. Department of Linguistics, University of Pennsylvania.

Lang, K. 1986. "A Language Theory of Discrimination." *Quarterly Journal of Economics* 405: 363–382.

Lazear, E. 1995. "Culture and Language." NBER Working Paper no. 5249.

Lewontin, R., L. Kamin, and S. Rose. 1985. *Not in Our Genes: Biology, Ideology, and Human Nature*. New York: Pantheon Books.

Liggett, T. 1985. *Interacting Particle Systems*. New York: Springer-Verlag.

Little, D. 1991. *Varieties of Social Explanation*. Boulder: Westview Press.

Magill, M., and M. Quinzii. 1996. *Theory of Incomplete Markets*. Cambridge, MA: The MIT Press.

Manski, C. 1993. "Identification of Endogenous Social Effects: The Reflection Problem." *Review of Economic Studies* 60: 531–542.

———. 1995. *Identification Problems in the Social Sciences*. Cambridge: Harvard University Press.

———. 1997. "Identification of Anonymous Endogenous Social Interactions." In *The Economy as an Evolving Complex System II*, ed. W. B. Arthur, S. Durlauf, and D. Lane. Menlo Park, CA: Addison-Wesley.

Mantel, R. 1974. "On the Characterization of Excess Demand." *Journal of Economic Theory* 7: 348–353.

McIntyre, L. 1996. *Laws and Explanations in the Social Sciences*. Boulder: Westview Press.

Morris, S. 1996. "Contagion." Mimeo. University of Pennsylvania.

Nozick, R. 1974. *Anarchy, State, and Utopia*. New York: Basic Books.

Perrow, C. 1984. *Normal Accidents: Living with High Risk Technologies*. New York: Basic Books.

Piattelli-Palmarini, M. 1994. *Inevitable Illusions*. New York: John Wiley.

Rauch, J. 1996. "Trade and Networks: An Application to Retail Entrepreneurship." Mimeo. UC San Diego.

Rochlin, G. 1997. *Trapped in the Net: The Unanticipated Consequences of Computerization*. Princeton: Princeton University Press.

Sagan, S. 1993. *The Limits of Safety*. Princeton: Princeton University Press.

Schelling T. 1971. "Dynamic Models of Segregation." *Journal of Mathematical Sociology* 1: 143–186.

Searle, J. 1993. *The Rediscovery of the Mind*. Cambridge, MA: The MIT Press.

Sonnenschein, H. 1973. "Do Walras' Identity and Continuity Characterize the Class of Community Excess Demand Functions?" *Journal of Economic Theory* 6: 345–354.

Topa, G. 1997. "Social Interactions, Local Spillovers and Unemployment." Mimeo. New York University.

Wardhaugh, R. 1995. *An Introduction to Sociolinguistics*. Oxford: Blackwell Publishers.

Young, H. P. 1993. "The Evolution of Conventions." *Econometrica* 61: 57–84.

———. 1998. *Individual Strategy and Social Structure*. Princeton: Princeton University Press.

———. 1999. "Diffusion in Social Networks." Mimeo. Johns Hopkins University and Brookings Institution.

3 Policy Interventions, Low-Level Equilibria, and Social Interactions

Robert A. Moffitt

Interest in social interactions, neighborhood effects, and social dynamics in the last several years has seen a revival. One reason is the widespread perception that many social indicators in the United States have worsened. The increase in wage and income inequality is one of the most prominent of these trends; a decline in the earnings and incomes of those at the bottom of the distribution is another, separate trend concerning absolute rather than relative changes; and an increase in the concentration of poverty and racial segregation is another. While there is a often a tendency to assume that everything is getting worse when this is not correct—a view usefully countered by Jencks (1992)—it is unquestionable that some measures of social well-being have deteriorated.

That inequality, concentration of poverty, segregation—and their continued persistence over time—might be a partial result of social interactions—that is, direct nonmarket interactions between individuals—that lead to low-level equilibria, or "traps," is an old idea that saw its last major discussion in the 1960s and early 1970s. That period saw extensive examination of the notion of a culture of poverty from which the poor cannot escape (Lewis 1966), of externalities in housing markets that lead to prisoner's dilemmas and Pareto inferior housing equilibria (Davis and Whinston 1961), of segregation as a natural sorting and self-reinforcing mechanism (Schelling 1971), and of peer-group effects in schools (Coleman 1966). The recent revival of interest in such models has come from a variety of sources. In sociology, the work of Wilson (1987) almost single-handedly brought the concept of neighborhood effects and role models back into general discussion, a discussion that has spilled over into all the social science disciplines. In economics, the work of Romer (1986), Lucas (1988), and others on the externalities in technology and human capital investment that promote economic growth has spilled over into more microeconomic concerns with neighborhoods, income inequality, and the like (Benabou 1993, 1996; Brock and Durlauf 1995, forthcoming; Durlauf 1996a,b, to cite the most influential works among many).[1] The growth of game theory in economics has also led to a branch dealing with the development of social norms and conventions as a natural outcome of group interactions (Young 1996).

The new theoretical literature on these issues in economics has spawned a number of papers demonstrating that, under specified conditions and model assumptions, certain policy interventions can be shown to possibly counter the effects of undesirable social interactions and can have social-welfare-improving consequences (e.g., Benabou 1996). In many cases, these interventions have been shown to permit an escape from the low-level equilibria resulting from those social interactions. A natural question is whether there is any empirical evidence that these, or other policy interventions that might be considered, would have the effects hypothesized, and for the reasons hypothesized, if they were in fact implemented. The answer to this question, in turn, naturally leads to an investigation of whether there have been any policy interventions in the past that have had, either intentionally or unintentionally, effects that have operated directly or indirectly on social interactions, and have been shown to produce positive effects of one kind or another. This is the motivating issue for this chapter.

Answering these questions necessarily requires addressing the prior issue of whether the existence of social interactions can be detected with empirical analysis in the first place, which is an obvious first requirement for estimating their magnitudes or whether policy interventions have affected them. This question has played a major role in the discussions in the empirical literature on social interactions— and not just in the recent literature, for there is almost no econometric issue in recent discussions that was not raised, even if much less formally, in the literature in the 1960s and early 1970s. However, the answers have been clarified, or at least formalized, in more recent years, and this has led to a clearer statement of the conditions for identification. Once one has established the conditions necessary for identifying the existence of social interactions, and for estimating their magnitude, one can then ask what the evidence from past policy interventions has to say about them and what kind of future policy interventions might be tested.

The chapter is organized into four sections. The first provides a general discussion of the issues involved in assessing the effects of interventions on social interactions. The second furnishes a discussion of the econometric identification issues surrounding social interactions and whether policy experiments can assist in that identification. That section demonstrates that identification is possible in many models of social interactions. The third briefly surveys the empirical evidence on the existence and magnitude of social interactions gathered from data on private actions in the absence of policy interventions, focusing on two types—peer-group effects in education and neighborhood effects in cities. The fourth section reviews the evidence on two policy interventions: (1) busing and desegregation, and (2) the Gautreaux and Moving to Opportunity (MTO) programs, which provide incentives to low-income families in inner-city neighborhoods to relocate.

3.1 Overview of the Issues

When considering some of the major social policy interventions in the United States since 1935—for example, the Social Security Act and the programs it spawned (Social Security, AFDC, unemployment insurance), other transfer programs like Food Stamps and Medicaid, the G. I. Bill, busing and school desegregation, Affirmative Action, and equal opportunity legislation—the most important basic distinction to be made for present purposes is whether the interventions operate through effects on private incentives—prices, incomes, and public goods—or through social interactions, or both. I shall call the private incentives the "fundamentals" and define them as those variables that an individual would employ in a purely private calculus of decision making, ignoring the characteristics or actions of other individuals.[2]

Most policy interventions operate on the fundamentals, and this generates an empirical problem for studying social interactions. The major transfer programs just noted, for example—the Social Security Act programs, Food Stamps, and Medicaid—are generally presumed to have had their major effects through prices and incomes, although in most cases there have been suggestions in the literature that the responses of recipients to those programs have generated, through social interactions, the establishment of norms or community responses that have independent effects of their own. Consequently, from the standpoint of assessing the evidence, simply establishing that these programs have had effects on the distribution of individual outcomes in U.S. society is obviously insufficient, in and of itself, to establish the mechanism by which those effects have occurred. A purely reduced-form policy intervention analysis, therefore, is not very useful for judging the importance of social interactions unless the intervention in question can be certified to have its effects solely, or at least mostly, operating through such interactions.

The interventions other than transfer programs share this problem. The G. I. Bill, which is regarded by some as the most successful social policy intervention in the U.S. postwar era, used as its policy lever a specific price (of education) and its initial effects operated solely through individual and private responses to that change in price, even if later eligible individuals were influenced by the large numbers of others going to college. Even the race-based interventions mentioned—Affirmative Action, equal opportunity legislation, busing, and school desegregation—affect the treatment of individual adults and children in specific situations and environments first and foremost by altering their workplace characteristics and educational inputs, and are not directly operating on social interactions.

A more recent example is the 1996 welfare legislation, which is generally considered to have changed the cash welfare system for single mothers in the most significant and fundamental way since the enabling Social Security Act of 1935. The supporters of the 1996 legislation clearly intended it to have effects operating through social norms—to "send a message" to young women that they should not have children out of wedlock and to change the "culture" of welfare expectations in low-income communities. However, there was very little in the legislation that directly did so, for the legislation primarily changed the prices and incomes faced by recipients and eligibles (i.e., the benefit formulas and eligibility rules and how they are applied).

These distinctions are also important for distinguishing the goals of theoretical and empirical work on social interactions. Many theoretical results in the literature demonstrate that, assuming the existence of social interactions of one type of another, a particular policy intervention that operates on the fundamentals—school finance equalization, for example, as in Benabou (1996)—may, under certain conditions, have beneficial effects on the distribution of individual outcomes and may change lower-level equilibria to higher-level equilibria. But if such a model were accepted and the recommended policy actually implemented, empirically observing that the intervention did indeed affect outcomes would establish nothing about whether social interactions were responsible, even in part, for those effects because they could have been solely a result of the change in the fundamentals.

The primary empirical implication of the existence of social interactions that work through changes in fundamentals is the presence of multiplier and contagion effects that can generate large responses to small changes in those fundamentals (Schelling 1978). One approach to detecting social interactions even when the fundamentals are the policy lever is to search for these multiplier and contagion effects. However, the difficulty with this approach is the inherent arbitrariness of what is "small" and what is "large," particularly in light of the fact that most population outcomes do not change very quickly regardless of the reason for change. A formal analysis of what the magnitude of the response should be in the absence of social interactions would seem to be necessary in this approach, and the assumptions built into that analysis about the way in which changes in fundamentals work themselves through the market and the society, the speed with which individuals adjust to changes in the fundamentals, and the existence of multiple equilibria are likely to be critical.[3] Consequently, while this approach should not be ruled out entirely, it would appear to be quite challenging to implement convincingly.

A more promising approach to establishing the existence and magnitude of social interactions through policy interventions is to search for interventions whose effects operate directly on those interactions, and not on the fundamentals, and for which no change in population outcomes at all should be expected in the absence of social interactions. At least three classes of such interventions would appear possible: (a) interventions that change group membership, either by forcibly reassigning individuals to schools, neighborhoods, or other groups, or that offer taxes or subsidies for voluntarily changing group membership; (b) interventions that alter the fundamentals for only a subset of a group with the intention of affecting the entire group; and (c) interventions that seek to operate directly on social norms.

Interventions that forcibly reassign group membership or that offer inducements to do so voluntarily alter the composition of groups without changing the fundamentals for any individuals and hence can identify the existence of social interactions by whether the population outcomes within groups are affected. Perhaps the best example of an intervention that forcibly reassigns group membership is court-ordered busing, an intervention that will be discussed further later in the

chapter. Assuming that who gets bused and who does not is exogenous, the remixing of individuals that results furnishes the opportunity to identify social interactions. At least two problems must be
circumvented for this means of identifying social interactions to
succeed, however. One is that the fundamentals for the individuals in
the population must be held fixed, for if those fundamentals change at
the same time as group membership changes, a difference in outcomes
could occur from that source alone. An example of this problem will
be given in the discussion of busing in section 3.4. A second problem
is that group membership will often, if not usually, be endogenous;
after being forcibly reassigned, individuals can simply move back to
where they began or otherwise adjust their behavior to compensate for
the change in location. If there is a unique equilibrium to the locational
distribution of individuals that is independent of initial conditions,
then any government alteration to locational decisions will be ineffec-
tive in the long run as the population merely returns to the old equilibrium. The detection of the effects of social interactions in this case
requires that the social interaction effects—that is, the responses of
individuals to the presence of different types of individuals in their
group—occur more quickly than the locational adjustment process.[4]

Policy interventions that tax or subsidize changes in group membership would appear to be more promising because they will alter the
equilibrium even when the locational process has a unique equilibrium. On a small scale, the Gautreaux and Moving to Opportunity
interventions that will be discussed in section 3.4 below are of this type.
In those interventions, families in inner-city low-income neighborhoods were offered housing in other, often higher-income areas. Once
again, however, several problems must be overcome for this approach
to succeed. One is that, as before, the fundamentals for the individuals
involved must be held fixed to avoid their having an independent effect
on outcomes. The second is that, again as before, the long-run equilibrium consequences of such a policy must be considered and the speed
of adjustment to the new equilibrium considered relative to the speed
of response to social interactions. Third, however, a more basic issue
would arise as to how the tax or subsidy to group membership would
be defined in equilibrium. If, for example, a subsidy for low-income
families to move to high-income areas is offered and sufficiently large
numbers of low-income families move to those areas—and possibly
high-income families move out—those areas will no longer be high
income. It would not make sense for the government to offer subsidies

for movement to specific geographic locations independent of the population living there, but if it offers subsidies for movement to areas on the basis of characteristics that are made endogenous by mobility, the equilibrium consequences of that policy are entirely unclear.

The second class of direct social-interaction intervention is that which seeks to change the fundamentals for a subset of the population in a group in an attempt to influence the outcomes of the others in the group. The change in fundamentals should affect the individuals directly involved but should not, in the absence of social interactions, affect the outcomes of other individuals (ignoring changes in market prices that might have an indirect effect). Although this type of intervention bears a superficial resemblance to the intervention mentioned above that seeks to identify large responses to small changes in fundamentals, the difference here is that no distinction between large and small is necessary, nor is the existence of nonlinearities necessary to identify the effects. It is necessary, however, that group membership itself not change quickly relative to the influence of social interactions, and in this respect this intervention shares the problems of those that change group membership more directly.

Interventions that are aimed directly at social norms are a third type of policy. The most common examples of such policies are mass media campaigns. Examples include campaigns to discourage young women from having children (especially out of wedlock), stay-in-school campaigns, antismoking campaigns, public-health campaigns in general, and the like. To some extent, these "hortatory" interventions can be viewed not as an attempt to change social norms but as an attempt to provide information—on the true consequences of teen childbearing, of smoking, or of dropping out of school, for example—on the presumption that, possibly because of the environment in which they are located, correct information is not available or perceived to the individuals targeted for the campaign.[5] But many are implicitly or explicitly attempts to actually change norms—that is, preferences—by attempting to convince the audience of the correctness of a different standard of behavior. However, a problem for inferring the existence of social interactions from the effects of these types of interventions is that they may simply work on individual preferences and not on norms per se. Consequently, a more credible test of social interactions would be hortatory interventions that target a subset of the population in an attempt to change their norms or behavior in the hopes that this will affect others in the population. Indeed, the literature on mass media campaigns is replete with strategies of this kind, such as interventions targeted at key actors, those in positions of authority or influence, opinion leaders, and so on (Katz and Lazarsfeld 1955; Rice and Atkin 1989). In this sense, these interventions are like those in the second class, for they operate on only a subset of the population, but in this case by changing the preferences, not the fundamentals, of that subset.

Although this discussion has entirely focused on policy interventions that can conceivably identify social interactions, they have direct implications for identifying those interactions from relationships in the data in the absence of such interventions as well. If we imagine randomized trials that could implement each of these three types of policy interventions correctly (i.e., in a manner to minimize the problems that have been revealed for each), then there necessarily exists a class of nonexperimental variables corresponding to each that replicate the experimental conditions nonexperimentally. These variables take the form of exclusion restrictions and instrumental variables in econometric models and constitute what are usually called natural experiments. Although the existence of such nonexperimental variation is not guaranteed, the policy intervention framework used here provides a natural framework within which to guide the search for alternative nonexperimental sources of identifying variation as well.

Subsequent sections of this chapter will formalize these arguments and review the empirical literature in a selected set of research areas in light of these principles. A theme, and conclusion, of the empirical review is that the principles here formulated have not been generally recognized and that serious attempts to identify social interaction effects using these approaches—either in the design of new policy interventions or in the design of econometric models with nonintervention data—have not been used very often or at least not successfully. While there is a certain amount of research attempting to use changes in group membership as a source of identifying information, it generally does not credibly avoid the problems that have been noted with that approach. Even less analysis has been conducted using the two second approaches, at least by econometric modelers (there is ample literature on the evaluation of mass media campaigns, however). Therefore, it would seem that much additional work could be performed along these lines.

Finally, apart from evidence from the empirical literature, what evidence is there for the existence and importance of social interactions, and therefore for their importance in affecting the response to policy interventions? Perhaps the strongest evidence for social interactions is now, as it always has been, the prima facie evidence on the high degree of stratification in the United States by income, education, race, and other characteristics across neighborhoods and schools, and the high variance across areas and schools that this strong sorting implies (Massey and Denton 1993; Jargowsky 1997). The persistence of this sorting over time is another piece of prima facie evidence in support of some type of self-reinforcing equilibrium mechanism, of which social interactions are one type. Ethnographic evidence (e.g., Anderson 1991) also supports the existence of strong social interactions. Yet another type of evidence in favor of the existence and magnitude of social interactions are "puzzles" in individual behavior that are difficult to explain with models of individual calculus. The $50 bill puzzle (see n. 5) and related behaviors is in this prima facie class, as is any evidence that individual actions taken by a socioeconomic group make them demonstrably worse off according to criteria that it is presumed they themselves would accept. Also in this class are sudden swings in time series trends in welfare participation, teen childbearing, and other social behaviors that cannot be explained by changes in prices and incomes.

This type of evidence is extremely important and not to be discounted, but it is nevertheless ultimately unsatisfactory. Establishing the existence of a large unexplained residual is not sufficient to establish the source of that residual, no matter how strong the a priori plausibility of one explanation over another. The type of evidence that is needed is instead harder evidence based on the testing of alternative hypotheses within models in which alternatives can be falsified. Empirical evidence of this type will be reviewed in sections 3.3 and 3.4.

3.2   Econometric Analysis

The inferential problems in detecting the existence and estimating the magnitude of social interactions have been subject to considerable and long-standing discussion. Here the problems of identification are formalized, and the role of policy interventions in assisting identification and providing a framework for nonpolicy intervention discussed in section 3.1 are presented.

The basic conceptual relationship in models of social interactions is the effect on one individual's actions of the actions of another individual or group of individuals. The archetypal empirical exercise in the literature therefore relates, usually through regression analysis, the behavior of an individual to the characteristics of some group to which the individual belongs. Thus regressions of educational attainment, teen childbearing, criminal behavior, and so on, on the individual's own characteristics but also the characteristics of a group, are typical. The traditional critique of such exercises is that the group characteristics are, in one sense or another, endogeneous or, more generally, correlated with unobservables in the equation. An issue is whether such endogeneity, if present, can be circumvented by some conventional technique such as instrumental variables or two-stage least squares, using some naturally occurring instrument (nonexperimental methods), or whether formal investigator-induced interventions (experimental methods) would permit identification of the parameters of interest. As noted in the last section, the approach here will be to initially determine whether any experiment is possible to identify social interactions effects.

While there are several ways in which endogeneity can arise, and more than one way in which even the same basic concept can be formulated, the major types of problems with estimating the effect of group characteristics on individual characteristics can be grouped into three categories:

- the simultaneity problem
- the correlated unobservables problem and the related errors-in-variables problem
- the endogenous membership, or mobility, problem

The third of these is perhaps the most commonly discussed. The first two problems can arise, however, even if group membership is exogenous.

3.2.1 Simultaneity

The simultaneity problem is mentioned occasionally in the empirical literature (e.g., Case and Katz 1991), although less frequently than the endogenous group membership and correlated unobservables problem, and has been considered formally recently by Manski (1993).[6] The problem arises if person A's actions affect person B's actions and vice versa. This generates a conventional simultaneous equations problem if we attempt to regress person A's actions on person B's or person B's on person A's. To illustrate the problem, suppose we have $g = 1, \ldots, G$ groups and that there are only two individuals ($i = 1, 2$) per group. Let y_{ig} be the outcome variable of interest for individual i in group g, x_{ig} be an individual socioeconomic characteristic of individual i in group g, and ε_{ig} be an unobservable. Assuming linearity for the relationship, the true structure is assumed to be

$$y_{1g} = \theta_0 + \theta_1 x_{1g} + \theta_2 y_{2g} + \theta_3 x_{2g} + \varepsilon_{1g} \tag{1}$$

$$y_{2g} = \theta_0 + \theta_1 x_{2g} + \theta_2 y_{1g} + \theta_3 x_{1g} + \varepsilon_{2g}. \tag{2}$$

We assume only that ε_{1g} and ε_{2g} are orthogonal to both x_{1g} and x_{2g} and that group membership is exogenous. The social interaction coefficients are represented by θ_2 and θ_3, which represent, respectively, the presence of endogenous and exogenous social interactions. The model could be made more realistic by considering more than two individuals per group, by adding a set of observable group-specific variables to the equation, and by other extensions, but this would not alter any of the results to be discussed here. Note as well that the linearity of the model implies that, in the absence of degenerate and other special solutions, there will be a single unique equilibrium, not multiple equilibria.[7]

Equations (1)–(2) constitute a simple linear simultaneous equations problem and can be analyzed using conventional rules for identification. As noted by Manski, the parameters in (1) and (2) are not identified.[8] This can be seen either by applying the usual exclusion condition rule—namely, the rule requiring that at least one exogenous variable be excluded from each equation (there are no such exclusions)—or by considering the reduced form, which is

$$y_{1g} = \alpha + \beta x_{1g} + \gamma x_{2g} + v_{1g} \tag{3}$$

$$y_{2g} = \alpha + \beta x_{2g} + \gamma x_{1g} + v_{2g}, \tag{4}$$

where

$$\alpha = \theta_0 (1 + \theta_2) / [1 - \theta_2^2] \tag{5}$$

$$\beta = (\theta_2 \theta_3 + \theta_1) / [1 - \theta_2^2] \tag{6}$$

$$\gamma = (\theta_2 \theta_1 + \theta_3) / [1 - \theta_2^2] \tag{7}$$

$$v_{1g} = (\varepsilon_{1g} + \theta_2 \varepsilon_{2g}) / [1 - \theta_2^2] \tag{8}$$

$$v_{2g} = (\varepsilon_{2g} + \theta_2 \varepsilon_{1g}) / [1 - \theta_2^2]. \tag{9}$$

The coefficients in equations (3) and (4) are the same and hence can be estimated consistently by pooling the data on the individuals and regressing the values of y_{ig} in the data set on each individual's own x and the x of the other individual in the group. But estimates of the three parameters α, β, and γ do not allow separate identification of the four parameters θ_0, θ_1, θ_2, and θ_3. Thus endogenous and exogenous interactions cannot be separately identified.

An important question is whether identification can be achieved using the covariance of the values of the residuals for different individuals within a group conditional on the values of x_{1g} and x_{2g}, namely, the covariance of v_{1g} and v_{2g}. Equations (8) and (9) imply this is possible only if ε_{1g} and ε_{2g} are independent, in which case θ_2 can be identified from that covariance (the individual variances of ε_{1g} and ε_{2g} can be simultaneously identified from the variances of v_{1g} and v_{2g}). For example, if $\theta_2 = 0$, that covariance is zero if ε_{1g} and ε_{2g} are independent. However, the difficulty is that ε_{1g} and ε_{2g} are probably strongly correlated in most applications, either because of endogenous group membership and the sorting of individuals across groups that results or, more generally, from the presence of the unobserved correlated effects that will be discussed momentarily. To assume independence of ε_{1g} and ε_{2g} is to implicitly assume that all of the correlation of values of y among individuals in a group who have the same x values arises from social interactions, and this ignores the basic identification problem in the model—namely, how to distinguish within group correlations that arise from social interactions from correlations that arise for other reasons.

Many studies in the literature assume one form of interaction only—endogenous or exogenous—and obtain identification by that restriction. Unfortunately, if the assumed form of interaction is incorrect, the resulting estimates are either biased or simply misinterpreted. For example, if exogenous interactions are assumed to be zero ($\theta_3 = 0$) when they are not, and if the system is estimated by two-stage least-squares using estimates of equations (3)–(4) to form instruments for the "other" y in equations (1)–(2), it can be shown that the coefficients on predicted "other" y in equations (1)–(2) are unbiased estimates of (γ/β) and hence are biased estimates of θ_2. On the other hand, if endogenous interactions are assumed to be zero ($\theta_2 = 0$) when they are not, then estimation of equations (1)–(2) leaving out the "other" y is equivalent to estimating the reduced form, and hence the social interaction coefficient—that on the "other" x—is an unbiased estimate of γ; this would be incorrectly interpreted as estimating θ_3.

A key point is, however, that the existence of social interactions in general is identified in this model (Manski 1993). The coefficient γ indicates whether any type of social interaction is present, for if $\theta_2 = \theta_3 = 0$ then $\gamma = 0$. Thus if the exogenous characteristics of individuals in a group are correlated with the values of y of others within the group (holding fixed own values of x), interactions must be present in this model, although one cannot determine whether it is because those characteristics have direct effects or they have indirect effects working through outcomes. To the extent, therefore, that it does not matter for the purposes at hand whether social interactions are of the endogenous or exogenous type, estimation of the reduced form equations (3)–(4) is sufficient. However, this form of inference will again founder on the presence of unobserved correlated effects or endogenous group membership, which will induce a relationship between y and x across individuals that arises from other sources.

It is useful to approach the question of identification by asking whether there are any randomized trials of policy interventions that could, even in principle, identify the model, a perspective not taken in the literature to date on social interactions. By "in principle", we mean randomized trials that use the observed and known values of all x and y of all individuals in a population (assumed free of measurement error), and their initial group membership, and that alter either x, y, or that group membership in different ways for different individuals. If we take group membership as fixed and seek to manipulate experimentally the values of x and y within groups, the structure of the model as given in equations (1)–(4) and the nonidentification results we have obtained for it necessarily imply that no such experiment is possible. In fact, the only experimentally manipulatable variables are the individual values of x_{1g} and x_{2g}, and we have already noted that this permits only the estimation of the reduced form in equations (3) and (4), which does not identify all the parameters (the experimental manipulation of these variables would merely break any correlation they have with the error terms, which is not the source of the problem we are discussing in this section). The values of y_{1g} and y_{2g}, like all endogenous variables in a model, cannot be directly experimentally manipulated; they are chosen by the individuals and, even if they could be temporarily altered by the government, would, if the system were allowed to adjust, simply return to their equilibrium values.[9]

Experimentally altering group membership, however, would allow identification. Randomly matching a set of $2G$ individuals into pairs of individuals would result in independence of ε_{1g} and ε_{2g}, and hence θ_2 could be identified from the correlation of residuals across individuals within a group. The identification of θ_2 permits the identification of θ_3 from the other reduced form coefficients. The randomization of group composition implies that any within-group correlation must be the result of endogenous social interactions. As noted in the last section, however, the ability of individuals to resort themselves if the assumption of exogenous group membership is relaxed is the main difficulty with this approach. We shall therefore return to this issue in the discussion of endogenous group membership below. We shall also consider at that point whether there are nonexperimental counterparts to random assignment of individuals.

It is possible that identification could be achieved if this linear model were made nonlinear in a way that permitted multiple equilibria (see, e.g., Brock and Durlauf 1995 and Durlauf 1996b for examples). For each of the stable equilibria there will be a reduced form counterpart to equations (3)–(4) that describes the relationship of the group distribution of x values to the y values, and nonlinearities may result in more parameter identification. A major problem with models of multiple equilibria is, however, detecting which equilibrium the observed data correspond to, assuming that the system is in equilibrium. This is a higher level of identification problem than any present in the linear, single-equilibrium model.[10]

While random assignment of group membership is a possible identification mechanism, there are, in fact, other policy interventions that can identify the model even without manipulation of group membership. However, the structure of the model must be changed. Specifically, partial-population experiments in which only a portion of the individuals within each group are given a treatment are in this class. Modifying equations (1)–(2) to introduce policy variables that affect one individual but not the other can be illustrated by letting p_{1g} be a government "price" (subsidy, tax, or other instrument) administered only to individual 1, a price variable that is independent of the unobservables in the model. Then we replace equation (1) with

$$y_{1g} = \theta_0 + \theta_1 x_{1g} + \theta_2 y_{2g} + \theta_3 x_{2g} + \theta_4 p_{1g} + \varepsilon_{1g}. \tag{10}$$

The absence of p_{1g} in equation (2) permits all parameters in the model to be identified. As can be seen from the reduced form (not shown), the parameter θ_2 is identified from the effect of p_{1g} on y_{2g}; this again leads to identification of θ_3 as well. The difference in this model and the previous one is that here there exists an exogenous variable that affects one individual directly but affects the other only through the endogenous social interaction. The identifying restriction is that individual 2 is not directly influenced by p_{1g} and there is no social interaction induced by that variable. Implicit in this restriction is the notion that the exogenous social interactions originally specified in equations (1)–(2) exist only for certain types of characteristics of individuals, and that the unique prices that some of them might face are not in that category. Indeed, this example suggests that there might be a larger class of exclusion restrictions consisting of characteristics of individuals that can be argued on some basis to not have a direct influence on others. Judging the plausibility of such restrictions, as well as that of the partial-population policy intervention suggested here, requires a more careful consideration of what is meant by exogenous social interactions and what the deeper source of such interactions is.

While the possibility of randomized trials of such policy interventions is reasonably clear, it is also possible that nonexperimental counterparts to such policy interventions exist. Any government program or any private market event that affects only a subset of the individuals in a group for reasons unrelated to the unobservables in the model (i.e., unrelated to y conditional on x) is a candidate in this class, if it can also be reasonably assured that such programs or events also have no direct social interaction effect on the other individuals in the community.

The hortatory policy interventions discussed in section 3.1 are also in this class, provided they aim to change the preferences of only a subset of the individuals with a group, and hence likewise can offer identification of the model parameters. Simply replace p_{1g} in equation (10) by a treatment dummy for a randomized trial of a hortatory campaign to affect the preferences of individual 1. As before, the additional restriction implicit in the approach is that being subjected to such a campaign is not a characteristic that has direct influence on the others in the group who are not subjected to it. Pure mass media campaigns that are directed at the entire population are consequently not in this class, but efforts to affect subsets of the population such as key influential persons are. In this case, however, there are no obvious natural experiment counterparts to mass media campaigns, although conceivably subsets of group populations might be discovered who were exposed to extra information for exogenous reasons.

3.2.2   Correlated Unobservables and Errors-in-Variables

The problem of correlated unobservables arises if there is some group-specific component of the error term, call it μ_g, that varies across groups and that is correlated with the exogenous characteristics of the individuals (x) (Manski 1993). The suggestion that the presence of such unobservables could account for much of the evidence on social interactions has a long history dating back to the 1960s (see section 3.3) and is one of the most common biases referred to in empirical studies. The unobservables could arise from a variety of sources and depend partly on the application. Often the unobservables are assumed to arise from unobserved preference components (neighborhoods) or abilities (classrooms) that are correlated across individuals within those groups. These correlations can be motivated by the endogenous group membership model, as described below—that individuals tend to locate where there are other individuals of the same type, in the most common case—but can in principle arise even in an exogenous group model. Alternatively, the unobservables may represent contextual, or environmental, influences that are measurable in principle but may not be in practice, such as school resources, crime rates, and employment opportunities in the neighborhood.

Modifying the previous model by allowing $i = 1, \ldots, N_g$ individuals per group, the reduced forms in equations (3)–(4) can be rewritten as

$$y_{ig} = \alpha + \beta x_{ig} + \gamma x_{(-i)g} + \mu_g + \eta_{ig} \qquad i = 1, \ldots N_g, \tag{11}$$

where $(-i)$ denotes the individuals in the group other than i and $x_{(-i)g}$ denotes a weighted mean of the values of x of the individuals in $(-i)$.[11] The component μ_g can be thought of as representing the covariance between ε_{1g} and ε_{2g} in equations (1)–(2) but modified for many individuals, that is, capturing an intraclass covariance. Then, assuming

$$E(x_{ig}\mu_g) \neq 0, \tag{12}$$

least-squares estimation of equation (11) will yield inconsistent estimates of both β and γ. In particular, it can be shown that the least-squares coefficient on $x_{(-i)g}$ is biased upward if the covariance between $x_{(-i)g}$ and μ_g is sufficiently larger than the covariance between x_{ig} and μ_g.[12] This is likely to be the case if $x_{(-i)g}$ represents some average across individuals that is more highly correlated with the unobservable than is any single observation. Thus in the presence of correlated unobservables even the weak form of identification obtainable from the reduced form in the simultaneity model—of the existence of any form of interaction, endogenous or exogenous—is lost.

A related model, not formally considered in the literature to this author's knowledge, arises if there are errors-in-variables in the measured individual characteristics x but the true values are correlated across individuals.[13] A typical example occurs where x_{ig} is the income of the family of child i in group g, $x_{(-i)g}$ is the mean family income in the rest of the group, and y_{ig} is some child outcome, but where x_{ig} measures transitory rather than permanent income and it is permanent income that matters. We can write the model as

$$y_{ig} = \alpha + \beta x_{ig}^* + \gamma x_{(-i)g}^* + v_{ig}, \tag{13}$$

$$x_{ig} = x_{ig}^* + \zeta_{ig}, \tag{14}$$

$$x_{ig}^* = \mu_g + \xi_{ig}, \tag{15}$$

where the variables with asterisks measure true but unobserved variables and those without asterisks are the observed, error-filled variables. Assuming all errors are independent across i and g and of each other, a correlation between x_{ig} and $x_{(-i)g}$ arises only from the presence of the common unobservable μ_g in equation (15). In the presence of that factor, it can be shown that a regression of y_{ig} on the observables x_{ig} and $x_{(-i)g}$ yields in the population a nonzero coefficient on $x_{(-i)g}$ even if $x_{(-i)g}^*$ does not truly affect y_{ig}. The simple reason for this result is that the other individuals' weighted mean of x serves as a proxy for μ_g. To be precise, the least-squares coefficient on $x_{(-i)g}$ in such a regression is biased upward if the variance of $\zeta_{(-i)g}$ is sufficiently smaller than the variance of ζ_{ig}, that is, if measurement error is smaller in the weighted mean $x_{(-i)g}$ than in the individual x_{ig}.[14]

Consistent estimation of γ requires in either model breaking the correlation between $x_{(-i)g}$ and μ_g. Consideration of policy interventions that might induce this result requires that thought be given to the source of μ_g and that a distinction be made between two generic sources of such correlated unobservables. The first is that which arises from sorting and endogenous group membership, and from preferences or other forces leading certain types of individuals to be grouped together. The second is that which arises from common environmental factors in the neighborhood such as crime, schools, and employment opportunities, which are different because their relationship to the population composition of a group is more complex. Crime, for example, may be partly a function of the fraction of group individuals with low income; school characteristics are determined through a political process where the influence of population composition is not entirely clear, particularly in cases where population in the area is fairly heterogeneous; and the proximity of employment opportunities to a neighborhood are likely fixed in the short run but will change over time as the population composition of a neighborhood changes if employer location decisions are affected by the location of workers.

For the first type of common unobservable, the randomized group assignment intervention discussed in the context of the simultaneity model will also eliminate the intragroup correlations that arise from endogenous group membership (with the same caveats regarding subsequent resorting). The additional element here is that it will also eliminate the correlation of $x_{(-i)g}$ and the reduced-form error term, which was not an issue in the simultaneity model. All structural parameters could be identified with this type of intervention and in this sense there is no difference between the simultaneity problem and the correlated unobservables problem. In addition, partial-population interventions that introduce a price or change the preferences of a subset of the population are likewise sufficient to identify the endogenous social interactions coefficient θ_2 even in the presence of correlated unobservables, so long as those policy interventions are constructed to be independent of all observables and unobservables. However, this is not sufficient to identify θ_3 because these interventions do nothing to remove the correlation of $x_{(-i)g}$ and the error term. For that purpose a randomized alteration of $x_{(-i)g}$ is necessary. It was not needed in the simultaneity model because $x_{(-i)g}$ was assumed uncorrelated with the error term in that case.

If the common unobservable is of the second type, identification is not so simple and, indeed, it is not even clear what the object of estimation is. This is because, in all the examples given, μ_g is a function of the distribution of x_{ig} (if not y_{ig}). If, for example, crime rates are a simple function of the low-income portion of the group population, then it is not clear that it will ever be possible to separate the effects of low income per se from the effects of crime. If a certain quality of local school necessarily follows the presence of sufficient numbers of high-income families, then it is not clear that it will ever be possible to separate the effects of high income per se from the effects of schools. One might take the position that such separation is not needed because it does not matter for policy purposes what the source of the influence of the low-income or high-income families is, but in fact there are policies that operate separately on the crime, schools, and other environmental

variables that do not work through the characteristics of the neighborhood population. These policies might be used to separate the effect of
the two, but this will be application-specific. There would not seem to
be any general solution to this problem that will work for all possible
environmental influences.

One possible line of attack to this generic problem is through the
assumption of nonlinearities in the relationship between μ_g and the
group population characteristics. If instead of $\mu_g = \delta x_{(-i)g} + \omega$, where ω
is a white-noise unobservable, we assume the relationship is nonlinear.
If school resources in a community are determined by the median
voter, for example, then changes in $x_{(-i)g}$ that do not change the identity of that voter will not change those unobserved resources; if variables like crime rates and employment opportunities are determined
by the value of $x_{(-i)g}$ in the dominant, or majority, part of the x distribution, then changes in $x_{(-i)g}$ that do not affect the composition of that
majority will not affect those rates and opportunities. The best example
of this latter case is one in which the values of x within a minority of
the population change, those within the majority remain fixed, and the
question is whether the values of y of the majority respond to changes
in the values of x among the minority.

Reliance on these types of nonlinearities for identification has the disadvantage of forcing reliance on assumptions that are difficult if not
impossible to test and also restricts the range of $x_{(-i)g}$ over which social
interactions can be tested (namely, only over ranges within which μ_g
does not change). It also makes the definition of groups even more
important than it usually is, for the choice of definition affects whether
a change in the values of x in a subpopulation within a group is "large"
or "small." If the distribution of x alters for only 1 percent of the individuals in a school district, and does not materially affect (unmeasured)
school resources in the district, it might still affect the residents in a particular block if the entire 1 percent whose x values have changed live in
that block; there they might constitute a majority and might affect the
values of different other types of μ_g on that block. The general problem
is that different types of effects, both arising from social interactions
($x_{(-i)g}$) and unobservables (μ_g), may have different group definitions.

3.2.3   Endogenous Group Membership

The endogenous group membership issues are particularly familiar
and have, again, been discussed since the 1960s. The simplest way to

set up the model is in the framework of the familiar two-equation switching regression model of econometrics consisting of an equation for outcomes y_{ig} conditional upon a group membership assignment of the population and an equation for the group membership assignment itself. An illustrative example of the first equation, again maintaining linearity, is

$$y_{ig} = \theta_0 + \theta_1 x_{ig} + \theta_2 y_{(-i)g} + \theta_3 x_{(-i)g} + \varepsilon_{ig}, \tag{16}$$

where we now, for simplicity, assume that $y_{(-i)g}$ and $x_{(-i)g}$ are the means of the individual values of y and x in each group excluding that of individual i. The reduced form of equation (16) is necessarily also linear and of the same form as considered previously, namely,

$$y_{ig} = \alpha + \beta x_{ig} + \gamma x_{(-i)g} + v_{ig} \tag{17}$$

As for the second equation, we define the utility to individual i from locating in a group g conditional on the locational decisions of the rest of the population and hence conditional on mean exogenous characteristics $x_{(-i)g}$ and mean structural residuals $\varepsilon_{(-i)g}$—we assume these residuals to be observed by individual i but not by the econometrician—in each group g as[15]

$$U_{ig} = f(x_{ig}, \varepsilon_{ig}, x_{(-i)g}, \varepsilon_{(-i)g}) + \eta_{ig}, \tag{18}$$

and with the following decision rule:

individual i chooses location g iff $U_{ig} \geq U_{ig'} \, \forall \, g'$. \tag{19}

The usual presumption is that the function f in equation (18) picks up conformity effects as individuals prefer to locate near individuals like themselves, but there is nothing in this general structure that requires it. Assuming that a unique locational equilibrium exists—that is, a single allocation of individuals to groups in which each individual's preferred location is consistent with that of all other individuals—equations (17)–(19) represent an internally coherent description of a social interactions model with endogenous group membership.[16]

That estimation of equation (17) on the assumption that x_{ig} and $x_{(-i)g}$ are independent of the error term in that equation yields inconsistent parameter estimates is familiar from the econometric literature on selection bias, for equation (18) clearly indicates that there will be a relationship between the error terms ε_{ig} and $\varepsilon_{(-i)g}$ (which are contained in the reduced form error term in that equation) and x_{ig} and $x_{(-i)g}$, which is induced by the locational decision mechanism.

The parameters of equation (16) or (17) are unidentified in this model just as they were in the correlated unobservables model discussed in the last section. The group membership selection equation gives specific form to such correlated unobservables, but the econometric implication is the same as any such model. However, this particular mechanism for the problem suggests a class of solutions along the conventional lines used for switching regression models, namely, exclusion restrictions. In this case, for identification of at least the coefficients of equation (17) (ignoring the intercept) a variable is needed that appears in equation (18) but not in equation (17), and no such variable appears (recall that the structural residuals terms ε_{ig} and $\varepsilon_{(-i)g}$ are not observed by the econometrician). A randomized trial of a policy intervention that offers subsidies (or penalties) to locate in groups g that differ across individuals i is sufficient for such a purpose. Denoting such a subsidy level as b_{ig}, we have

$$U_{ig} = f(x_{ig}, \varepsilon_{ig}, x_{(-i)g}, \varepsilon_{(-i)g}, b_{ig}) + \eta_{ig}. \tag{18'}$$

We suggest that the presence of such a variable should permit identification of the coefficients in equation (17), although without demonstrating it formally.[17] We also suggest that it is certainly possible that there exist nonexperimental counterparts to these subsidies in the form of differential moving costs across individuals and other constraints on mobility that differ cross-sectionally.

A major question surrounding this approach concerns the design of the subsidies b_{ig} and how they are tied to the characteristics of the areas g (they are presumably not tied literally to the index variable g itself, which is arbitrary and meaningless). How the subsidies are designed will affect the equilibrium of the model and make the analysis of identification more complicated still. For example, as noted in section 3.1, if subsidies are based on the population composition of the group, those will change as individuals change group, and hence the value of the subsidies will not stay fixed as the system moves toward equilibrium.

As will be noted in the review of empirical work below, the most common approach to this problem is to ignore the equilibrium implications of the model and simply analyze the effects of moving a small subset of the population from one location to another, holding the locations of the rest of the population fixed. As also noted in section 3.1, this is not an unreasonable strategy but does require that the speed of locational adjustment that results be slower than the speed at which the social interactions take form and have their influence. It also requires an a priori judgement on what constitute "small" versus "large" changes in the population composition of a group.

3.2.4 Summary

The identification method that works most often in all of these situations we have discussed is by means of a randomized policy intervention that provides subsidies or taxes to group membership or that otherwise induces changes in group membership unrelated to the sorting motivations that occur in the absence of such interventions. Nonexperimental counterparts that achieve the same end are also candidate approaches. Such interventions break the correlation between observed and unobserved group characteristics, and they generate independence of errors within groups that can identify endogenous social interactions. The major unresolved problem in this approach is the presence of environmental variables that are unobserved but tied to the distribution of group characteristics themselves, and here the best approach is to rely on nonlinearities that are plausibly related to specific theories of concrete environmental variables.

Partial-population price interventions and partial-population hortatory interventions are also candidates for identifying some of the social interaction parameters. These methods do rely on exogenous group membership and are therefore candidates if population reallocations occur more slowly than within-group social interaction influences. The relative speeds of adjustment issue comes up sufficiently often in the discussion of identification approaches that it would probably be fruitful to model those dynamics explicitly, which has rarely been done in the literature, and to search for testable implications of the types of dynamics assumed.

3.3 Evidence: Private Actions

For lack of a better term, I denote studies of social interactions that arise naturally in society and without any exogenous government intervention as studies of private actions. In this category, two literatures on social interactions stand out in size relative to all others; these are the literatures on peer-group effects in education, and on neighborhood effects in cities. Both literatures are sizable and both, especially that on peer group effects, have already been surveyed or summarized multiple times. I will survey the surveys, as it were, but also note specific studies that are either representative or unusual in some respect.[18]

3.3.1   Peer-Group Effects in Education

The literature on peer-group effects in education dates from the publication of the Coleman report (Coleman et al. 1966). Coleman's analysis of U.S. schools indicated that educational achievement of black students was positively related to the fraction of students in their school that were white. This was one of the most controversial findings of the Coleman report—among many that were controversial—and has been held primarily responsible for the subsequent movement toward forced busing in the United States in the late 1960s and early 1970s (Heckman and Neal 1996).[19]

From the standpoint of the detection difficulties described above in section 3.2, such a peer-group association has the all the problems noted above except the simultaneity problem (because the percent of a school that is white is an x, not a y, in such a model). It is quite possible, in fact extremely plausible, that greater-percentage white schools have better (unmeasured) resources and inputs than lesser-percentage white schools, that the percentage white might be correlated with unmeasured characteristics of black students, and that the types of black students whose parents choose to get them into high-percentage white schools are systematically different than other black students in unmeasured ways; in short, that the biases discussed in section 3.2 are all present.

These points are sufficiently obvious that they constituted a theme repeatedly made in the subsequent volume on the Coleman report published not long afterward (Mosteller and Moynihan 1972). Individual papers by Christopher Jencks, Eric Hanushek and John Kain, David Armor, Marshall Smith, and David Cohen, Thomas Pettigrew, and Robert Riley all mentioned these possible biases and interpretative problems with Coleman's result.

However, the papers in the Mosteller-Moynihan volume went further than this in their critiques of the Coleman peer-group finding. First, several authors (Jencks; Cohen, Pettigrew, and Riley; Armor) found that the peer-group effect became either insignificant or inconsequential in magnitude once individual and family background characteristics like family SES were controlled for (which Coleman had not done). Second, and even more damaging, a replication of Coleman's work by Smith revealed that Coleman had made a coding error that greatly affected the estimated peer group effect; namely, it became insignificant when the error was corrected.

The importance of these early findings cannot be underestimated because the biases noted above and by the authors of the Mosteller-Moynihan volume are likely still present and hence the effects estimated by such methods are arguably an upper bound; therefore, a small estimated effect could easily reflect a true zero effect.

Since the Mosteller-Moynihan volume, a large number of studies of peer group effects have been conducted. Most of those in the education literature are summarized in a recent review by Schofield (1995), who surveys the surveys as well as updates them (some of the more widely cited earlier surveys are those by Cook et al. 1984; Mehard and Crain 1983; St. John 1975; and Weinberg 1977). For someone whose expectation is that peer effects are likely to be strong, the literature Schofield surveys will be surprising because of the extremely weak nature of the findings. Many, if not a majority, of studies find small or weak effects of peers. The findings are fragile and nonrobust to specification and to the inclusion of other controls. Schofield concludes her survey by stating that "research suggests that desegregation has had some positive effect on the reading skills of African-American youngsters. The effect is not large, nor does it occur in all situations" (Schofield 1995, 610). She also finds that there is no evidence for any effect on mathematics skills.[20]

In the economics literature, which overlaps somewhat but not completely with that surveyed by Schofield, the majority of studies again find weak or nonexistent peer group effects. Two exceptions are the studies by Summers and Wolfe (1977) and Henderson, Meiszkowski, and Sauvageau (1978), the first of whom found positive effects on the test scores of a sample of Philadelphia students of the achievement levels of the other students in the school, and the second of whom found similar effects in a study of Montreal schools. It is easy to note the biases that could lead to such positive correlations, but this does not explain why these studies yielded stronger effects than the majority of other studies, which also were subject to those biases. Henderson, Meiszkowski, and Sauvageau speculated that one reason for the difference of their results with those in U.S. schools was the extreme social and cultural homogeneity of their French-speaking population.[21]

This literature continues and is thriving in economics. The major difference between the newer studies and the older ones is that the former regularly use instrumental variables to account for endogeneity of the characteristics of the peer group. However, thus far the instruments chosen have generally been ad hoc in nature and not based on a strong, or at least explicitly formulated, theory, and not on the types of identifying variables discussed in this chapter. A typical example is Gaviria and Raphael (1997), who regress various student social outcomes (drug and alcohol use, cigarette smoking, etc.) on the characteristics of students in their schools, but instrumenting the latter with whether the families are long-term or recent residents of the area. The argument is that long-term residents are less likely to be selected because they moved sufficiently far in the past as not to be affected by current locational characteristics. Not only does this ignore the fact that long-term residents are a self-selected set of families who have chosen *not* to move out of the area, it presumes them to be out of equilibrium, an assumption that needs defense and demonstration, at best. It also assumes incorrectly that the instrumental variables technique will correct for student self-selection, and it ignores most of the correlated unobservables problem.

3.3.2   Neighborhood Effects

As noted in the introduction, perhaps the strongest evidence for neighborhood effects thus far is simply the prima facie descriptive evidence on strong sorting within U.S. cities by neighborhood, as well as its persistence and the actual increase in isolation of minority poor (Massey and Denton 1993; Wilson 1996; Jargowsky 1997). [22] Considering instead the literature testing falsifiable hypotheses for the existence and magnitude of social interactions, it should again be noted that much of the empirical literature on neighborhood effects was spawned by the work of Wilson (1987) who suggested that disadvantaged black familes left behind in inner-city neighborhoods have no successful role models to emulate (his argument is much more complex than this simplistic description implies). A large body of literature has ensued, the vast majority of which has consisted of simple regressions of family outcomes on own characteristics and some measure of the characteristics of the other families in a localized area. Once again, the problems in doing so have been recognized in the literature, even if relatively little has been done about them. A survey of the literature up to 1990 is provided by Jencks and Mayer (1990), who find the evidence to be surprisingly weak and fragile, in light of the presumed bias toward stronger effects (not that there are not many studies that show positive correlations).[23] Subsequent studies that similarly make no adjustment for potential bias include those of Crane (1991), Mayer (1991), Corcoran et al. (1992), Brooks-Gunn et al. (1993), Solon, Page, and Duncan (forthcoming), and many others. While many of these studies find positive neighborhood effects, it is difficult to conclude that anything at all has been learned except that raw intraneighborhood correlations often hold up when individual characteristics are controlled (though some studies such as Solon, Page, and Duncan (forthcoming) find that most of the effect goes away when such controls are added).[24]

A small number of studies have attempted instrumental variable methods but, once again, with problematic choice of instruments. Case and Katz (1991) instrument the neighborhood variables with lagged x variables; Evans, Oates, and Schwab (1992) instrument school composition with citywide variables for the unemployment rate, median income, and the like; and Cutler and Glaeser (1997) instrument a racial segregation index with a variety of variables, including prior residence and citywide governance variables. What is absent in these discussions is any formal description of a residential choice model that could justify the instruments, a dynamic model that could justify the use of lags, an accounting for both correlated unobservables and area selection effects, or, in some cases, simply a good defense for why the variables should not affect the outcome variable directly. The instruments have an ad hoc flavor because they are not based on any explicit theory or model.

3.4   Evidence: Policy Interventions

The number of policy interventions that can be fairly described as having effects on social interactions as a major goal is quite small, and the number that have been evaluated or studied seriously is even smaller. In this section, I will focus on two upon which a considerable amount of ink has been spilled: school desegregation and busing, and the Gautreaux/MTO programs. While this is not an exhaustive list of those that have been studied, these two will illustrate the issues involved in using policy interventions to study social interactions. In addition, I will note two additional types of policy interventions that are germane to the estimation of social interactions but less widely known (hortatory campaigns and I Have a Dream programs).

3.4.1 School Desegregation and Busing

Perhaps the most dismaying feature of the literature on the effects of school desegregation and busing on student achievement is that it greatly overlaps with the literature on peer-group effects in education. In particular, the majority of studies of school desegregation consist of studies regressing black student outcomes on the racial composition of their schools, and thus do not examine directly the effect of the intervention in question (namely, the intervention of school desegregation). In these studies, the differences in school racial composition that generate the independent variable of primary interest occasionally arise from court-ordered desegregation plans; they more frequently arise from voluntary residential location patterns and school choice patterns; from school board rezoning decisions; and from student transfers subsequent to school openings or closings. From a program evaluation standpoint, only variation that directly arises from court-ordered desegregation plans provides direct evidence on the policy intervention of interest. Yet this issue appears to have escaped most of the analyses in the literature, which rarely note that it matters which source of variation in generating the treatment variable of interest is utilized for estimation.

To be sure, there would be problems in studying court-ordered desegregation by itself because most of those orders are by now twenty years old and one could only conduct historical studies (though this would certainly be of interest). In addition, studying current outcomes in areas that were once under court order is problematic because significant resegregation of those school districts has occurred, exactly as a sorting-equilibrium model with a single stable equilibrium would predict (Schofield 1995, 598). In any case, based on the studies that have been conducted, the literature has concluded that the effects of school desegregation, like those of peer effects, are at best modest and at worst zero, as described previously.

There are exceptions to the methodological objection that has been made here. A good example is the study by Boozer, Krueger, and Wolkon (1992) whose treatment variable of interest is also racial composition but who instrument it with a dummy breaking the data into pre-1964 and post-1964 periods, which is a good indicator of when court-ordered desegregation began. The authors found that using this instrument reduced the coefficient on racial composition to insignificance. Thus, at least for this one study, an improvement in the methodology did not change the general empirical conclusions from the prior literature.

While the literature hence suggests relatively few effects of desegregation, it should be noted for the purposes of this chapter that court-ordered desegregation is a problematic treatment for the evaluation of peer effects in education in the first place. The treatment in this case is transferring a disadvantaged minority student to a majority-white school. Because majority-white schools differ in many ways from the schools from which the minority students came, school resources by themselves differ and are therefore part of the treatment; this is the problem of correlated unobservables noted in section 3.2. Solving this problem, it could be argued, would require an experiment in which white students were bused to minority schools, not the other way around; in that type of experiment, the general school environment of minority students would not change, and the effects of being in the same classroom or school with white students could be more readily isolated.[25] But on top of this are the effects of transportation to school by bus itself on student functioning, as well as any short-run stigma or social adjustment effects experienced by minority students bused into majority white schools. Both of these effects could have deleterious effects on achievement and hence could mask positive peer effects.

3.4.2 Gautreaux/MTO Programs

The well-known Gautreaux program in Chicago was the result of a housing discrimination lawsuit settled in the 1970s (Rosenbaum 1992; Rosenbaum and Popkin 1991; Popkin, Rosenbaum, and Meaden 1993). In the program that followed the settlement of the suit, public housing residents who volunteered for the program were put on a waiting list and offered new housing in other parts of the city that were less than 30 percent black as such housing became available. Rosenbaum has argued that the locations of the offered apartments were randomly assigned and that residents therefore randomly ended up in different types of neighborhoods. Rosenbaum's analysis has shown that those who ended up in suburban neighborhoods had more successful outcomes on a number of dimensions (employment rates, wage rates, school attendance and completion, etc. for either adults or children) than those who ended up in city neighborhoods.

The Gautreaux program has the usual set of biases that are associated with almost any social experiment. Only volunteers were enrolled,

for example; the offered housing was obtained by the program opera-
tors only from landlords who agreed to participate; and some of
the families moved back to the city or attrited from the experiment
(Rosenbaum 1995). But aside from these biases, the Gautreaux program
has properly received considerable attention from researchers and pol-
icymakers who have seen it as a reasonable attempt to experimentally
alter group membership.[26]

Partly as a result of the success of the program, the U.S. Housing and
Urban Development (HUD) has mounted an ambitious set of randomized trials in five cities to test a similar program. These programs,
called Moving to Opportunity (MTO), offer inner-city public housing
residents who volunteer one of two options—a voucher to use for
housing in a high-income area of the city, and a voucher to use any-
where in the city. Public housing residents are randomly assigned one
of these options, and a third group is randomly assigned to control
status. The evaluations are still being conducted but the early results
show positive effects on some outcomes (Katz, Kling, and Liebman
1999; Ludwig, Duncan, and Hirschfield 1999; Ludwig, Duncan, and
Pinkston 2000). HUD has termed the MTO demonstrations "the most
significant social experiment HUD has implemented in the last 25
years" (Goering and Feins 1997).

While the Gautreaux and MTO programs have the strongly desirable feature of randomization or quasi-randomization (in the case of
Gautreaux), they do have problems as a test of the presence of neighborhood effects. For example, while the Gautreaux/MTO programs
remove sorting bias, they do not solve the correlated environmental
unobservables problem because the neighborhoods into which the participants move differ from their old neighborhoods in more ways than
simply the socioeconomic composition of their neighbors. Differences
in labor market opportunities, in school quality, in crime rates, and
even in housing quality (the new units are presumably better quality
than the old) exist. In fact, with regard to the first of these, the programs are motivated as much by the spatial mismatch problem (i.e., job
opportunities) as by social interactions. While it is sufficient for some
policy purposes to know simply the composite and net effect of all
these factors taken together, the multiplicity of factors hinders the
detection of effects of social interactions per se.

Once again, a better strategy to measure social interactions would
be to measure the change in the outcomes of the initial residents of
the areas into which the inner-city public housing residents moved,

for it could be argued that the contextual-environment factors were approximately fixed for them before and after the change.[27] Unfortunately, the evaluations of the programs appear not to have collected data on that population. One could argue that the MTO movers are such a small part of their new neighborhoods that their effect on aggregate moments of the destination neighborhood distributions would be negligible, but this ignores the issue noted in section 32 that some types of neighborhood effects may be quite local (e.g., on a single city block). The crude proxies for neighborhood effects that are used in the empirical literature, which are solely the result of data limitations, should not lead to a conclusion that no social interactions are present in smaller geographic areas. More generally, the theory is consistent with a small intervention affecting only a small number of individuals.

A larger, more difficult problem to solve is the possibility of subsequent residential mobility of both MTO participants and initial residents of the destination areas. While these considerations may be discounted because they are require long-run adjustments, implying that the programs can at least measure short-term responses, it must also be considered whether the most important social interaction effects are not also long-run in nature. In addition, as just discussed, the relevant mobility of the initial residents of the destination areas may be that of those on a particularly city block, not those in the rest of the neighborhood.

3.4.3 Other Policy Interventions

Much literature on policy interventions works through diffusion and network processes and other forms of social interactions, but two are worth mentioning here given the types of substantive applications we are primarily concerned with. One is the substantial literature on media campaigns as well as interventions that intend to have effects working through social networks (Katz and Lazarsfeld 1955; Rice and Atkin 1989; Valente and Saba 1998). In the sociological literature, the most well-known model of network effects is that of Granovetter (1973), who argued that there is "strength of weak ties" in the sense that information can flow rapidly in communities even if the social ties between individuals are weak. Models of diffusion in this literature tend to be more specific in their modeling of how individuals within a community interact than those in the economics literature, and they often model the influence of individual opinion leaders and followers, for example, as well as quantifying the "density" of personal information networks by the closeness of the ties between individuals (Valente 1995).

However, the evaluation of these interventions appears to be in its infancy. While there has been substantial work on advertising, commercial marketing, public relations, and public health campaigns, relatively little work has been conducted within the framework of randomized trials or quasi-experiments. By and large the evaluation method of choice has been a simple before-and-after, or evaluation by means of a crude comparison group, with consequent weak inferences. The microstructure of the diffusion of change induced by such campaigns also appears to be rarely evaluated by formal methods.

Another well-known intervention that has not been evaluated much is the I Have a Dream program. The initial program was begun by Eugene Lang in 1981, a businessman-turned-philanthropist who offered to help pay the college expenses of a group of disadvantaged sixth-grade students in a New York school if they would complete high school. The program attracted considerable media attention and led to the formation of a Foundation that currently oversees about 160 projects in 63 cities. The programs all follow the original idea of offering college financial assistance to elementary school students if they finish high school. Unfortunately, relatively few evaluations of these programs have occurred to date, and those that have been conducted have not attained a high level of rigor. Other similar programs have also sprung up to provide aid to students for higher education (U.S. General Accounting Office 1990), but these have have likewise seen little evaluation effort. Nevertheless, these programs all clearly fall into the class of interventions whose intended effect is to provide examples of successful educational completion to other students and hence to work through social interactions.

3.5   Conclusions

In the literature on social interactions, theory has run considerably ahead of empirical testing, the development of policy interventions that work through social interactions, and the evaluation of such interventions. Although strong prima facie evidence for the existence of social interactions is present in many different types of evidence, the importance and magnitude of those interactions remain largely unknown, and hence the desirability of developing policy interventions aimed primarily at those interactions has not yet been established. While there has been considerable empirical work on social interactions, particularly in the areas of peer group effects in education and neighborhood effects, the literatures have not successfully confronted the several basic identification and estimation problems summarized here and in much prior work. In addition, several relevant major policy interventions—desegregation and busing, for example, and the Gautreaux/MTO programs—have not been properly designed, or the appropriate outcome data collected, to measure social interactions per se.

Despite the rather discouraging empirical record to date, however, several methods of identifying social interactions and estimating their magnitude have been presented here. Methods for inducing exogenous variation in group members, and methods for inducing partial-population price and hortatory variation often permit the separate identification of exogenous and endogenous interactions. These methods have not been seriously applied in the empirical literature to date.

In addition, while past policy interventions have not been well designed to measure social interactions per se, some of the many opportunities to do so are outlined in the chapter. Some of the interventions that seem most promising for social interaction effects (e.g., the I Have a Dream programs) have not been evaluated at all. In designing new interventions, the most difficult problem is controlling for the presence of unmeasured contextual-environmental unobservables, but interventions that hold those unobservables relatively constant but that alter group composition in such a way as to allow measurement of social interactions to appear quite feasible. In addition, more attention must be paid to data collection at the local level, and to a more careful theoretical framework in mind, in order to make significant progress on many of the policy interventions of interest. These possibilities offer the prospect of learning much more about social interactions than is now known.

Notes

Presented at the Colloquium on Social Dynamics, Brookings Institution, January 22–23, 1998. The author would like to thank Gary Burtless, Bruce Hamilton, Christopher Jencks, Charles Manski, and Thomas Valente for comments.

1. See also Pollak (1976) for a well-known study of interdependent preferences, which is another form of social interaction.

2. Individual actions do, of course, influence other actions through the market (determination of prices, etc.) but these are not what are usually defined as social interactions, which occur through direct nonmarket influences.

3. The possible existence of multiple equilibria is especially important because it could be regarded as the key feature of social interactions models. The empirical difficulty in detecting the existence of multiple equilibria solely from the observation of nonlinear responses to small policy interventions is that it is unclear in general what size of stimulus is needed to move a society from one equilibrium to another. Indeed, one's intuition is that a particularly massive intervention may be necessary to move a society off of a long-established low-level equilibrium.

4. If there are multiple equilibria, then the population will settle down to a new equilibrium, and it is more likely that social interactions can be detected from the change in population outcomes.

5. This problem is related to the "$50 bill puzzle." A $50 bill lies on the sidewalk and the individual does not pick it up—why not? Most calculations show the return to additional education to be extremely high, even for disadvantaged youth, but their actions do not appear to respond to it. One hypothesis is that the youth do not correctly perceive the payoff.

6. See also Manski (1997) for several extensions.

7. We ignore the issue of how groups are defined and take that as exogenous. Manski (1993) emphasizes that the need to know group composition a priori is a fundamental problem in social interaction models. This requirement is driven by the need to exclude the group identifiers themselves from x, a requirement implicitly assumed in this model. An example of the problems that arise when this requirement does not hold is given below in the discussion of unobserved correlated variables.

8. The notation and model setup here differ somewhat from those of Manski. The most important difference is that Manski replaces y_{2g} and x_{2g} in equation (1), and y_{1g} and x_{1g} in equation (2), by their expected values in the group. The reduced form of such a model would be the same as equations (3) and (4) except that the reduced-form error terms would not contain the "other" error, namely, ε_{2g} would not appear in equation (8) and ε_{1g} would not appear in equation (9). As noted below, these error terms cannot be used for identification of social interactions in any case without unacceptable independence restrictions, so there is no important difference in the models in this respect. The analysis of identification on the basis of reduced-form coefficients is essentially the same here as in Manski (although Manski does treat correlated unobservables using a different notation; these are not considered here until section 3.2).

9. It is conceivable that the government may have the means to manipulate residuals, an issue that will be further discussed below. But knowledge of the residuals v_{1g} and v_{2g}, which the government could presumably estimate, do not identify the underlying residuals ε_{1g} and ε_{2g}, and hence manipulation of v_{1g} and v_{2g} would be meaningless.

10. If the system is thought to be out of equilibrium, more possibilities for identification are possible if there are lags. However, once again, it is unclear how a determination is made whether the data describe an in-equilibrium or out-of-equilibrium state. Assuming the incorrect equilibrium to describe the data will result in incorrect inference.

11. Most of the analysis here could be generalized to allow $x_{(-i)g}$ to be a nonlinear function of the x values in the set. However, the reduced form in that case would not be linear.

12. This assumes that the covariance in equation (12) is positive. The exact bias is [Cov $(x_{(-i)g}, \mu_g)\text{Var}(x_{ig}) - \text{Cov}(x_{ig}, \mu_g)\text{Cov}(x_{ig}, x_{(-i)g})]/A$, Where A is a positive number.

13. Although not formally considered, it is nevertheless frequently mentioned in the empirical literature. For recent examples of such reference, see Datcher (1982) and Case and Katz (1991).

14. This assumes $\beta > 0$. The exact bias in the coefficient on $x_{(-i)g}$ is $[\beta\text{Var}(\zeta_{ig})\text{Var}(\mu_g) - \gamma\text{Var}(\zeta_{(-i)g})\text{Var}(x_{ig})]/A$, where A is a positive number. In the absence of the term μ_g, least squares still produces an inconsistent estimate of γ but this is solely from the presence of measurement error and the direction of bias is toward zero.

15. The mean $y_{(-i)g}$ is not appropriate because it will be affected by whether individual i does or does not choose to join group g.

16. These models often have multiple equilibria, however, which raises the issues discussed earlier in the context of the simultaneity problem.

17. This model is more complex than the standard switching regression model because the actions of others are not exogenous and will themselves respond indirectly to the set of b_{ig} faced by all other individuals. A more formal analysis would require working out the equilibrium of the model, which is beyond the scope of this chapter.

18. I should stress that while these two literatures are larger than others in volume, this section does not do justice to the extensive literature across many social science disciplines where the concept of social interactions, or related concepts, has been discussed.

19. An earlier study of Coleman (1961) reported the results of an extensive examination of social cliques in schools and presaged his interest in peer effects.

20. For a similar conclusion in a recent survey, see Jaynes and Williams (1989, 374).

21. On the other hand, Henderson, Mieszkowski, and Sauvageau also had data at the classroom level, unlike most other studies.

22. The study of Glaeser, Sacerdote, and Scheinkman (1996) should be considered to fall within this descriptive class, for that study decomposes the unexplained residual from a group-level outcome regression into a portion due to social interactions and a random portion, using parametric restrictions on the form of each to separately identify them, rather than constructing a testable hypothesis for social interactions.

23. "Our first and strongest conclusion is that there is no general pattern of neighborhood or school effects that recurs across all outcomes" (174).

24. See the volume edited by Brooks-Gunn, Duncan, and Aber (1997) for more studies of this kind. See also the chapter by Duncan, Connell, and Klebanov (1997) for a discussion of the biases in studies of neighborhood effects.

25. Alternatively, one could examine the effect on white students in schools where minority students were bused in, on the presumption that the contextual unobservables were fixed and hence any change in the outcomes for white students would likely reflect social interactions. The school peer-group effects literature indicates that there were relatively few effects of minority racial composition on white achievement scores (Schofield 1995).

26. A special problem in Gautreaux was that some of the moved minority families experienced harassment by white families after the move, which compounded the adjustment

problems of moving to a new environment (Rosenbaum 1995). The important question for evaluation is whether these effects are long-run or short-run, and whether they would be greater or smaller if a different number of families have moved in.

27. As in the desegregation case, a better experiment to detect social interactions might be to move a large number of white residents into a minority-dominant public housing unit.

References

Anderson, E. 1991. "Neighborhood Effects on Teenage Pregnancy." In *The Urban Underclass*, ed. C. Jencks and P. Peterson. Washington: Brookings.

Benabou, R. 1993. "Workings of a City: Location, Education, and Production." *Quarterly Journal of Economics* 108 (August): 619–652.

———. 1996. "Equity and Efficiency in Human Capital Investment: The Local Connection." *Review of Economic Studies* 63 (April): 237–264.

Boozer, M., A. Krueger, and S. Wolkon. 1992. "Race and School Quality Since Brown v. Board of Education." *Brookings Papers on Economic Activity: Microenomics* 269–338.

Brock, W., and S. Durlauf. 1995. "Discrete Choice with Social Interactions I: Theory." Working paper 5291. Madison: Social Science Research Institute.

———. Forthcoming. "Interactions-Based Models." In *Handbook of Econometrics*, Vol. IV, ed. J. Heckman and E. Leamer.

Brooks-Gunn, J., G. Duncan, and J. Aber, eds. 1997. *Neighborhood Poverty*, Vols. I and II. New York: Russell Sage Foundation.

Brooks-Gunn, J., G. Duncan, P. Klebanov; and N. Sealand. 1993."Do Neighborhoods Influence Child and Adolescent Development?" *American Journal of Sociology* 99 (September): 353–395.

Case, A., and L. Katz. 1991. "The Company You Keep: The Effects of Family and Neighborhood on Disadvantaged Youths." NBER Working paper no. 3705. Cambridge, MA.

Coleman, J. et al. 1996. *Equality of Educational Opportunity*. Washington, DC: Government Printing Office.

———. 1961. *The Adolescent Society: The Social Life of the Teenager and Its Impact on Education*. New York: Free Press of Glencoe.

Cook, T., eds. 1984. *School Desegregation and Black Achievement*. Washington DC: National Institute of Education.

Corcoran, M., R. Gordon, D. Laren, and G. Solon. 1992. "The Association between Men's Economic Status and Their Family and Commnity Origins." *Journal of Human Resources* 27 (Fall): 575–601.

Crane, J. 1991. "The Epidemic Theory of Ghettos and Neighborhood Effects on Dropping Out and Teenage Childbearing." *American Journal of Sociology* 96 (March): 1226–1259.

Cutler, D., and E. Glaeser. 1997. "Are Ghettos Good or Bad?" *Quarterly Journal of Economics* 112 (August): 827–872.

Datcher, L. 1982. "Effects of Community and Family Background on Achievement." *Review of Economics and Statistics* 64 (February): 32–41.

Davis, O., and A. Whinston. 1961. "The Economics of Urban Renewal." *Law and Contemporary Problems* 25 (Winter): 105–117.

Durlauf, S. 1996a. "A Theory of Persistent Income Inequality." *Journal of Economic Growth* 1 (March): 75–93.

————. 1996b."Statistical Mechanics Approaches to Socioeconomic Behavior." NBER Technical Working paper no. 203. Cambridge, MA.

Duncan, G., J. Connell, and P. Klebanov. 1997. "Conceptual and Methodological Issues in Estimating Causal Effects of Neighborhoods and Family Conditions on Individual Development." In *Neighborhood Poverty*, ed. J. Brooks-Gunn, G. Duncan, and L. Aber. New York: Russell Sage Foundation.

Evans, W., W. Oates, and R. Schwab. 1992. "Measuring Peer Group Effects: A Study of Teenage Behavior." *Journal of Political Economy* 100 (October): 966–991.

Gaviria, A., and S. Raphael. 1997. "School-Based Peer Effects and Juvenile Behavior." Mimeo. University of California at San Diego.

Glaeser, E., B. Sacerdote, and J. Scheinkman. 1996. "Crime and Social Interactions." *Quarterly Journal of Economics* 111 (May): 507–548.

Goering, J., and J. Feins. 1997. "The Moving to Opportunity Social 'Experiment': Early Stages of Implementation and Research Plans." *Poverty Research News* 1 (Spring): 4–6.

Granovetter, M. 1973. "The Strength of Weak Ties." *American Journal of Sociology* 68 (May): 1360–1380.

Heckman, J., and D. Neal. 1996. "Coleman's Contributions to Education: Theory, Research Styles and Empirical Research." In *James Coleman*, ed. J. Clark. London and Washington: Falmer Press.

Henderson, V., P. Mieszkowski, and Y. Sauvageau. 1978. "Peer Group Effects and Educational Production Functions." *Journal of Public Economics* 10 (August): 97–106.

Jargowsky, P. 1997. *Poverty and Place: Ghettos, Barrios, and the American City.* New York: Russell Sage Foundation.

Jaynes, G., and R. Williams, eds. 1989. *A Common Destiny: Blacks and American Society.* Washington, DC: National Academy Press.

Jencks, C. 1992. *Rethinking Social Policy: Race, Poverty, and the Underclass.* Cambridge: Harvard University Press.

Jencks, C., and S. Mayer. 1990. "The Social Consequences of Growing Up in a Poor Neighborhood." In *Inner-City Poverty in the United States*, ed. L. Lynn and M. McGeary. Washington, DC: National Academy Press.

Katz, E., and P. Lazarsfeld. 1955. *Personal Influence: The Part Played by People in the Flow of Mass Communications.* New York: Free Press.

Katz, L., J. Kling, and J. Liebman. 1990. "Moving to Opportunity in Boston: Early Impacts of a Housing Mobility Program." Mimeo. Harvard University.

Lewis, O. 1966. *La Vida: A Puerto Rican Family in the Culture of Poverty*. New York: Random House.

Ludwig, J., G. Duncan, and P. Hirschfield. 1999. "Urban Poverty and Juvenile Crime: Evidence from a Randomized Housing-Mobility Experiment." Mimeo. Georgetown University.

Ludwig, J., G. Duncan, and J. Pinkston. 2000. "Neighborhood Effects on Economic Self-Sufficiency: Evidence from a Randomized Housing-Mobility Experiment." Mimeo. Georgetown University.

Lucas, R. 1988. "On the Mechanics of Economic Development." *Journal of Monetary Economics* 22 (July): 3–42.

Manski, C. 1993. "Identification of Endogenous Social Effects: The Reflection Problem." *Review of Economic Studies* 60 (July): 531–542.

———. 1997. "Identification of Anonymous Endogenous Interactions." In *The Economy as an Evolving Complex System*, ed. W. B. Arthur, S. Durlauf, and D. Lane. Reading, MA: Addison-Wesley.

Massey, D., and N. Denton. 1993. *American Apartheid*. Cambridge: Harvard University Press.

Mayer, S. 1991. "How Much Does a High School's Racial and Socioeconomic Mix Affect Graduation and Teenage Fertility Rates?" In *The Urban Underclass*, ed. C. Jencks and P. Peterson. Washington, DC: Brookings.

Mehard, R., and R. Crain. 1983. "Research on Minority Achievement in Desegregated Schools." In *The Consequences of School Desegregation*, ed. C. Rossell and W. Hawley. Philadelphia: Temple University Press.

Mosteller, F., and D. Moynihan. 1972. *On Equality of Educational Opportunity*. New York: Random House.

Pollak, R. 1976. "Interdependent Preferences." *American Economic Review* 66 (September): 309–320.

Popkin, S., J. Rosenbaum, and P. Meaden. 1993. "Labor Market Experiences of Low-Income Black Women in Middle-Class Suburbs: Evidence from a Survey of Gautreaux Program Participants." *Journal of Policy Analysis and Management* 12 (Summer): 556–573.

Rice, R., and C. Atkin, eds. 1989. *Public Communication Campaigns*. Newbury Park: Sage.

Romer, P. 1986. "Increasing Returns and Long Run Growth." *Journal of Political Economy* 94: 1002–1037.

Rosenbaum, J. 1992. "Black Pioneers—Do Their Moves to the Suburbs Increase Economic Opportunity for Mothers and Children?" *Housing Policy Debate* 2: 1179–1213.

———. 1995. "Changing the Geography of Opportunity by Expanding Residential Choice: Lessons from the Gautreaux Program." *Housing Policy Debate* 6: 231–269.

Rosenbaum, J., and S. Popkin. 1991. "Employment and Earnings of Low-Income Blacks Who Move to Middle-Class Suburbs." In *The Urban Underclass*, ed. C. Jencks and P. Peterson. Washington: Brookings.

St. John, N. H. 1975. *School Desegregation: Outcomes for Children*. New York: Wiley.

Schelling, T. 1971. "Dynamic Models of Segregation." *Journal of Mathematical Sociology* 1: 143–186.

———. 1978. *Micromotives and Macrobehavior*. New York: Norton.

Schofield, J. 1995. "Review of Research on Desegregation's Impact on Elementary and Secondary School Students." In *Handbook of Research on Multicultural Education*, eds. J. Banks and C. Banks. New York: Macmillan.

Solon, G., M. Page, and G. Duncan. Forthcoming. "Correlations between Neighboring Children in Their Subsequent Educational Attainment." *Review of Economics and Statistics*.

Summers, A., and B. Wolfe. 1977. "Do Schools Make a Difference?" *American Economic Review* 67 (September): 639–652.

U.S. General Accounting Office. 1990. *Promising Practice: Private Programs Guaranteeing Student Aid for Higher Education*. Washington, DC: Government Printing Office.

Valente, T. 1995. *Network Models of the Diffusion of Innovations*. Cresskill, NJ: Hampton Press, Inc.

Valente, T., and W. Saba. 1998. "Mass Media and Interpersonal Influence in a Reproductive Health Communication Campaign in Bolivia." *Communication Research* 25: 96–124.

Weinberg, M. 1977. *Minority Students: A Research Appraisal*. Washington, DC: Government Printing Office.

Wilson, W. J. 1987. *The Truly Disadvantaged: The Inner City, the Underclass, and Public Policy*. Chicago: University of Chicago Press.

Wilson, W. J. 1996. *When Work Disappears: The World of the New Urban Poor*. New York: Knopf.

Young, P. 1996. "The Economics of Convention." *Journal of Economic Perspectives* 10: 105–122.

4

Measuring Social Interactions

Edward L. Glaeser and
José A. Scheinkman

4.1 Introduction

A growing literature has argued that many economic actions—crime, education choice, labor force participation, out-of-wedlock births—are marked by social interactions (see, e.g., Akerlof 1997; Becker 1997; Bernheim 1994; Young 1997).[1] These social interactions imply that the net private benefits from pursuing a particular activity rise as others also pursue this activity. For example, working hard in school might be less painful for a young student if his friends are also studying, both because his friends can help him learn and because his friends are not available for other leisure activities. These interactions can take many forms, ranging from pure physical externalities (while one person is being arrested, the police find it harder to arrest someone else), to learning from one's neighbors, to stigma (the more people who are committing a particular crime, the less likely is that crime to be a negative signal) to pure taste externalities (individuals just enjoy imitating others). We will discuss the many forms of these externalities at length in section 4.2, but the primary focus of this essay is on measuring the extent of social interactions, not on determining which mechanisms are most important in generating them.

Social interactions are particularly important because they can help explain striking shifts in aggregate outcomes over time and space. There are a large number of variables where shifts over time and space seem far too large to be explainable with standard economic forces. For example, Levitt (1997) shows that only 25 percent of the massive crime increase from 1960 to 1975 can be explained by demographic shifts. Mulligan (1995) argues that massive female labor force participation in World War II cannot be explained by changes in either wages or the opportunity cost of time. Likewise, the dramatic change in divorce rates or the rise in out-of-wedlock births (see Akerlof, Katz, and Yellen 1996) all seem to be only partially connected to visible shifts in observable variables.[2]

Social interactions help explain these changes, because of the strategic complementarities inherent in social interactions. These strategic complementarities imply that even if changes in fundamentals create only a small change in the level of activity for each individual, each individual's small change will then raise the benefits for everyone else pursuing the activity. The societywide effect of a small change in fundamentals, because of these ripple effects, may therefore be quite large. Small changes in fundamental variables can set off a cascade in individual behavior so that large shifts in outcomes may result from tiny changes in fundamentals.

The rapid shifts in the variables that we mentioned earlier are of prime policy interest. The rise in female labor force participation is probably the most important single shift in the postwar labor market. The rise in crime over the 1960–75 period led to a tenfold increase in reported crime in many areas. The rise in out-of-wedlock births and the rise of divorce appear to have caused deep changes in our society. To the extent that theory and measurement of social interactions enables us to understand these massive changes, the study of social interactions potentially has major policy relevance. Furthermore, since social interactions usually imply the existence of externalities, the presence of these interactions often suggests some scope for government action.

Indeed, we believe that nonmarket interactions between people represent most of the human experience. These interactions play a critical role in determining behavior, preferences, and utility. Social interactions models of the type discussed in this chapter and in this volume are one way of understanding the features of nonmarket interactions that make them different from more standard interactions that work through market transactions. This chapter focuses on one empirical approach to these interactions.

4.1.1 Measuring Social Interactions—A Brief Literature Review

This chapter focuses on a narrow set of issues in empirically measuring the size and nature of social interactions. Several empirical approaches to understanding these interactions exist. There is a literature that includes Crane (1991), Case and Katz (1991), Evans, Oates, and Schwab (1992), Rauch (1994), Borjas (1995), O'Regan and Quigley (1996) and many others that uses microdata to examine these connections. The basic structure of this research often involves regressing an action of a person on the average action of a person's "neighbors," where neighbors can mean members of the individuals census tract or some self-reported social group.

There are three problems with this methodology, which are discussed at length by Manski (1993). First, if a person is affected by his neighbors, he also affects his neighbors. As such the supposedly independent variable (the neighbors' actions) is a function of the dependent variable (the individual's actions). Most recent research in this area (see Case and Katz 1991) addresses this problem by instrumenting for the independent variable using the average levels of other neighbors' characteristics that are supposedly exogenous (such as neighbor's parents characteristics). Second, there may be omitted variables in a particular area that affect the returns to the activity in that area and that would induce a spurious correlation between individuals and neighbor's actions, even if all individuals are immobile. This problem is also potentially treatable using exogenous neighbor's characteristics as instruments for neighbor's actions.

Third, individuals choose their neighborhoods and individuals who are likely to do the same things may choose to live close to one another, perhaps because of social interactions. Evans, Oates, and Schwab (1992) address this problem by modeling the choice of peer group as an endogenous variable. They argue that standard peer group effects disappear once the endogeneity of peer groups has been properly treated.

General solutions to all of these problems are enormously difficult to find in the absence of controlled experiments, such as Gautreaux or Moving-to-Opportunity, where individuals are actually randomized across neighborhoods. Even these experiments often suffer from the fact that we only observe individuals who chose to join in the experiment or who decide not to turn down the opportunity to move to a new neighborhood. When individuals are selected based on moving, the results are clearly biased because only persons who benefit from moving will choose to move.

Even clever solutions to this bias that use only the randomized part of the experiment are problematic. For example, consider an experiment where randomized individuals (perhaps those who draw an even number) are given the opportunity to move to a new neighborhood and others aren't given that opportunity (perhaps those who draw an odd number). By using the number that the individual is given as an instrument for neighborhood movement (thus not using whether or not the individual actually moved), some of the worst part of the bias is eliminated. Nevertheless, since the only people who move are those who benefit from moving, the experiment never tracks the full sample of possible movers. Even the randomized treatment effect must be interpreted as estimating the benefit of having an option to move, not the benefit of actually moving.

Brock and Durlauf (1997) represents a particularly comprehensive and careful discussion of the use of microdata to estimate social interactions. In particular, they focus on discrete choice problems often in a panel setting. They present a thorough discussion of when discrete choice models with social interactions are actually identifiable, a major contribution to research in this area. Again, though, they show identification to be extremely difficult in many cases, especially when unobserved heterogeneity is particularly important.

Another empirical approach to measuring social interactions relies on using only aggregate information (see Brock and Durlauf 1995; Glaeser, Sacerdote, and Scheinkman 1996; Gaviria 1997; Topa 1997). The intuition of this approach is that since social interactions create high levels of variance across space and time, by using the variance of aggregates, one can measure the extent of these interactions. This approach is free of the most basic endogeneity or reflection problem, because the approach explicitly acknowledges that all individuals affect each other. However, it is free of neither the problem of omitted variables that vary across space, nor the problem of selection of different types of people into different areas.

Alternative approaches have been proposed by Glaeser, Sacerdote, and Scheinkman (1996) to address these problems. We implicitly control for an area specific fixed effects that eliminates some or most of the omitted variables problem. We examine groups that are more or less mobile to see if there appears to be a connection between mobility and measured social interactions, which there would be if measured social interaction just reflected location choice. We use "scaling" rules predicted by the theory that should allow us to differentiate between sorting and direct interaction. Finally, we use the variance of observables to determine the range of reasonable estimates for the importance of unobservables. While these corrections are far from perfect, they do suggest that there are ways that this methodology can be made useful. We believe strongly that given the importance of estimating social interactions, all possible methodologies should be used. Even if the classic approach discussed first was better in 90 percent of the cases (which we do not believe), there is still significant value in using alternative methodologies that do not share exactly the same set of problems (although they have problems of their own).

Topa (1997) also uses aggregate-level variables to study social spillovers in employment status. Formally, he writes down a nonhomogeneous version of a contact process in which the probability of becoming employed depends on both individual characteristics and the number of one's neighbors who are employed. The probability of becoming unemployed depends only on individual characteristics. The nonhomogeneity allows Topa (1997) to differentiate spatial sorting from spillovers, but it also stops him from explicit derivations of the stationary distribution of the employment process. Instead, he uses the process of indirect inference where parameters are estimated by minimizing a distance between actual data and simulations of the structural model for different parameter values. A principle feature of the Topa model is that the covariance between individuals—the degree of social interaction—is determined by spatial distance. He estimates large quantities of spillovers using Chicago Census Tract level information for 1980 and 1990. He finds that spillovers are strongest for minorities and individuals with less education.

Brock and Durlauf (1995) do not present estimation based on aggregates, but rather a variety of theoretical results that are introduced as a first step toward empirical work. They focus on a global interactions model and produce results on the existence of multiple equilibria and the existence of threshold effects.

4.1.2 Overview

Our focus is on measuring the size and nature of social interactions. Our particular interest is in interactions where one person's taking a particular action increases the likelihood of another person also taking the same action. We will generally use the term *positive social interactions* to refer to just this type of situation. Most of the peer effects and interaction models discussed above (and discussed below) can be said to have this basic structure.

Our primary interest is in empirically determining the size and nature of these positive social interactions. We are interested in the extent to which one person's action will affect his neighbor's action.

We are interested in the extent to which this sort of influence decays with geographic and social distance. We are interested in the extent to which individual interactions are increased and reduced as individuals choose the social milieu in which they exist. In principle, if social interactions are to be a major piece of positive economics or policy prescriptions, this type of information is crucial.

This chapter extends our previous methodology is four ways, starting with section 4.3. First, we introduce a social interactions model with a continuous rather than a discrete one-zero choice variable. This change is useful for considering many variables where outcomes are continuous rather than discrete. If we believe that the action is continuous but that the econometrician only observes a discrete outcome, then this continuous interaction model can be used for thinking about discrete variables. We present a new set of empirical results measuring the extent of social interactions for these continuous variables. One primary difference between continuous and discrete variables is that to use continuous variables it is necessary to have a separate estimate of the population variance of outcomes from microdata (in the case of discrete variables with known mean level p, the population variance is always $p(1 - p)$).

Our second section extends our previous work to include both local and global interactions. A local interaction occurs across neighbors. A global interaction occurs through an aggregate. Classic examples of local interactions may include learning from neighbors (as in Ellison and Fudenberg 1995) or joint neighbor production of non-work-related activities. Global interactions may include communitywide norms or effects that work through the price mechanism. Like local interactions, global interactions produce high variances. Unlike local interaction models, global interactions also naturally produce multiple equilibria, which local interactions do not as long as the interaction from neighbor-to-neighbor decays sufficiently quickly. We demonstrate an empirical methodology for considering multiple equilibria and other social interactions jointly. This methodology finds the existence of multiple equilibria for many variables, but notes that the bulk of the variance across areas remains even after we have allowed for the existence of multiple equilibria. Actually separating local from global interactions requires subarea aggregates or microdata where individuals are matched to a peer group below the global level.

Our third section presents a version of the model with both local interactions and locational selection. Individuals choose their areas to maximize utility based on possibly limited information about their own tastes. The variance across areas is then based on the combination of locational decisions and social interactions (of course, the local decisions are also based on the existence of social interactions). The identification of selection versus social interaction hinges again on a scaling rule. In other words, if we know that people are selecting between sets of areas with different population sizes, then it is possible to differentiate between the two sources of cross-area variation.

Finally, we examine local and global interaction models in a dynamic context. Following a large body of work on technology adoption, we note that the level of social interaction determines the extent to which adoption is linear or S-shaped. We present a simple means of testing for the extent of social interaction in dynamic processes, but we do not show how to determine between local and global interactions outside of using simultaneously cross-sectional and time series information. We present a ranking across a number of dynamic processes of that appear to be the most interactive. In general local interactions seem to generate somewhat slower dynamic change, and in principle it may be possible to differentiate between the two theories just using time series information given sufficient assumptions on functional form.

Our overall conclusion is that there appears to be substantial social interaction in a large number of variables. Some of this interaction creates multiple equilibria, but most of the variance that social interaction creates occurs beyond these equilibria. Differential selection into different areas is clearly particularly important, but there is still variance beyond that caused by selective migration.

4.2   Discussion of Interactive Mechanisms

There is no shortage of the mechanisms that may generate social interactions of either the local or the global variety. Furthermore, while we will stress "positive" social interactions, namely, interactions where an individual's action positively influences his neighbors' actions, there are also many well-known cases of negative social interaction. For example, competition for scarce resources is a form of a global negative interaction that operates through the price system. As one individual decides to consume more of a particular commodity, that individual drives up the price and drives down consumption of all others who also face that price. Because of this force, we generally expect to find positive social interactions in actions where there are not scarce resources for which individuals are competing. We loosely divide the mechanisms that generate social interactions into four primary categories: physical, learning, stigma and taste-related interactions.

One reason to care about the different reasons why social interactions occur is that different policy implications are associated with different interactions. For example, if one person's level of education increases his neighbor's education through dissemination of learning, then it makes sense to subsidize education. There is a socially desirable spillover that should be subsidized. However, different policy implications appear if one person's level of education increases his neighbor's education for signaling reasons—namely, as one person gets more education the other person must also get more education or be thought inferior. In that case, there is a socially undesirable spillover that should not be subsidized. While we will not be able to delve into methods of differentiating the sources of spillovers in this chapter, this section stresses the wide range of possible mechanisms and the extreme policy importance of recognizing the different ways in which positive interactions might occur.

4.2.1 Physical and Learning Interactions

Many forms of physical social interactions exist, even just within a single activity. For example, social interactions may occur in crime because of congestion in law enforcement (as in Sah 1991). This force surely plays a significant role in riots, where the large number of rioters lowers the probability of arrest (see DiPasquale and Glaeser 1998). Increases in crime may lower the opportunity cost of legal activity (because legal actors are being robbed) and may therefore lower the opportunity cost of time and raise further the amount of criminal activity (as in Murphy, Shleifer, and Vishny 1991). These interactions may either be local or global depending on the range of criminals and police. For example, if criminals attack legal businesses throughout the area, then this interaction is global. If criminals only attack very close legal operations, then the interaction is local.

Network externalities are a classic physical interaction. In these externalities, it is more valuable to use a technology when others are using it as well. For example, telephones and e-mail become more valuable when others also have these communication devices. Cities themselves are networks and the existence, growth, and decline of urban agglomerations depend to a large extent of these interactions.

The presence of investment also can generate these physical interactions. Investing in learning the QWERTY keyboard may only make sense when a large percentage of keyboards follows this configuration. Investing in an IBM versus a Macintosh or a Betamax versus a VHS video recorder depends on the presence of complements to use such as software or videocassettes. These complements are much more likely to abound when others are also using the technology. As a result there is a positive, global interaction that moves the nation to the extreme of using one or the other technology (as in the case of VHS vs. Beta; see Arthur 1989 for a discussion of "historical lock-in") or an uneasy coexistence between two technologies (as in the case of IBM and Macintosh). In these cases, it has often been argued that suboptimal equilibria often continue to exist supported by social interactions.

Other social interactions based on learning may occur if individuals actually help each other learn (as in Benabou 1993). In Young (1993), individuals learn by observing past actions and learning produces convergence of strategies to a Nash equilibria. Having neighbors who are taking an action makes it easier to learn about this action. This learning may take the form of just learning that a new technology exists (as in Griliches 1958) or learning how to operate a technology correctly or learning the returns of this technology. Again, depending on how the technology operates, the interaction may either be local or global. Ellison and Fudenberg (1993) explicitly consider global learning where people interact with random members of a broad population. Ellison and Fudenberg (1995) examine local learning where people interact with their near neighbors. Fads and herding are other examples of behavior where learning-related externalities can create social interactions (Banerjee 1992; Bikhchandani, Hirshleifer, and Welch 1992).

4.2.2 Signaling and Taste Interactions

Interactions can also be generated through the desire to resemble outwardly the group that is taking a particular action. When actions are signals, then there is a natural interaction that comes about because the value of a signal is a function of who else is taking that signal. For example, Rasmusen (1996) develops a model of stigma and criminal behavior where more criminality tends to lower the stigma associated with criminality. As a result, more people become criminals. Glaeser (1992) argues for positive social interactions in labor market mobility, where more people changing firms in high mobility countries (such as the United States) eliminates the stigma associated with rapid mobility in low mobility countries (such as Japan).

Of course, the presence of signaling doesn't necessarily yield positive interactions. For some actions (particularly snob goods), greater participation necessarily means that the action goes from being a positive signal to being a negative signal (see, e.g., Pesandorfer 1996). As more people perform the action or consume the snob good, there is less of a signaling demand for the product. There is an inherent asymmetry between actions that are demanded because they are positive signals and actions that are avoided because they are negative signals. As more individuals perform actions that are positive signals, the signal dissipates and the value of the action disappears. As more individuals perform actions that were once negative signals, again the signal dissipates, but in this case the demand for the action will rise with the disappearance of the signal.

To make this point clearly, consider the following simple model where individuals choose a discrete one-zero action. There is a distribution of "quality" across people, denoted θ, and individuals want to resemble high quality individuals. The value of the action is a function (denoted $W(.\,,.)$) of the average quality of people consuming the action (denoted $\hat{\theta}$) and the quality of the individual (denoted θ_i). This value function is a reduced form that is meant to capture the signaling value of the action. Assuming that $W(.\,,.)$ is monotonic with respect to individual quality, equilibria will be defined with a marginal individual, denoted with θ^*, who is indifferent over taking the action, namely, $W(\theta^*,\hat{\theta}) = 0$.

We can discuss two possible equilibria. First, if $\partial W/\partial \theta_i$ is always greater than zero, then only individuals with quality greater than θ^* will take this action. In this case, an increase in the number of individuals who are taking the action (i.e., a reduction in θ^*) will lead to a reduction in the average quality level and an overall reduction of demand for the action. In this case, social interactions will lower variation in levels of the action over space. If $\partial W/\partial \theta_i$ is everywhere negative, then only individuals with quality less than θ^* will take the action. An increase in the number of people taking the action will raise θ^* and increase demand for the action. In this case, social interactions are positive. The implication is that social interactions should be particularly important in generating large variances across time and space for actions that stigmatize rather than elevate.[3]

A second type of stigma model involves a community norm of behavior where deviations are punished by the community (the rationality of this punishment strategy is generated by repeated game or Folk theoremlike arguments). This community norm may serve to eliminate negative externalities from particular types of behavior. In this case, as more people participate in the action, fewer people become available to participate in the punishment and the costs of deviation become smaller. Again, a positive social interaction occurs because costs decline with the number of individuals taking the action.

A variety of literature has also argued for the possibility that interactions enter directly into the utility function. Bernheim (1994) argued for a taste for conformity where individuals experience a loss in utility just for deviating from the norms of the crowd. Akerlof (1997) examines a more general set of preferences where social choices enter into the utility function. Clearly, if the number of users of a commodity enters directly into one's taste for a commodity, then there will be social interactions.

Much of the more casual discussion of these taste-based preferences often hinges upon people adopting the norms of behavior from others. For example, individuals think that certain types of behavior are "acceptable" because they see others also following these forms of behavior. By and large these stories can often be captured well with learning models where agents learn optimal behavior from their neighbors or with community-punishment type models. However, some observers tend to think that there is too much adherence to learned community norms to be justified by this type of model.

One alternative model assumes that individuals maximize a utility function that is the sum of utility from standard consumption and from one's living up to one's ideal self (this follows a long Freudian literature and is close to Akerlof and Kranton 1997), or $Utility = U(X) + V(Z,\bar{Z})$, where X represents standard consumption variables and Z is a stock variable that captures one's identity (i.e., Z could include years of education or not being a liar or being thin).

There exists a vast variety of things that individuals could care about being like (i.e., in principle anything could influence Z), so in practice parental and community norms must then determine which norms matter. In the utility function, this is accomplished with the $\bar{Z}$ term that is meant to capture the inputs from outside sources that determine which actions individuals should base their self-image upon (i.e., how important is it to be hard-working or clever or attractive or decent).

Social interactions occur because through learning this ideal behavior, individuals influence each other. Natural examples of this type of effect occur in crowd behavior where individuals seem to completely forego what is commonly thought of as civilized behavior because they are sanctioned by the crowd (see, e.g., the extensive literature on the motivation of Nazis).

Of course, in any of these taste-based theories we must try to understand what function these tastes would be playing in an evolutionary setup. Evolution should optimally just give individuals the actual evolutionary utility function (maximize DNA propagation) and enough intelligence to do this well. Clearly evolution isn't able to do this exactly, and every set of combinations of tastes and computing ability is some solution to a second-best problem. Interdependent preferences, if they exist, are surely solving some evolutionary problem. In particular, they may be acting to help get the optimal degree of social learning. However, without a better idea of the costs that stymie evolution just making people optimal social learners, we cannot tell why this particular form of utility would have evolved.

4.3   A Simple Model of Local Interactions

The following model description somewhat generalizes the model in the text of Glaeser, Sacerdote, and Scheinkman (1996) in allowing for a richer action space on the part of individuals. Individual i now chooses an action $A(i)$ from a subset of the line. Individuals are arranged on a one-dimensional lattice (a circle or line), and the choice of an individual's action is based entirely on his own taste for the action and for imitating his predecessor on the line. More precisely, a measure of individuals $(1 - \pi)$ receive sufficient utility from copying their predecessor that they will imitate exactly their predecessor's actions. The remaining individuals will choose their action independently; we will refer to these individuals as fixed agents. The mean action taken by these fixed agents is μ_A and the variance is σ_A^2.

If the probability of being a fixed agent is i.i.d. over the lattice, then in the equilibrium of this model two agents who are separated by K other agents will either do exactly the same thing if there are no fixed agents between them (which occurs with probability $(1 - \pi)^K$) or choose their actions independently if there is a fixed agent between them (which occurs with probability $1 - (1 - \pi)^K$). Thus, the covariance between two such agents equals $(1 - \pi)^K$ times σ_A^2. Using this fact, elementary algebra reveals that the sum of the city's actions, when divided by the square root of the city size, satisfies

$$\frac{1}{\sqrt{N}}\sum_{i=1}^{N}(A(i)-\mu_A)\xrightarrow{N\to\infty}N\left(0,\frac{2-\pi}{\pi}\sigma_A^2\right). \tag{1}$$

This implies that the variance of normalized city averages will go to σ_A^2 in the case where there are only fixed agents or go to infinity in the case where there are no fixed agents.

4.3.1 An Alternate Model

An alternative and equivalently simple model, which is somewhat more appealing in its assumptions about individual behavior, but is somewhat less appealing in its restrictions on the action space assumes that the action space is the real line. In this case, we can assume that individuals' utility is a function of their own tastes, their actions, and their predecessors' actions:

$$U(A_i, A_{i-1}, \Theta_i) = \Theta_i A_i - \frac{1-\alpha}{2}A_i^2 - \frac{\alpha}{2}(A_i - A_{i-1})^2, \tag{2}$$

so that the marginal utility of the action for individual i is directly influenced by an idiosyncratic taste shock Θ_i, and by his neighbors' action, A_{i-1}. In order to incorporate observable individual characteristics into the formula, we define $\Theta_i = \theta_i + f(X_i)$, where θ_i has mean zero and variance σ_θ^2 (which is constant across cities), and X_i is the individual's set of observable characteristics that may include individual level characteristics (e.g., age and gender) and city-level characteristics (e.g., spending on welfare). We write $\overline{f(X)}$ for the mean level of the function $f(.)$ and $\overline{f(X)}_j$ for the mean level of the function $f(.)$ in city j.

In this case, the individual's action is defined by $A_i = \theta_i + f(X_i) + \alpha A_{i-1}$, or equivalently

$$A_i - \overline{A}_j = \theta_i + f(X_i) - \overline{f(X)}_j + \alpha(A_{i-1} - \overline{A}_j), \tag{3}$$

where $\overline{A}_j$ is the mean action level in city j. The variance of an individual's actions can be found by noting that equation (3) and the fact that conditional on city j, $f(X_i)$ is independent of A_{i-1} (this uses our assumption that there is no sorting across neighborhoods within cities):

$$Var(A_i - \overline{A}_j) = \sigma_\theta^2 + Var_j^{f(X)} + \alpha^2 Var(A_{i-1} - \overline{A}_j) = \frac{\sigma_\theta^2 + Var_j^{f(X)}}{1 - \alpha^2}, \tag{4}$$

since in equilibrium $Var(A_i - \overline{A}_j) = Var(A_{i-1} - \overline{A}_j)$, and where $Var_j^{f(X)}$ refers to the variance of $f(X)$ within city j. As long as the X variables are independently distributed, then the correlation coefficient between individuals who are separated by K other individuals is now α^K. As N grows large, a version of equation (1) again holds:

$$Var\left(\frac{1}{\sqrt{N}} \sum_{i=1}^{N}\left(A(i) - \frac{\overline{f(X)}_j}{1 - \alpha}\right)\right) \xrightarrow{N \to \infty} \frac{\sigma_\theta^2 + Var_j^{f(X)}}{(1 - \alpha)^2}. \tag{5}$$

In general, we will assume that $Var_j^{f(X)}$ is constant across cities.

In order to determine the underlying parameters, if the econometrician observed the variance of

$$\frac{1}{\sqrt{N}} \sum_{i=1}^{N}\left(A(i) - \frac{\overline{f(X)}_j}{1 - \alpha}\right) \text{ (denoted } Var_{agg})$$

and the population variance of A within cities (denoted Var_{ind}—which is assumed to be constant across cities), then it is clear that in the limit

$$\alpha = \frac{Var_{agg} - Var_{ind}}{Var_{agg} + Var_{ind}},$$

and given our estimate of α and $Var_j^{f(X)}$, it is possible to estimate σ_θ^2.

This model requires more modification for discrete action spaces. One interpretation is to assume that there is a latent continuous variable that expresses only in measurable discrete units. For example, individuals may choose a continuous quantity of criminality that displays itself in a discrete value, whether or not the individual has been arrested. Another example is that individuals choose a continuous level of sexual behavior that displays itself in the number of out-of-wedlock births. For this model to be technically correct, it must be true that neighbors observe and make their decisions based on the actual continuous variable, not the discrete outcome.

4.3.2   Methodological Discussion

The fundamental empirical idea of this methodology is to use the relationship between the variance of community-level aggregates and the variance of individual data to estimate the size of the social interactions. Our first step is to estimate the variance of action levels within cities. To do this, we allow for city-specific means and just estimate a common variance of the action around these city-specific means.

Next we assume the $f(X) = \beta'X$ and we estimate $\dfrac{\beta'}{1-\alpha}$ by regressing sample average action outcomes on sample average city-level characteristics (including state effects that should eliminate the effect of state-level laws and regulations.):

$$\hat{A}_j = \frac{\beta'\hat{X}_j}{1-\alpha} + \varepsilon_j. \tag{6}$$

Using the predicted value from this regression, we obtain a value of $\dfrac{\beta'\hat{X}_j}{1-\alpha}$. With these estimates, the predicted levels of outcomes across cities based on city-level variables, we can estimate the variance of

$$\frac{1}{\sqrt{N}} \sum_{i=1}^{N} \left(A(i) - \frac{\overline{f(X)}_j}{1-\alpha} \right).$$

This aggregate variance and the individual variance are sufficient to estimate α.

If we are interested in differentiating between variance caused by observables ($Var_j^{f(X)}$) and variance caused by idiosyncratic tastes (σ_θ^2), we must then assume that there is no sorting within the city. Then we can estimate the regression using the 1990 Census Public Use Micro Sample to estimate a regression of the form $A_i = City\ Fixed\ Effect + \beta'X_i + \varepsilon_i$. The city fixed effect will eliminate any bias that comes from differential sorting of individuals across cities.[4] With this regression, we have now estimated the coefficients β, on individual-level characteristics. Given these coefficients, we form a value of $\beta'X$ for the all individuals and we can calculate the value of $Var_j^{f(X)}$, by calculating the variance of this predicted action level within cities.

4.3.3 Some Results

Table 4.1 presents our first set of results for female-headed household rates. This variable represents the share of all families that are headed by a woman. This can be thought of as roughly the share of women who "choose" to have a family without a husband, conditional upon

Table 4.1
Estimation of Strength of Social Interactions Affecting Female Headship Rates
in Families

	Var_{ind}	Var_{agg}	α[a]
Unadjusted female headship rate[b]	0.134	171.53	0.998
Rate controlling for city-level observables[c]	0.132	52.09	0.995
Rate controlling for state effects and city-level observables[d]	0.132	19.52	0.987

Source: Individual-level data are from the 1990 Census Public Use Micro Sample. Aggregate data are from the 1990 Census Summary Tape Files.

a. $\alpha = \dfrac{Var_{agg} - Var_{ind}}{Var_{agg} + Var_{ind}}$.

b. Var_{ind} is the individual-level variance. It is the raw variance of the female headship rate among families in the United States. Var_{agg} is the adjusted variance of the city aggregate rate. It is the variance of $\sqrt{N_c}(A_c - \overline{A})$ where N_c is the number of families in the city, A_c is the average action in the city, and $\overline{A}$ is the average action in the United States.

c. The individual variance is the variance of the female headship rate, controlling for city fixed effects. The aggregate variance is the variance of

$$\sqrt{N_c}\left(A_c - \frac{\beta' X_c}{1-\alpha}\right),$$

where $\dfrac{\beta_c}{1-\alpha}$ is estimated from a city-level regression of A_c on median family income, the number of people under age 18 per family, and on the fraction of the population of families that is black, Hispanic, a high school dropout, a college graduate, in poverty, and headed by someone aged 15–24, 25–34, 35–44, 55–64, or 65–100. All variables are defined for the population of family heads except the education variables, which are defined for the population over 18 years old.

d. The individual variance is the variance of the female headship rate controlling for city fixed effects. The aggregate variance in this row is calculated in the same way as in the second row of the table except that every raw variable is replaced with its deviation from the state mean.

choosing to have a family (there are very few male-headed households without a woman). All of our data comes from the 1990 census summary tape files. Our unit of observation is the metropolitan statistical area (MSA or when applicable the primary metropolitan statistical area).

Our goal is to estimate α—the parameter that captures the degree of social interaction. This basic formula for this parameter is that

$$\alpha = \frac{Var_{agg} - Var_{ind}}{Var_{agg} + Var_{ind}},$$

where Var_{agg} and Var_{ind} are the aggregate- and individual-level variances described above.

The first row in table 4.1 shows the individual- and aggregate-level variances when no observables are allowed as control variables. The individual-level variance is the variance from a national mean. In this case we find an α value of 0.998, which is extremely close to one and quite far from zero.

The second row shows results where we have controlled for city-level variables in calculating the city aggregate variance and calculated the individual-level variances from a city-level mean. A wide battery of city-level variables have been included that are described in the table. While many of these variables may be endogenous, our goal is to control for as much as possible rather than to include only exogenous variables. Both the individual variance and the aggregate variance decline, but the aggregate variance declines by much more. The estimate of α thus falls to 0.995, which still represents quite sizable levels of social interaction. This level of α implies that the actions of individuals who are separated by one hundred other individuals have a correlation coefficient of 0.606.

The third row gives results where we calculate the aggregate variance controlling for city-level variables and state-level fixed effects. These state-level fixed effects should control for any omitted state-level legal variables affecting this outcome variable. As expected, the aggregate variance declines substantially, beyond our controls for city-level variables. The individual-level variance is still estimated around city-level means, and the overall value of α declines to 0.987, which implies that the correlation coefficient of actions of individuals who are separated by one hundred other individuals is 0.27.

4.3.4 An Aside on Multidimensional Interaction Models

Glaeser, Sacerdote, and Scheinkman (1996) presents a variant on the voter model of physics (e.g., Kindermann and Snell 1980). Agents were located at points on a one-dimensional lattice and chose one of two possible actions. In our model, there were fixed agents who choose their actions at random. The other type, imitative agents, copied the action of one of their two neighbors with equal probability. Without fixed agents, the voter model in one (or two) dimensions produces unanimity in the long run and this unanimity is clearly inaccurate empirically for many variables. More precisely, suppose the agents are in Z_d, the set of points in R^d with integer coordinates, and that each agent chooses at time t, an action $a_i^t \in \{0,1\}$. At time zero, each agent chooses an action that is independent of other agents with $\mathrm{Prob}\{\alpha_i^t = 1\} = p$. The neighbors of an agent $i \in Z_d$ are given by $N(i) = \{j \in Z_d: \max_{l=1,\ldots,d}|i^l - j^l| = 1\}$. For each $i \in Z_d$ there exists a Poisson process P_i with rate γ with P_i independent of P_j and such that at each epoch τ, the agent revises his action. Assume in addition that if agent i revises his action, then $a_i^\tau = a_j^\tau$ with probability $1/(\#N(i))$ for each $j \in N(i)$. That is, i copies the action of one of his neighbors at each epoch τ. If $d = 1$, 2 for any $i \in Z_d$, $j \in Z_d$ there exists an $\varepsilon > 0$ and a T such that if $t > T$, $\mathrm{Prob}\{a_i^t = a_i^t\} > 1 - \varepsilon$. In other words, in one or two dimensions, agents behavior will eventually be unanimous.

However, if $d \geq 3$, unanimity no longer holds and there exists a stationary measure $\mu(p)$ and

$$\text{if } S_n = \sum\nolimits_{|i| \leq n} \frac{a_i - p}{\left((2n+1)^d\right)^{1/2+1/d}}, \text{ then } S_n \rightarrow N[0, \sigma^2].$$

This formula suggests that empirically one could in principle estimate the number of dimensions that explain the observed variance of group-level average actions. The larger the dimension of the interactions, the lower is the exponent $(1/2 + 1/d)$ that must be used to normalize to get a normal distribution. In the limit as d grows, the exponent approaches $1/2$. Thus, the higher-dimension lattices increasingly resemble the case where decisions are independent. Intuitively, sufficiently large amounts of interaction eliminate the tendency of interaction to produce all-or-nothing out-comes. Another way of generating scaling rules other than scaling by $1/2$ involves models with long spatial dependency (Glaeser and Scheinkman 1997).

4.4 Combining Local and Global Interactions

In this case, we assume that utility depends both upon the actions of a neighbor and of the community as a whole. The community average can either increase or decrease the incentives to engage in the particular level of behavior. A globally high level of crime may mean that many voters are criminals who do not want to pay for police expenditures. Alternatively, a high communitywide level of crime may reduce the incentives to engage in crime. Also perhaps, as more people are criminals, there may be fewer potential victims, so the returns to crime in the community may fall (again this is only a global interaction if criminals choose their victims from a global rather than a local pool).

To treat global interactions formally, we again assume that action levels are continuous and that individuals choose their actions treating the global levels as exogenous to maximize:

$$U\left(A_i, A_{i-1}, \frac{\sum_{\ell \neq i} A_\ell}{n}, \Theta_i\right) = \Theta_i A_i - \frac{1-\alpha}{2} A_i^2 - \frac{\alpha\varphi}{2}(A_i - A_{i-1})^2$$
$$- \frac{\alpha(1-\varphi)}{2}\left(A_i - g\left(\frac{\sum_{\ell \neq i} A_\ell}{n}\right)\right)^2 \tag{7}$$

which implies

$$A_i = \Theta_i + \alpha\varphi A_{i-1} + \alpha(1-\varphi)g\left(\frac{\sum_{\ell \neq i} A_\ell}{n}\right). \tag{8}$$

Both α and φ are strictly less than one and greater than zero (when $\varphi = 1$ this is the pure local interactions model discussed above). As before to make the system symmetric $A_0 = A_n$. We will also treat two separate assumptions about the taste shocks. First, we assume that $\Theta_i = \theta_i$ where θ_i is i.i.d., with a mean that we normalize to zero and variance σ_θ^2. Second, we assume that $\Theta_i = \theta_i + f(X_i)$, where θ_i is again i.i.d. with mean zero and variance σ_θ^2, and X refers to observable characteristics of the individual. In both cases, the variable Θ_i is assumed to have a bounded support. The function $g(.)$ is bounded and continuously differentiable with a bounded derivative.

For any given sequence $\{\Theta_i\}_{i=1}^n$, we can define a function $F: R^n \to R^n$ that maps the vector $(A_0, \ldots, A_{n-1})$ by

$$F(A_0, \ldots, A_{n-1}) = \left(\Theta_i + \alpha\varphi A_0 + \alpha(1-\varphi)g\left(\frac{\sum_{\ell \neq i} A_\ell}{n}\right), \ldots, \Theta_n + \alpha\varphi A_{n-1}\right.$$
$$\left. + \alpha(1-\varphi)g\left(\frac{\sum_{\ell \neq n} A_\ell}{n}\right)\right). \tag{9}$$

Here $A_0 = A_n$. As $\alpha < 1$, $\varphi < 1$, and $g(.)$ is bounded, the function will have at least one fixed point that will solve equation (5). In general, however, there is no guarantee that this fixed point is unique. It is entirely possible that multiple solutions exist for equation (8). Further, the optimal action of agent i depends on the total population size n, and we denote this dependence by writing A_i^n for the action taken by individual i.

Summing equation (8) and writing $\hat{A}_n = \dfrac{\sum_{i=1}^{n} A_i^n}{n}$, we find

$$(1-\alpha\phi)\hat{A}_n - \frac{\alpha(1-\phi)}{n}\sum_{i=1}^{n}\left[g\left(\frac{\sum_{k\neq i} A_k^n}{n-1}\right)\right] = \frac{\sum_{i=1}^{n}\Theta_i}{n}. \tag{10}$$

Further iteration of equation (8) yields

$$A_i^n = \alpha^i\phi^i A_0 + \sum_{\ell=1}^{i}\alpha^{i-\ell}\phi^{i-\ell}\left[\Theta_j + \alpha(1-\phi)g\left(\frac{\sum_{k\neq\ell} A_k^n}{n}\right)\right]. \tag{11}$$

At this point, we will separate our discussion into two sections, based on our two assumptions about Θ.

Case 1: $\Theta_i = \theta_i$

We will assume that there are a finite number of solutions to the equation

$$g(x) = \frac{1-\alpha\varphi}{\alpha(1-\varphi)}x$$

and that at each such solution

$$g'(x) \neq \frac{1-\alpha\varphi}{\alpha(1-\varphi)}.$$

This is a "generic" assumption.

In the appendix, we show that the sequence $\hat{A}_n$, of average actions in a population of size n, converges, as $n \to \infty$, to a solution of the equation

$$g(\overline{A}) = \frac{1-\alpha\varphi}{\alpha(1-\varphi)}\overline{A}. \tag{12}$$

We denote $a_i^n = A_i^n - \overline{A}$, and we also show in the appendix that

$$\sum_{i=1}^{n}\frac{a_i^n}{\sqrt{n}} \to N\left(0, \frac{\sigma_\theta^2}{(1-\alpha\varphi-\alpha(1-\varphi)g'(\overline{A}))^2}\right). \tag{13}$$

Within city variance (using equation 8) is $\sigma_\theta^2/(1 - \alpha^2\varphi^2)$. It is somewhat meaningless to try to determine between the effects of α, φ, and $g'(\overline{A})$, but even if we attempt to distinguish between σ_θ^2, and $\alpha(1 - \varphi)g'(\overline{A})$, it is impossible to do so without more information. Essentially we have three variables and only two equations.

If we had an additional variable, for example the covariance of actions of individual i and $i - 1$ within a city, then we could back out these three variables. Within a given city, $\text{cov}(A_i, A_{i-1}) = \alpha\varphi \text{Var}(A_{i-1}) = \dfrac{a\varphi\sigma_\theta^2}{1 - a^2\varphi^2}$. This covariance can be found either directly (if microdata is available) or by city subaggregates (i.e., neighborhood level averages). In this case, $\alpha\varphi$ equals the correlation coefficient of two neighbor's actions, and by using the variance, σ_θ^2 can be found. With these two parameters, it is possible to determine the size of the global interaction by looking at variances across cities.

Alternatively, one could identify the model by examining the variance of neighborhood-level averages within a single city. If a neighborhood has size h, then conditioning on the city level mean,

$$Var\left(\frac{\sum_{j=i}^{i+h} A_j}{\sqrt{h}}\right) = \frac{\sigma_\theta^2}{(1 - \alpha\varphi)^2}.$$

The only difference between this expression and equation (13) is that all neighborhoods within a city are affected by the same global interaction term, so there are no terms involving $g'(A)$.

If it is desirable to control for observables and still use this simpler framework, a simple assumption is that observed action $Y = A + f(X)$, where Y is the observed action and $f(X)$ is a function of observables. Thus A can be inferred by subtracting $f(X)$ from Y, if $f(X)$ is known (and given our assumption, there is no reason why it cannot be estimated from either micro-level or aggregate-level regressions). All of the statements about A are unchanged with this assumption. Empirically, it is necessary to work with $Y - f(X)$, the residuals from a first stage regression. This framework allows for a simple manner of controlling for observables. However, it is not satisfying in that we are assuming that one's influence on one's neighbors is only a function of unobservable factors. The next section introduces a more complicated setup, where we allow observables to influence neighbors.

Case 2: $\Theta_i = \theta_i + f(X_i)$

In this case, we assume that taste shocks contain an individual-specific, i.i.d. component, a component that is based on an individual's observable characteristics, and a component based on city-level characteristics (which may include both individual-specific and city-specific attributes). We assume that Θ_i has a second moment. Using a similar logic to the one used in case 1, and making an analogous assumption concerning the finiteness of the set of solutions to the equation $(1 - \alpha\varphi)x - \alpha(1 - \varphi)g(x) = \overline{f(X)}_j$ one can show that, in the limit, the mean level of the action in city j must satisfy

$$(1 - \alpha\varphi)\overline{A}_j - \alpha(1 - \varphi)g(\overline{A}_j) = \overline{f(X)}_j. \tag{14}$$

Equation (14) typically has many solutions for each value of $\overline{f(X)}_j$. From now on, we condition on a "branch" of the solution and note that except for a finite set of values of $\overline{f(X)}_j$, the solutions will vary smoothly with $\overline{f(X)}_j$ within each branch. Importantly, for each value of $\overline{A}_j$, there exists at most one $\overline{f(X)}_j$ that solves the equation. Thus, in principle one can estimate $\overline{f(X)}_j$ as a function of $\overline{A}_j$.

Using the implicit function theorem and differentiating (14) implies

$$\frac{\partial \overline{f(X)}_j}{\partial \overline{A}_j} = (1 - \alpha\varphi) - \alpha(1 - \varphi)g'(\overline{A}_j). \tag{15}$$

Thus the derivative of predicted value with respect to outcome level will yield an estimate of $(1 - \alpha\varphi) - \alpha(1 - \varphi)g'(\overline{A})$. The connection between realized outcome and predicted outcome based on microlevel variation gives us an estimate of the extent to which there are spillovers.

If we assume that the distribution of X is constant across neighborhoods such that the average level of $f(X)$ in each neighborhood within city j is $\overline{f(X)}_j$, then

$$Var\left(\sum_{i=1}^{h} \frac{A_i - \overline{A}_j}{\sqrt{h}}\right) \to \frac{\sigma_\theta^2 + Var_j^{f(X)}}{(1 - \alpha\varphi)^2}, \tag{16}$$

where h again indexes the members of the neighborhood. Furthermore, the variance of action levels within the city will again equal $\dfrac{\sigma_\theta^2 + Var_j^{f(X)}}{1 - (\alpha\varphi)^2}$. The variance of neighborhoods and the variance of individual level actions within cities allows us to identify $\alpha\varphi$. Thus, as we learn $(1 - \alpha\varphi) - \alpha(1 - \varphi)g'(\overline{A}_j)$ from the aggregate regressions, we are able to separate the extent to which spillovers come from local and global sources, after we condition in an equilibrium.

Unfortunately, this approach requires us to assume that there is no sorting by observables across neighborhoods. If we actually were able to run individual-level regressions within cities with neighborhood-level fixed effects, we could then drop this assumption. Then we could note that $(1 - \alpha\varphi)(\overline{A}_h - \overline{A}_j) = \overline{f(X)}_h - \overline{f(X)}_j$, where quantities with the h subscript indicate neighborhood-level outcomes. The relationship between predicted outcomes and actual outcomes then provide a separate estimate of $(1 - \alpha\varphi)$.

4.4.1   A Discrete Version

Since many of our variables are discrete, it makes sense to consider an analogous model where only two actions $\{0, 1\}$ are possible. For simplicity we only describe the model in the case without observables. In this case, assume that a city has n agents on a circle. With probability α, agent i bases his actions exclusively on the actions of agent $i - 1$, and we again identify agent zero with agent n. With probability $1 - \alpha$, agent i bases his action on the global average. In this case, the probability that agent i chooses action 1 is given by $g\left(\dfrac{\sum_{j\neq i} A_j}{n-1}\right)$ where $g(.)$ is a continuously differentiable function defined for $x \in [0, 1]$ with $1 > g(x) > 0$. Following a similar reasoning to that of the previous model, we may conclude that the average action in a city must converge as $n \to \infty$ to some solution of the equation $\overline{A} = g(\overline{A})$. Furthermore, the variance of normalized city-level averages satisfies

$$Var\left(\frac{\sum_{j=i}^{i+n} a_j}{\sqrt{n}}\right) = \frac{1+\alpha}{1-\alpha} \times \frac{\overline{A}(1-\overline{A})}{1-g'(\overline{A})}.$$

The variance of normalized neighborhood-level averages

$$Var\left(\frac{\sum_{j=i}^{i+n} a_j}{\sqrt{h}}\right) = \frac{1+\alpha}{1-\alpha}\overline{A}(1-\overline{A}).$$

Of course, the variance of any one individuals action is $\overline{A}(1 - \overline{A})$. These three equations allow us to empirically identify the model. We will estimate the parameters for discrete variables as if they were continuous variables in the next section, but more properly discrete variables need to be treated differently using this particular formulation.

4.4.2 Empirical Implementation

This section employs two distinct methodologies. The first methodology assumes that observable variables do not create spillovers and can just be controlled for and then ignored. The second methodology assumes that observable variables create their own spillovers. For both methodologies, we can estimate the value of $(1 - \alpha\varphi)$ by using the micro-level variance and the variance of neighborhood averages. If we assume that the observables can just be subtracted, we begin by regressing outcomes on observables (in a micro-level regression) and then using those coefficients to subtract the effect of observables from any aggregate.

Methodology 1—Social Influence Comes Only from Unpredictable Elements of Decisions
The first methodology relies upon the assumption that we can ignore the effect of observables on social interactions. In this case, we first regress our micro-outcome variable (does the family have a single head?) on a battery of family-level characteristics including city-level fixed effects. This regression furnishes us with estimates of the effect of observable characteristics on the outcome variable, and using these estimates we correct tract-level and city-level outcome variables for observable characteristics. As discussed earlier, because of sorting across cities, observable characteristics may be correlated with the action of one's neighbors and as such either city-level regressions or micro-level regressions that do not control for city-level fixed effects may well be biased. Of course, we are unrealistically forced to assume that there is no sorting within cities.

Thus, all further procedures within this methodology are done using corrected female-headed household rates where the effect of observable characteristics has been eliminated (except for the row marked Raw Female Headship Rate in Families and table 4.2a). Using the corrected city-level female headship rates, we then determine how much of the variance across cities can be plausibly explained by the existence

Table 4.2a
Female Headship Rate of Families
Multiple Equilibria Model[a] (Three-Component Distribution Is Optimal)

	Components of Distribution of Adjusted City Female Headship Rates of Families					Average Aggregate Variance[b]	$g'(\overline{A})\alpha(1-\varphi)$[c]
	First	Second	Third	Fourth	Fifth		
Mean	-2.93					171.02	0.0250
Variance	171.02						
Weight	1.00						
Means	-4.58	15.740				139.89	0.0250
Variances	55.50	1097.40					
Weights	0.92	0.08					
Means	-3.35	-5.17	32.75			126.98	0.0250
Variances	120.77	12.52	1680.20				
Weights	0.55	0.42	0.03				
Means	-5.02	-5.04	3.75	142.50		96.06	0.0250
Variances	77.76	12.17	307.44	0			
Weights	0.42	0.38	0.19	0			
Means	-8.18	-5.32	-1.96	4.38	142.50	89.32	0.0250
Variances	71.40	10.22	46.21	306.07	0		
Weights	0.25	0.31	0.25	0.19	0		

Source: 1990 Census Summary Tape Files.
a. The adjusted PMSA female headship rate defined as $\sqrt{N_c}(A_c - \overline{A})$ where N_c is the city population of families, A_c is the city female headship rate among families, and $\overline{A}$ is female headship rate in the United States, is modeled as a random variable distributed as a mixture of normals. The mixtures are estimated using the EM algorithm. The Akaike Information Criterion is minimized by the three-component distribution.
b. The average aggregate variance is the weighted average of the variances of the components of the overall distribution.
c. As in Table 4.3, $g'(A)\alpha(1-\varphi) = 1 - \alpha\varphi - \sigma_\theta^2/Var_{city}$. $\alpha\varphi$ and σ_θ^2 are estimated in row 1 of table 4.3, and Var_{city} is the average aggregate variance calculated in this table.

Table 4.2b
Female Headship Rate of Families: Controlling for Individual Traits and City Fixed Effects Multiple Equilibria Model[a] (Three-Component Distribution Is Optimal)

	Components of Distribution of Adjusted City Female Headship Rates of Families					Average Aggregate Variance[b]	$g'(\overline{A})\alpha(1-\varphi)$[c]
	First	Second	Third	Fourth	Fifth		
Mean	-2.72					83.44	0.0728
Variance	83.44						
Weight	1.00						
Means	-4.77	5.35				66.49	0.0728
Variances	22.60	242.07					
Weights	0.80	0.20					
Means	0.90	-4.99	55.75			56.72	0.0727
Variances	126.15	16.98	497.29				
Weights	0.32	0.67	0.01				
Means	-3.33	-4.88	18.65	51.73		42.51	0.0726
Variances	63.07	11.00	15.03	541.84			
Weights	0.50	0.45	0.04	0.01			
Means	-3.42	-9.35	-4.44	18.61	51.74	41.88	0.0726
Variances	61.33	1.38	8.45	15.12	541.72		
Weights	0.53	0.04	0.39	0.04	0.01		

Source: 1990 Census Summary Tape Files.

a. The adjusted PMSA female headship rate controlling for individual traits and city fixed effects is defined as $\sqrt{N_c}(\hat{A}_c - \hat{A})$ as in row 2 of table 4.3. This random variable is modeled as a random variable distributed as a mixture of normals. The mixtures are estimated using the EM algorithm. The Akaike Information Criterion is minimized by the three-component distribution.

b. The average aggregate variance is the weighted average of the variances of the components of the overall distribution.

c. As in table 4.3, $g'(\overline{A})\alpha(1-\varphi) = 1 - \alpha\varphi - \sigma_\theta^2 Var_{city}$. $\alpha\varphi$ and σ_θ^2 are estimated in row 2 of table 4.3, and Var_{city} is the average aggregate variance calculated in this table.

Table 4.2c
Female Headship Rate of Families Controlling for Individual Traits and State Effects Multiple Equilibria Model[a] (Two-Component Distribution Is Optimal)

	Components of Distribution of Adjusted City Female Headship Rates of Families					Average Aggregate Variance[b]	$g'(\bar{A})\alpha(1-\varphi)$[c]
	First	Second	Third	Fourth	Fifth		
Mean	-1.98					36.12	0.0726
Variance	36.12						
Weight	1.00						
Means	-2.81	1.03				33.76	0.0726
Variances	8.97	121.67					
Weights	0.78	0.22					
Means	-0.48	-2.92	50.59			26.54	0.0724
Variances	67.86	7.10	0				
Weights	0.32	0.68	0				
Means	-2.62	-3.03	-0.46	50.59		26.62	0.0724
Variances	9.96	6.08	69.34	0			
Weights	0.24	0.45	0.31	0			
Means	-14.51	-8.71	-2.95	0.41	23.10	21.57	0.0723
Variances	16.39	0.16	6.57	46.29	347.86		
Weights	0.02	0.01	0.66	0.29	0.01		

Source: 1990 Census Summary Tape Files.
a. The adjusted PMSA female headship rate controlling for individual traits and state effects is defined as $\sqrt{N_c}(\hat{A}_c - \hat{A})$ as in row 3 of table 4.2. This random variable is modeled as a random variable distributed as a mixture of normals. The mixtures are estimated using the EM algorithm. The Akaike Information Criterion is minimized by the two component distribution.
b. The average aggregate variance is the weighted average of the variances of the components of the overall distribution.
c. As in table 4.3, $g'(\bar{A})\alpha(1-\varphi) = 1 - \alpha\varphi - \sigma_\theta^2/Var_{city}$, $\alpha\varphi$ and σ_θ^2 are estimated in row 3 of table 4.3, and Var_{city} is the average aggregate variance calculated in this table.

Table 4.2d
Parameter Estimates for Global vs. Local Interactions Model

	$\alpha\varphi$	σ_θ^2	$g'(\overline{A})\alpha(1 - \varphi)$
Female headship rate in families	0.905775	0.001737	0.247777
Fraction of population over 5 in same house as 1985	0.991719	0.000017	0.004193
Unemployment Rate	0.959802	0.000093	0.076921
Fraction not in labor force	0.983460	0.000061	−0.015368
Fraction on welfare	0.978419	0.000030	0.061562
Fraction in poverty	0.992624	0.000011	0.014454
Fraction of housing owner occupied	0.992535	0.000012	0.026431
Number of cars	−0.921217	16280.685916	−1.091941
Average rent	0.9999996172960	0.00000000000015	0.000002

Source: Aggregate estimates are from the 1990 Census PMSA data. Individual estimates are from the 1990 Census Public Use Microsample.
Note: Variable of interest is sqrt(city population)*(city-level rate − country-level mean).

of multiple equilibria (of normalized city averages) and how much can be determined by the variance of cities within each of these equilibria. While the variance created by the multiple equilibria is not the only variance due to global interactions, in our model it represents one component of the global interactions.

Of course, this result is due to the assumption that the global interaction may be nonlinear while the local interaction is linear. If the global interaction were linear, then it could not generate multiple equilibria. If the local interaction were nonlinear, then even in the absence of global interactions multiple equilibria could still exist. Perhaps it is therefore wiser to interpret the amount of variance created by multiple equilibria as the variance associated with nonlinearities in the interaction process rather than as the outcome of global interactions.

We allow for the presence of multiple equilibria by using the EM algorithm to fit a mixture of normal distributions to the observed distribution of corrected city-level headship rates. Tables 4.2a, 4.2b and 4.2c show the results of estimating multiple equilibria via the EM algorithm for female-headed household rates. This algorithm allows us to estimate that each city is drawn from up to five distributions with different means and standard deviations. Since the data is always fit better by more distributions, a loss function must be specified so that we allow more distributions only if a sufficiently large amount of explanatory power is generated by allowing for an extra distribution. We implement this loss function using the Akaike Information Criterion, which allows us to compare across numbers of distributions to determine which one gives us the most explanatory power relative to its criterion.

In table 4.2a, we estimate the number of distributions for percent of households that are female-headed without any additional controls. In this case, the Akaike Information Criterion is minimized with three component distributions. The first distributions, which contains 55 percent of the cities, has a low mean and a variance roughly comparable to the aggregate variance. The second distribution has 42 percent of the distribution and a much lower variance, which leads to a correspondingly lower value of social interactions for this group. The third distribution has only 3 percent of the cities, but it also has an extremely high mean and variance.

In table 4.2b we again control for city-level variables in estimating the aggregate variance term. The EM algorithm is used on the distribution of female-headed household rates across cities after we have first orthogonalized these rates to a battery of city level characteristics. In this case, the three-component distribution again minimizes the Akaike Information Criterion. In table 4.2c, we orthogonalize city-level female headed household rates with respect to city-level variables and with respect to state-level fixed effects. The average aggregate variance is reduced much less by allowing for the presence of multiple equilibria. In this case, the Akaike Information Criterion is minimized with two component distributions. The first distribution has 78 percent of the cities and the second distribution has 22 percent of the cities.

Once we have estimated the number of distributions that best fit the data, we use the variance of the city-level aggregates around each distribution to estimate the degree of local and global interactions. Notice that the reduction in variance created by allowing the presence of multiple equilibria is already one sign that global equilibria matter. Table 4.2d shows the results from this procedure for female headship rates. We use the average city-level variance rather than the variance for each one of the component distributions in order to produce a single set of results. We use the three formulas

$$Var_{tract} = \frac{\sigma_\theta^2}{(1-\alpha\varphi)^2},$$

$$Var_{ind} = \frac{\sigma_\theta^2}{1 - \alpha^2 \varphi^2}, \text{ and}$$

$$Var_{city} = \frac{\sigma_\theta^2}{(1 - \alpha\varphi - \alpha(1-\varphi)g'(\overline{A}))^2}$$

to estimate the key parameters of the model: $\alpha\varphi$ (which captures the importance of local interactions) and $\alpha(1 - \varphi)g'(\overline{A})$ (which captures the importance of global interactions, after we condition in an equilibrium).

Our findings, shown in table 4.2d, are that allowing for multiple equilibria and global interactions substantially reduces the importance of local interactions in female headship rates. The value of $\alpha\varphi$ is comparable to the value of α in table 4.1, with only local interactions, and it is clear that including global interactions has lessened the importance of social interactions. However, after conditioning in an equilibrium, the importance of local interactions is much higher than the importance of global interactions. We find that an increase in your neighbor's action is more than twelve times more important than an increase in the city-level average (which is found by comparing $\alpha\varphi$—the effect of the neighbor—with $\alpha(1 - \varphi)g'(\overline{A})$ the effect of the city-level average). Of course, we are really differentiating between city-level and tract-level interactions, and we are referring to tract-level interactions as local interactions. It might be that tract-level interactions are not actually local as described by our model, namely, neighbor-to-neighbor. Instead, the tract-level interactions that we identify as local might occur equally across the tract, namely, individuals are influenced by the average level of behavior in their tract. Table 4.3 exhibits parameter estimates for global vs. local interaction models for several other variables.

Methodology 2—Allowing Control Variables to Influence Interactions

The previous methodology assumes that only the unpredictable component of actions creates social interactions. In this section, we rely upon the fact that the component of individuals' actions that are attributable to observable characteristics will have exactly the same social interaction effect as the components of individuals' actions that are not attributable to any observable characteristics. If observable characteristics influence neighbors, but not as strongly as unobservable charac-

Table 4.3
Female Headship Rate: Local vs. Global Interactions

	Var_{ind}	Var_{tract}	Var_{city}	$\alpha\varphi$[a]	σ_θ^{2}[a]	$g'(\overline{A})\alpha(1-\varphi)$[a]
Raw female headship rate in families[b]	0.134	10.74	171.53	0.975	0.0017	0.025
Female headship rate controlling for individual traits and city-fixed effects[c]	0.111	2.94	83.69	0.927	0.016	0.073
Female headship rate controlling for individual traits and state effects[d]	0.111	2.92	36.23	0.927	0.016	0.073

Source: 1990 Census Summary Tape Files and Public Use Microsample.

a. $\alpha\varphi = \dfrac{1 - Var_{ind}/Var_{tract}}{1 + Var_{ind}/Var_{tract}}$ $\sigma_\theta^{2} = Var_{ind}(1 - \alpha^2\varphi^2)$ $g'(\overline{A})\alpha(1-\varphi) = 1 - \alpha\varphi - \sigma_\theta^{2}/Var_{city}$

b. Var_{ind} is the individual variance from row 1 of table 4.1. Var_{tract} is the average across cities of the variance of adjusted tract averages: $\sqrt{N_t}(A_t - A_c)$ where N_t is the population of families in the tract, A_t is the female headship rate in the tract, and A_c is the average in the city. Var_{city} is the aggregate variance from row 1 of table 4.1.

c. Var_{ind} is the variance of the residual from the following microregression: $A_i = \beta'X_i + \varepsilon_i$, where A_i is the deviation of the female headship rate from the city mean and X_i is a vector of deviations of individual traits from city means. These traits include income and number of children and a set of dummies indicating whether the family head is Black, Hispanic, a high school dropout, a college graduate, aged 18–24, 25–34, 35–44, 55–64, 65–100, and in poverty. Var_{tract} is the average across cities of the within-city variance of $\sqrt{N_t}(\hat{A}_t - \hat{A}_c)$ where $\hat{A}_t = A_t - \beta'X_t$, $\hat{\beta}$ is the vector of parameter estimates from the micro-level regression, X_t is the vector of tract-level averages of individual traits (not deviated from city means), and $\hat{A}_c$ is the within-city average of $\hat{A}_t$. Finally, Var_{city} is the variance of $\sqrt{N_c}(\hat{A}_c - \hat{A})$ where, as for the tract-level variables, $\hat{A}_c = A_c - \beta'X_c$ and $\hat{A}$ is the national average of $\hat{A}_c$.

d. The variables in row 3 of the table are calculated in an analogous manner to those in row 2 except that the aggregate variances are calculated controlling for state fixed effects.

teristics, then neither one of these procedures is correct and some mixture of the two procedures is best.

Table 4.4 presents an estimation of the strength of global interactions for female headship rates. To estimate $\alpha\varphi$ we use exactly the same procedure as we did above. First we regress micro-outcomes on observables, and then we use the parameter estimates from this regression to correct for observable characteristics. We then estimate the individual-level variance and the tract-level variance, and using $Var_{tract} = \sigma_\theta^{2}/(1 - \alpha\varphi)^2$, and $Var_{ind} = \sigma_\theta^{2}/(1 - \alpha^2\varphi^2)$ we form an estimate of $\alpha\varphi$.

Table 4.4
Estimation of Strength of Social Interactions: Global vs. Local Interactions
Using Regression of Predicted City-Level Female Headship Rate on Actual City-Level
Rate

	Var_{ind}^a	Var_{tract}^b	$\overline{\dfrac{\partial f(X)}{\partial A}}^{c}$	$\alpha\varphi^d$	$\sigma_\theta^2 + Var_j^{f(x)d}$	$g'(\overline{A})\alpha(1-\varphi)^d$
Female headship rate controlling for individual traits and city fixed effects	0.111	2.94	0.792 (0.052)	0.927	0.016	−0.719
25th percentile^c			0.386 (0.176)			−0.178

Source: Individual-level data are from the 1990 Census Summary Tape Files. Aggregate-level data are from the 1990 Census Public Use Microsample.

a. Var_{ind} is the variance of the residual from the following micro-regression: $A_i = \beta'X_i + \varepsilon_i$ where A_i is the deviation of the female headship rate from the city mean and X_i is a vector of deviations of individual traits from city means. These traits include income and number of children and a set of dummies indicating whether the family head is Black, Hispanic, a high school dropout, a college graduate, aged 18–24, 25–34, 35–44, 55–64, 65–100, and in poverty.

b. Var_{tract} is the average across cities of the within-city variance of $\sqrt{N_t}(\hat{A}_t - \hat{A}_c)$ where $\hat{A}_t = A_t - \hat{\beta}'X_t$, $\hat{\beta}$ is the vector of parameter estimates from the micro-level regression, X_t is the vector of tract-level averages of individual traits (not deviated from city means), and $\hat{A}_c$ is the within-city average of $\hat{A}_t$.

c. $\overline{\dfrac{\partial f(X)}{\partial A}}$ is the slope estimated from a spline-regression of $\hat{A}_c = \hat{\beta}'X_c$ on the actual rate, A_c
Row 1 is the estimate of the slope for those cities above the 25th percentile. Row 2 is the estimate of the slope for cities below the 25th percentile.

d. $\alpha\varphi = \dfrac{1 - Var_{ind}/Var_{tract}}{1 + Var_{ind}/Var_{tract}}$ $\sigma_\theta^2 = Var_{ind}(1 - \alpha^2\varphi^2)$ $g'(\overline{A})\alpha(1-\varphi) = 1 - \alpha\varphi - \overline{\dfrac{\partial f(X)}{\partial A}}$.

Our estimate of global interactions is more difficult. As discussed above, we use the parameter estimates from the microregression to create a predicted outcome level for each city based on the city-level observables and the parameter estimates from the micro-level regression. We then regress this citywide predicted action level on the action. If there were substantial nonmonotonicities in this function, then multiple equilibria would be a possibility. As it is, the function is completely monotonic and thus this procedure does not confirm the existence of multiple equilibria at the city level.

Intuitively, the result of regressing predicted outcomes on actual outcomes can be best thought by considering the null hypothesis of no social interactions. In that case, we would expect the predicted outcome level to move one-for-one with the actual outcome level (on average). However, as we see we find that the predicted outcome level moves less than one-for-one, which means that large changes in the actual outcome level are associated with smaller changes in the predicted outcome level. This finding is quite supportive of the existence of social interactions.

However, our formula is that $(\partial \overline{f(X)})/\partial \overline{A} = 1 - \alpha\varphi - \alpha(1 - \varphi)g'(\overline{A})$. Our point estimates of $(\partial \overline{f(X)})/\partial \overline{A}$ range from 0.386 to 0.792, but our estimate of $\alpha\varphi$ (from the micro-level and tract-level variance) is 0.927. As such, the global interaction terms must be negative (although in one case, the global interaction term is not statistically different from zero). There are two possible ways of interpreting this result. First, it is possible that the global interaction terms are negative.

Second, and we think more realistically, problems are associated with the fact that we are cobbling together two different procedures to estimate the global and local interaction. In principle it would be possible to estimate $\alpha\varphi$ by regressing average tract-level predicted outcome on average tract-level outcome. If there is any tendency of the unobservable causes of actions to create more social interaction than the observable components, then our current estimate of $\alpha\varphi$ will be much higher than it would be using this alternative method. Moreover, if unobservable causes of actions matter more, then our use of two procedures will lead to many more estimation problems than using a common procedure to estimate both components of local and global interactions.

This section has been highly exploratory, and we hope that future work will extend this approach. However, we have argued that there are two distinct methodologies for estimating local and global interactions. First, it is possible to use aggregate variances and compare these variances with micro-level variances. Second, it is possible to use the connection between average predicted level outcome and average outcome. While this second point is similar to micro-level estimation techniques (see, e.g., Case and Katz 1991) that look for social interactions by using neighbors characteristics as instruments, our procedure is essentially novel in many ways and needs more development before it can be counted on to produce reliable results.

4.5 Selection into Locations

We now revert back to our simpler local interactions model and assume

$$U(A_i, A_{i-1}, \theta_i, P_z) = \theta_i A_i - \frac{1-\alpha}{2} A_i^2 - \frac{\alpha}{2}(A_i - A_{i-1})^2 - P_z, \tag{2'}$$

where P_z represents the cost of living in city z. As before, individuals choose their actions so that $A_j = \theta_i + \alpha A_{i-1}$. In this model, however, individuals choose their city as well as their action. Furthermore, they will choose their city before observing who their neighbor will be or even exactly what their value of θ_i will be. One justification for this is that individual tastes will change over time (so individuals are unsure as to what their tastes will be). We further assume that no one knows who his neighbor will be. However, individuals will have a guess as to what sort of people are selecting into the city.

To implement the idea that individuals have some imperfect knowledge about their own tastes, we assume $\theta_i = \hat{\theta}_i + \varepsilon_i$, where $\hat{\theta}_i$ and ε_i are both mean zero, i.i.d. random variables with variances $\sigma_{\hat{\theta}}^2$ and σ_ε^2, and suppose γ solves $(1 - \gamma)\sigma_{\hat{\theta}}^2 = \gamma\sigma_\varepsilon^2$. The term $\hat{\theta}_i$ represents tastes that are known ex ante and may include the effect of observable individual characteristics. The term ε_i represents individual tastes that are only known after migration, which are assumed to be independent of all other individuals' taste shocks. There are a fixed number of C cities labeled 1 to C, and all of these cities are ex ante identical (this represents a simplification over the previous models). Furthermore, while it is possible to endogenize the size of communities (as long as cost of living rises sufficiently quickly with population size, there will always be interior solutions for city size), we will assume that the fractions of the population $(k_1, \ldots, k_C)$ are exogenous.

Using the fact that individual i knows that he will choose his actions optimally so that $A_i = \theta_i + \alpha A_{i-1}$, the expected utility of individual i who chooses city after observing $\hat{\theta}_i$ will be

$$E(U_i|z) = \frac{\hat{\theta}_i^2 + \sigma_\varepsilon^2}{2} + \alpha\hat{\theta}_i E(A_{i-1}|z) - \frac{(1-\alpha)\alpha}{2} E(A_{i-1}^2|z) - P_z. \tag{17}$$

The key point in this equation is that there is a strategic complementarity between an individual's expected proclivity toward the action ($\hat{\theta}_i$) and the tendency in the city to follow the action. For example, if agent i weakly prefers city z to city z', where $E(A_{i-1}|z) > E(A_{i-1}|z')$, then any agent i' for whom $\hat{\theta}_{i'} > \hat{\theta}_i$ will prefer z strictly to z'. This fact implies that there will be strict sorting of individuals across cities, unless the cities are exactly identical (as in Benabou 1993). Without getting into more detailed dynamic issues, usual ad hoc notions of stability assure us that these symmetric equilibria will be unstable. The intuition of this is that if one of two initially symmetric cities becomes slightly higher in expected action levels, then all of the individuals with higher $\hat{\theta}_i$s will tend toward that city. Because of this instability of the symmetric equilibria cases, we will focus exclusively on the stable complete sorting equilibria.

The determination of which cities will be high action and which will be low action is not determined by the model. We will normalize and order the cities so that expected action levels rise monotonically with z. We let λ_z denote the highest skill level in city z. Naturally, $\lambda_z < \lambda_{z+1}$ and in equilibrium if $\hat{\theta}_i \in (\lambda_{z-1}, \lambda_z)$, then individual i lives in city z. For simplicity, we will assume that the distribution $\hat{\theta}_i$ has a density function $f(.)$, so we will not worry about individuals at the boundary. Since individuals at the boundary need to be indifferent between the two cities, if mass points are present we may assign a convenient fraction of the agents of that type to each city.

Formally, an equilibrium is a vector $Inf(\hat{\theta}) = \lambda_0, \lambda_1, \lambda_2, \ldots, \lambda_{C-1}, \lambda_C = Sup(\hat{\theta})$ and a vector $p_1, p_2, \ldots, p_{C-1}, p_C$ such that (1) if $\hat{\theta}_i \in [\lambda_{z-1}, \lambda_z]$ then $E(U_i|z) \geq E(U_i|z')$ for each $z' = 1, \ldots, C$, and (2) Probability ($\hat{\theta}_i \in [\lambda_{z-1}, \lambda_z]$) $= k_z$ for each $z = 1, \ldots, C$. The existence of an equilibrium is easy to show. The model does not pin down the level of property values, only the difference of housing costs across cities, so we will normalize $p_1 = 0$.

We denote $\bar{\theta}_z = E(\hat{\theta}_i|z) = E(\theta_i|z)$ and $\bar{A}_z = E(A_i|z)$. Using the first-order condition $A_i = \theta_i + \alpha A_{i-1}$, since $E(A_i|z) = E(A_{i-1}|z)$, it follows that $\bar{\theta}_z = (1 - \alpha)\bar{A}_z$. We further let A_i^z (θ_i^z) denote the action (taste shock) associated with individual i in city z and note that city z has $n_z = k_z T$ inhabitants, where T denotes the total population of the country. Since $\hat{\theta}_i$ has a finite variance, it follows that

$$\sum_{i=1}^{n_j} \frac{A_i^z - \bar{A}_z}{\sqrt{n_z}} - \frac{1}{1-\alpha} \sum_{i=1}^{n_z} \frac{\theta_i^z - \bar{\theta}_z}{\sqrt{n_z}} \to N\left(0, \frac{\sigma_z^2}{(1-\alpha)^2}\right), \tag{18}$$

where σ_z^2 is the overall variance of θ_i^z. We know that $\sigma_z^2 = \hat{\sigma}_z^2 + \sigma_\varepsilon^2$, where $\hat{\sigma}_z^2$ is the variance of the signal θ_i^z in city z, which must satisfy

$$\hat{\sigma}_z^2 = \int_{\lambda_{z-1}}^{\lambda_z} \left(\hat{\theta} - \bar{\theta}_z\right)^2 \frac{f(\hat{\theta})}{k_z} d\hat{\theta} = \int_{\lambda_{z-1}}^{\lambda_z} \hat{\theta}^2 \frac{f(\hat{\theta})}{k_z} d\hat{\theta} - \bar{\theta}_z^2.$$

We now let

$$\omega_z = \frac{1}{1-\alpha} \sum_{i=1}^{n_z} \frac{\theta_i^z}{\sqrt{n_z}} = \frac{1}{1-\alpha} \sum_{i=1}^{n_z} \frac{\theta_i^z - \bar{\theta}_z}{\sqrt{n_z}} + \frac{\bar{\theta}_z \sqrt{n_z}}{1-\alpha}.$$

This term reflects the weighted average of taste shocks in city z. By analogy to equation (18), the variance of ω_z is equal asymptotically to the variance of the normalized sum of the deviations of actions of individuals in city z from the average action of the population. We assume that the ratio of any one's city population to the average city population (denoted $\hat{n}_z$) is bounded from above and below by two constants K_1 and K_2, so that $K_1 < \frac{n_z}{\hat{n}_z} < K_2$.

The variance of the random variable $\sqrt{n_z}\,\omega_z = \sqrt{k_z T}\,\omega_z$, the weighted variance of the ω_z terms, equals

$$CVar(\sqrt{k_z}\,\omega_z) = C\frac{TVar(k_z\bar{\theta}_z)}{(1-\alpha)^2} + CE\left(\frac{k_z\sigma_z^2}{(1-\alpha)^2}\right). \tag{19}$$

In this equation, the moments can be computed against the measure that attributes probability $1/C$ to each of the C cities.

The second term of the right-hand side of equation (19), equals

$$\frac{\sigma_\varepsilon^2 + E(\hat{\theta}^2) - \sum_{z=1}^{C} k_z\bar{\theta}_z^2}{(1-\alpha)^2}.$$

It then follows that

$$Var(C\sqrt{k_z}\,\omega_z) = \frac{1}{(1-\alpha)^2}\left[\sigma_\varepsilon^2 + E(\hat{\theta}^2) + \sum_{z=1}^{C}(n_z-1)k_z\bar{\theta}_z^2\right]. \tag{20}$$

Intuitively, this equation makes it clear that the variance of weighted city-level averages is determined by the overall level of interaction, the variance of taste shocks, and the amount of sorting across cities.

The first two terms in brackets are generally invariant with respect to increases in C. The third term is generally of order T/C (which is average city size). If the support of θ is bounded, then the last term is at most of order T/C. Further, as $K_1 < \frac{n_z}{\hat{n}_z} < K_2$ implies that $K_1/N < k_z$ we can place a lower bound on $\bar{\theta}_z$ provided that $j \leq N/4$ or $j \geq 3N/4$. Hence the last term in brackets is at most of order T/C.

4.5.1   Empirical Approaches

While in principle there could be many different approaches to estimating the share of the cross-city variance that comes from sorting and
the share that comes from local interaction, we focus on the last implication of the model. The taste- and local-interaction-related variance
terms are not of order T/C (i.e., they do not change with average city
size), while the sorting source of variance is of order T/C. In principle,
if we compared across sets of locations, where there is no migration
between each set of cities but within each set of cities, where the
average city size differs then we could determine the extent to which
sorting determines the variance across cities. For example, if we found
that the variance was much higher in areas with larger city sizes, then
we would attribute much of the variance to sorting and less to local
interaction.

   While in practice it is impossible to perform this sort of exercise perfectly, we will present a crude facsimile using U.S. states. Of course, for
this estimation to be perfectly correct we would need to assume that
all sorting occurs within states not across states. However, the estimation procedure would still be basically unbiased if the means of the
underlying taste distribution differed across states but the variance of
the taste distribution stayed constant or at least did not change in a
way that was systematically related to average city size.

   We estimate the variance of weighted outcome variables $Var(C\sqrt{k_z}\,\omega_z)$
within each state, using the relationship between this variance and the
variance of the normalized sum of the deviations of actions of individuals in city z from the average action of the population, and then regress
this variance on the average city size within the state. The amount that
remains in the intercept can be interpreted as the amount of variance
that can properly be attributed to social interaction. Table 4.5 shows our
estimates for three variables. As a test case, in the third row of table 4.5
we used percent nonwhite, which should reveal variance only due to
sorting. The intercept in this case was negative and statistically insignificant, which means that the methodology is not inappropriately identifying social interaction in this case.

   In the case of female-headed households and the crime rate, we
find positive levels of social interaction and significant levels of sorting.
In both cases, the sorting effect is significantly positive. In the case of
the crime rate, the social interaction effect is significantly positive. In
the case of female-headed households, the social interaction effect is

Table 4.5
Sorting Equilibria: Results from Regression Analysis
Equation Estimated Is $var_j(N\sqrt{k_j}\,\eta_j) = \beta_0 + \beta_1(n_j/N_j) + \varepsilon_j$

	β_0	β_t	R^2	Var_{ind}	α
Female headship rate of families	39.42	0.005	0.169	0.16	0.992
	(146.76)	(1.5E-05)			
Crime rate	30.88	2.6E-04	0.095	0.06	0.996
	(11.44)	(1.2E-04)			
Percent non-white	−299.39	0.018	0.201	1.88E-06	—
	(508.47)	(0.005)			

Sources: Regression data and the variances of crime and percent non-white are derived from the County and City Data Book 1994 . The female headship rate data is from the 1990 Census Public Use Microsample.
Note: Standard errors are in parentheses. η was estimated as $\sqrt{\overline{N}}\,(A_i - \overline{A})$ where $\overline{N}$ is the average city size, A_i is the action, and $\overline{A}$ is the average of A_i. k_j is $1/$number of cities in the state. a is calculated using the formula, $\alpha = \dfrac{Var_{agg} - Var_{ind}}{Var_{agg} + Var_{ind}}$, where the intercept, β_0, is used for Var_{agg} and Var_{ind} is the individual-level variance of the action in the United States.

not statistically significant, but it is economically sizable. As a result, we must conclude that this procedure shows promise but is far from precise.

Of course, it is worthwhile to stress that sorting itself only occurs because of social interactions. Similar individuals would not choose to locate near each other if there weren't social interactions. Hence, our results should be seen as estimating the extent to which social interactions operate through sorting or through interaction after sorting.

4.6   Dynamic Models

Many of the sorting problems just discussed disappear when considering time series variation. While we lose sources of variation, we do eliminate some of the hardest problems of estimating social interactions. In this case, we consider a simple class of models in which all individuals start in a particular state and then may choose to switch to another state (or action). The switch is assumed to be irreversible, which admittedly it will not be in many cases. We have in mind choosing a particular technology or moving to a new country or perhaps women entering the labor market (although in this case, the decision is clearly reversible).

Descriptively, we will focus on the last example, despite the reversibility issue. There are many reasons to suspect that substantial social interactions are involved in women entering the labor market. As more women entered they lowered the stigma of work, reduced the discrimination against women in the workplace, and eliminated the social network that facilitated not working in the formal labor market.

We model a single location with population n. Each agent is indexed by an integer $i = 1, 2, 3, \ldots, n$. At time t an individual i is in one of two states. The state $s_t^i = 0$, if the agent has not entered the labor market, otherwise $s_t^i = 1$. We will assume that entering the labor market is irreversible—that is, if $s_t^i = 1$, and $t' > t$, then $s_{t'}^i = 1$.

Agent i's flow of utility per period depends on his type $\tau \in \{0, 1, 2\}$, and on his own state. In addition if $s_t^i = 1$, the utility also depends on the states of agents in a set $N(i)$ of "friends" of i, at the last time t_1 such that $s_{t_1}^i = 0$. In order to simplify the forecasting problem of agents, we assumed that although new workers benefit from the presence of older entrants into the labor market that are their friends, the reverse is not true.[5] We will begin by assuming that $N(i) = \{i - 1, i + 1\}$. For symmetry we identify 0 with n and $n + 1$ with 1; that is, we set $N(1) = \{n, 2\}$ and, $N(n) = \{n - 1, 1\}$. At each time t if $s_t^i = 0$, we assume that agent i will be given, with probability p a choice to enter the labor market. She then must compare the value of staying with the value of working that is a function of her type and the states of her friends. Let $v_{t+1} = s_t^{i-1} + s_t^{i+1}$ and $V(\tau, v)$ denote the value of entering the labor market, as a function of the type τ and the value v of the sum of the states in $N(i)$ as of the preceding period. Since it is only the value v, in the period before entering the labor market that matters, if δ is the discount factor per period then $V(\tau, v) = \dfrac{\delta}{1-\delta} h(\tau, v)$, where here $h(\tau, v)$ is the per-period utility of an individual that works, as a function of her type τ, and the value v of the sum of the states in $N(i)$, in the period before she worked. Similarly, let $U(\tau, v)$ denote the value of staying, as a function of the type τ and the value v of the sum of the states in $N(i)$, in the preceding period. Elementary dynamic programming implies that

$$U(\tau, v_{t-1}) = g(\tau) + \delta[(1-p)E(U(\tau, v_t) + pE(\max\{U(\tau, v_t), V(\tau, v_t)\})], \quad (21)$$

where $g(\tau)$ is the per-period utility of an individual that stays outside the labor market as a function of his type τ and E denotes the expected value over the value of v_t conditional on v_{t-1}. Individuals work whenever $U(\tau, v_t) < V(\tau, v_t)$. Since an agent has a choice of never working, we know that $U(\tau, v_t) \geq \dfrac{1}{1-\delta} g(\tau)$.

We make three assumptions: (A1) $h(0, v) < g(0)$, for any $0 \leq v \leq 2$, (A2) $h(1, 0) = h(1, 1) = h(1, 2) > g(1)$, and (A3) $h(2, 0) < g(2) < h(2, 1) = h(2, 2)$. Assumption A1 states that agents of type 0 get a higher flow of utility by not working. Assumption A2 states that agents of type 1 do not care about the number of friends that work, but always get a higher utility by working. Assumption A3 states the additional benefit to a type two agents from the previous working of a second friend. In addition, the utility of a type 2 agent not working is larger than that of working by herself, but lower than that of working, if at least one friend works. These assumptions make the behavior of individuals quite simple to determine. Type 0 will never work. Type 1 will always work when she is given a chance. Type 2 will not work if none of her friends work. Obviously we can weaken the qualities assumed in the assumptions and still retain the solution to problem 1.1 by combining hypotheses about the function h and g with hypotheses about the discount factor δ and the probability p. Each agent is type τ with probability q_τ, independent of the type of all other agents.

Given any i, let $i-$ be the largest integer less than i such that $\tau_{i-} \neq 2$, and let $i+$ be the smallest integer greater than i such that $\tau_{i+} \neq 2$. Here, again we identify n as the predecessor of 1 and 1 as the successor of n. As $t \to \infty$, $s_t^i \to 1$ unless $\tau_{i-} = \tau_{i+} = 0$ in which case $s_t^i = 0$ for all t. We write s^i for the asymptotic value of s_t^i. The asymptotic distribution of states can be derived in a manner similar to the derivation of the steady state distribution in the models of Glaeser, Sacerdote, and Scheinkman (1996). In particular, the expected fraction of workers converges to

$\mu \equiv 1 - q_0 - (1 - q_0 - q_1) \dfrac{q_0^2}{(q_0 + q_1)^2}$, where q_0 and q_1 are the fractions of type zero and type one respectively. Furthermore, under the asymptotic distribution, if m_n denotes the fraction of workers in population of size n the $(m_n - \mu)\sqrt{n} \to N(0, \sigma^2)$.

To establish this central limit behavior, it is enough to observe that if $j > j'$ and $A_{j,j'}$ is the event that at least for two values of $j > i > j'$, $\tau_i \in \{0, 1\}$, then conditional on $A_{j,j'}$, s^j is independent of $s^{j'}$. Since the probability of the complement of $A_{j,j'}$ goes to zero exponentially as $j - j'$ does to infinity, we know that m_n displays central limit behavior. Furthermore, the variance of the limit random variable σ^2 can be computed in a standard way by calculating the covariance between s^j and $s^{j'}$ on the complement of $A_{j,j'}$. The variance, σ^2, can be made arbitrarily large if we let the fraction of type 2 individuals converge to one—the presence of individuals who are sensitive to social interactions increases the variance across populations.

The dynamics are also possible to compute. The expected number of workers in the first period is npq_1; the expected number of entrants in the second period is $np(1 - p)q_1 + 2np^2q_1q_2$. Hence if $q_2 > 1/2$, the expected number of entrants in the second period is larger than in the first period. This fact means that if q_2 is large then the expected cumulative migration starts as a convex function of time. Eventually, the expected number of workers converges to $n\left(1 - \dfrac{q_0^2}{(q_0 + q_1)^2}\right)$. This indicates that an S-shaped cumulative entrant curve is to be expected.[6]

Unfortunately we do not have closed form solutions that would allow us to estimate these curves at this time. Instead, we will present some results based on a simpler method of estimating social interactions in a dynamic setting.

While this dynamic local interactions model needs further investigation, using simulations it appears to be quite close to a dynamic global interactions model, many of which have been studied extensively theoretically and empirically as well (as pioneered by Griliches 1958; see also Besley and Case 1991). While global interactions models have appeared regularly in the literature on technological adoption so our presentation is in no sense novel, in the spirit of collecting together a wide number of approaches to measuring social interactions, we present a particularly simple model here, without any claims to innovation. We assume that in each time period a fraction of individuals (which is denoted $\beta - X$, where $X(t)$ is the state variable for the number of workers) receiving exogenous shocks inducing them to work. Likewise all workers also interact with another individual, who is drawn randomly from the pool of individuals. If a nonworker interacts with a worker, then the nonworker will begin working. Thus, there are two sources of growth in the working population—an exogenous rise due to idiosyncratic shocks and a rise due to interactions, which will be global since individuals meet with each other randomly (if individuals always only met their neighbors, then this would be a local interactions model). Given these two processes, at each point in time the measure of nonworkers who begin to work is $a_0 + a_1 X(t)$.

While this differential equation is not that actually suggested by the previous model, we know that we can fit the simulations of the model quite well (r_s^2 typically over 99.9%) with a differential equation of this form, so we believe that this functional form is reasonable and provides us with a convenient measure of the degree of social interaction. We thus have a differential equation of the form

$$\dot{X}(t) = (\alpha_0 + \alpha_1 X(t))(\beta - X(t)) = a + bX(t) + cX(t)^2. \tag{22}$$

This equation is meant to be flexible. Simulations showed that the time series predicted by the previous model is captured well by a differential equation of this form. The relative importance of the α_1 term gives us the importance of social interactions (or contagion) in the process; the relative importance of the α_0 dictates the importance of nonsocial related forces. One interpretation of this equation, in the context of technology adoption, is that a fraction of those individuals who haven't adopted (but will eventually adopt) adopts each period, and a fraction adopts if and only if they meet someone who has already adopted. The solution for this equation (conditional on knowing the initial value) is

$$X(t) = \frac{\alpha_1\beta - \alpha_0 - (\alpha_1\beta + \alpha_0)Tanh\left[-\frac{1}{2}Log\left[\frac{\alpha_0 + \alpha_1 X(0)}{\alpha_1\beta - \alpha_1 X(0)}\right] - \frac{\alpha_1\beta + \alpha_0}{2}t\right]}{2\alpha_1}.$$

$$\tag{22}$$

where $X(0)$ is the initial value. This equation can itself be fit using maximum likelihood.

The estimate of β describes the final level of the action. The α_0 term tells us about flat growth; the α_1 term tells us about interactive growth. When comparing dynamic processes, if we compare a process that takes fifty years and a process that takes one year to get close to β, both α terms will be much bigger in the faster process. To avoid these issues, we normalize assuming a common T, for $X(T) = Z\beta$, where Z is a parameter fixed by the econometrician (perhaps 0.95). This normalization essentially means that each process is normalized so that it takes exactly the same amount of time to run its course. The normalization also means that only one free parameter (chosen to be α_1) other than β

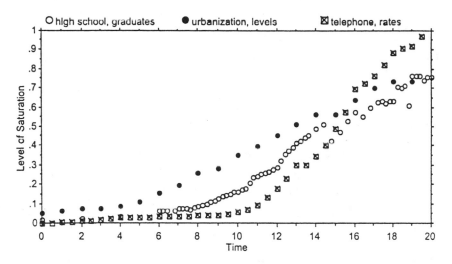

Figure 4.1
Time paths of schooling, telephones, urbanization.

remains. Different values of $\alpha_1 = 0$. Figure 4.1 shows how different values of this free parameter influences the S-shaped form of the process. When $\alpha_1 \approx 0$, the curve is concave. As there is more interaction (α_1 increases), the adoption curve becomes more S-shaped.[7]

To show the efficacy of this estimation procedure, we estimate curves for three time processes that seem to be one-sided and social. The first variable of interest is to consider urbanization in the United States, which moved from 5.1 percent to 75 percent between 1790 and 1980. Taking 1790 as year zero, and estimating 0.83 for β, and normalizing the period of urbanization to twenty years (which will be our standard normalized period), our estimates become $\alpha_0 = -0.007[.001]$ and $\alpha_1 = 0.33[0.01]$.[8] The share of seventeen-year olds who graduate from high school rises from 2 percent in 1870 to approximately 75 percent in 1970, again following an S-shaped curve. With 1870 as the base year, normalizing and estimating 0.79 for β, we find that we estimate that $\alpha_0 = -0.077[0.005]$ and $\alpha_1 = 0.49[0.01]$. Using the third variable, the ratio of phones to households, we normalize and find that we estimate that $\alpha_0 = -0.0005[0.00003]$ and $\alpha_1 = 0.56[0.01]$. The normalized rankings suggest that phones are more interactive than schooling, which is more interactive than urbanization. The following graph shows the results in the raw data. The curve closest to the y-axis shows the results for urbanization. The second curve shows the schooling results and the final curve shows the results for telephones.

4.7 Conclusion

This chapter has presented a tour of primary issues in estimating social interactions. A first issue is estimating the extent to which the high variance of different processes should be thought of as the result of multiple equilibria or high variances around those equilibria. Following our first estimation technique, which essentially asks whether the distribution of city variances is best fit by one or more distributions, we found that multiple distributions fit the data better. Our second estimation technique, which involves examining the connection between prediction and actual city-level outcomes, reveals no evidence of multiple equilibria. In both cases, we found that there was usually a large component of the variance that was not explained by the existence of multiple equilibria.

A second issue is the extent to which interactions are due to local or global interaction processes. We show that the key to estimating which processes operate are to have data at the subcity level. Using subcity data tends to support the importance of local (tract- or sub-tract-level) interactions relative to city-level interactions.

A third issue is the extent to which interactions reflect sorting on tastes and the extent to which they reflect social interactions after sorting occurs. Of course, sorting itself reflects the presence of some social interaction that induces like individuals to be with each other. We found large evidence of sorting behavior.

Finally, we examined a simple dynamic model and used a simple methodology that lets us compare the degree of social interactions across different dynamic processes.

Appendix

In this appendix, we establish for the model in section 4.3 that (i) the average action in a population of size n, $\hat{A}_n$, converges, as $n \to \infty$, to a solution of the equation:

$$g(\overline{A}) = \frac{1 - \alpha\phi}{\alpha(1 - \phi)} \overline{A}, \tag{A1}$$

and (ii) if $a_i^n = A_i^n - \overline{A}$, then

$$\sum_{i=1}^{n} \frac{a_i^n}{\sqrt{n}} \to N\left(0, \frac{\sigma_\theta^2}{(1 - \alpha\varphi - \alpha(1 - \varphi)g'(A))^2}\right). \tag{A2}$$

Define B by

$$B = \left(\frac{1}{1-\alpha\phi}\right)\left(\frac{\sup(|\theta|)}{1-\alpha\phi} + \frac{\sup(|g|)}{\alpha\phi}\right). \tag{A3}$$

It follows from equation (8) in section 4.3 that, since $A_0^n = A_n^n$, then $A_0^n \leq B$ and if $|A_i^n| \leq B$ then $|A_{i+1}^n| \leq B$. Hence for each n, i, $|A_i^n| \leq B$, and $|\hat{A}_n| \leq B$. Also for each $i \leq n$,

$$\left|\frac{\sum_{k \neq i} A_k^n}{n-1} - \hat{A}_n\right| \leq \left|\frac{\hat{A}_n}{n-1} - \frac{A_i^n}{n-1}\right| \leq \frac{2B}{n-1}. \tag{A4}$$

Since $|g'(A)| \leq K$ for some K, we have that

$$\left|\frac{1}{n}\sum_{i=1}^{n} g\left(\frac{\sum_{j \neq i} A_j^n}{n-1}\right) - g(\hat{A}_n)\right| \leq \frac{2BK}{n-1}. \tag{A5}$$

Using equation (10) from section 4.3 and the strong law of large numbers,

$$(1-\alpha\phi)\hat{A}_n - \frac{\alpha(1-\phi)}{n}\sum_{i=1}^{n} g\left(\frac{\sum_{k \neq i} A_k^n}{n-1}\right) \rightarrow 0 \text{ with probability one.}$$

Hence using (A5) we have that with probability one,

$$(1-\alpha\phi)\hat{A}_n - \alpha(1-\phi)g(\hat{A}_n) \rightarrow 0. \tag{A6}$$

Since $\hat{A}_n$ is a bounded sequence, it must have limit points. From equation (A6), we have that any such limit point $\overline{A}$ must satisfy

$$g(\overline{A}) = \frac{1-\alpha\phi}{\alpha(1-\phi)}\overline{A}, \text{ that is, (A1).}$$

Since $|\hat{A}_n - \hat{A}_{n-1}| \leq \dfrac{2B}{n}$ and since equation (A1) has a finite number of fixed points, all the limit points of a given sequence must coincide. Hence $\hat{A}_n$ must in fact converge to some $\overline{A}$ that solves (A1), which establishes the first claim of this appendix.

Combining equations (A1) and (10) from section 3 and multiplying by $\sqrt{n}$, we obtain

$$\sqrt{n}(1-\alpha\phi)(\hat{A}_n - \overline{A}) - \sqrt{n}\alpha(1-\phi)[g(\hat{A}_n) - g(\overline{A})]$$

$$= \frac{\sum_{i=1}^{n} \theta_i}{\sqrt{n}} + \sqrt{n}\alpha(1-\phi)\left[g(\hat{A}_n) - \frac{\sum_{i=1}^{n} g\left(\frac{\sum_{k \neq i} A_k^n}{n-1} \right)}{n} \right]. \qquad (A7)$$

Equation (A5) implies that the second term in the right-hand side of (A7) converges to 0. Hence the Central Limit Theorem guarantees that the right-hand side of (A7) converges to a normal random variable with mean zero and variance σ_θ^2.

We can now establish

PROPOSITION 1 $\sqrt{n}(\hat{A}_n - \overline{A})$ is bounded with probability 1.

Proof   The right hand side of equation (A7) is bounded with probability 1. Suppose that a subsequence n_k has the property that $\sqrt{n_k}|\hat{A}_{n_k} - \overline{A}| \to \infty$. Dividing both sides of equation (A7) by $\sqrt{n_k}|\hat{A}_{n_k} - \overline{A}|$ and taking the limit as $n_k \to \infty$, we establish that $g'(\overline{A}) = \frac{1-\alpha\phi}{\alpha(1-\phi)}$, which is a contradiction. We denote $a_i^n = A_i^n - \overline{A}$. We know that

$$\sqrt{n}(1-\alpha\phi)(\hat{A}_n - \overline{A}) - \sqrt{n}\alpha(1-\phi)g'(\overline{A})(\hat{A}_n - \overline{A}) + \sqrt{n}\alpha(1-\phi)o(\hat{A}_n - \overline{A})$$
$$\to N(0, \sigma_\theta^2). \qquad (A8)$$

Proposition 1 implies that $\sqrt{n}o(\hat{A}_n - \overline{A}) \to 0$. Hence the second claim of this appendix is established.

Notes

Both authors acknowledge financial support from the National Science Foundation. Glaeser also thanks the Sloan Foundation. Andrea Eisfeldt and Lars Nesheim provided excellent research assistance.

1. Many of these ideas had antecedents in the classics works on social interactions, such as Schelling (1978), which presents a discussion of a wide range of social interactions, and Duesenberry (1949) who first formalizes interdependent preferences. Jovanovic (1987) is also a particularly prescient formalization of a social interactions model.

2. Akerlof, Katz, and Yellen (1996) actually specifically link the rise in out-of-wedlock births with changes in abortion and birth control, but this link is indirect and works through the stigma associated with being an unwed mother or a delinquent father.

3. Possible exceptions to this might occur when $\partial W/\partial\theta_i > 0$ if individuals don't want to take the action if no one else is taking the action, because it has no signaling value in

that case. In that case, some consumers are necessary for there to exist a positive sorting equilibrium. Of course, well-established theory about reasonable beliefs when no one is taking an action argues that people's beliefs about off-the-equilibrium path behavior should ensure that the action still has positive signaling value when no one is taking the action.

4. Furthermore, it will eliminate the effect of any variables that are city rather than individual-specific. Of course, it will not eliminate the problems of sorting across neighborhoods. That problem can only be solved with neighborhood fixed effects.

5. In general, this will still leave a forecasting problem for agents since they may be better off waiting for their friends to act. However, in our model we will assume that the gains from acting are such that each type will either never act or act as soon as a certain percentage of their friends have acted.

6. We can also obtain an S-shaped curve where every agent interacts equally with every other agent. Under a global interactions model, we lose the variance across populations over and above the characteristics of the populations.

7. There is a literature on this topic that we are not referencing. We apologize at this point for failing to survey the technology adoption literature adequately at this point. This excellent and lengthy literature is, of course, connected to this topic but too far afield from our basic interest to be given significant page space.

8. These errors are biased because we have treated the observations as independent; further work will deal with the variety of standard time series issues involved in estimating this nonlinear trend. The r^2, which is again somewhat misleading is 99.62 percent, is typical for these estimates.

References

Akerlof, G. 1997. "Social Distance and Social Decisions." *Econometrica* 65(5): 1005–1028.

Akerlof, G., and R. Kranton. 1997. "The Economics of Identity." Mimeo. Brookings Institution.

Akerlof, G., M. Katz, and J. Yellen. 1996. "An Analysis of Out-of-Wedlock Childbearing in the United States." *Quarterly Journal of Economics* 111(2): 277–318.

Arthur, W. B. 1989. "Increasing Returns, Competing Technologies and Lock-in by Historical Small Events: The Dynamics of Allocation under Increasing Returns to Scale." *Economics Journal* 99(1): 116–131.

Banerjee, A. 1992. "A Simple Model of Herd Behavior." *Quarterly Journal of Economics* 107: 797–818.

Becker, G. 1997. "Social Economics." Mimeo. University of Chicago.

Benabou, R. 1993. "Workings of a City: Location, Education and Production." *Quarterly Journal of Economics* 108: 619–652.

Bernheim, D. 1994. "A Theory of Conformity." *Journal of Political Economy* 102(5): 841–877.

Besley, T., and A. Case. 1994. "Diffusion as a Learning Process: Evidence from HYV Cotton." Mimeo. Princeton University.

Bikhchandani, S., D. Hirshleifer, and I . Welch. 1992. "A Theory of Fads, Fashions, Customs, and Cultural Change as Information Cascades." *Journal of Political Economy* 85: 365–390.

Borjas, G. 1995. "Ethnicity, Neighborhoods and Human Capital Externalities." *American Economic Review* 85: 365–390.

Brock, W., and S. Durlauf. 1995. "Discrete Choice with Social Interactions I: Theory." NBER Working Paper #2591.

————. 1997. "Discrete Choice with Social Interactions II: Econometrics." Mimeo. University of Wisconsin.

Case, A., and L. Katz. 1991. "The Company You Keep: The Effect of Family and Neighborhood on Disadvantaged Youth." NBER Working Paper #3708.

Crane, J. 1991. "The Epidemic Theory of Ghettos and Neighborhood Effects on Dropping Out and Teenage Childbearing." *American Journal of Sociology* 96: 1226–1259.

DiPasquale, D., and E. Glaeser. 1998. "The L.A. Riot and the Economics of Urban Unrest." *Journal of Urban Economics* 46(1): 52–78.

Duesenberry, J. 1949. *Income, Saving and the Theory of Consumer Behavior*. Cambridge: Harvard University Press.

Ellison, G., and D. Fudenberg. 1993. "Rules of Thumb for Social Learning." *Journal of Political Economy* 101: 612–643.

————. 1995. "Word-of-Mouth Communication and Social Learning." *Quarterly Journal of Economics* 110(1): 93–126.

Evans, W., W. Oates, and R. Schwab. 1992. "Measuring Peer Group Effects: A Model of Teenage Behavior." *Journal of Political Economy* 100(5): 966–991.

Gavaria, A. 1997. "Increasing Returns and the Evolution of Violent Crime: the Case of Columbia." Mimeo. UC San Diego.

Glaeser, E. L. 1992. "Two Essays on Information and Labor Markets." Ph.D. diss. University of Chicago.

Glaeser, E. L., and J. Scheinkman. 1997. "Social Interactions and Long-Range Dependence." Mimeo. Princeton University.

Glaeser, E. L., B. Sacerdote, and J. Scheinkman. 1996. "Crime and Social Interactions." *Quarterly Journal of Economics* 111(2): 507–548.

Griliches, Z. 1958. "Research Costs and Social Returns: Hybrid Corn and Related Innovations." *Journal of Political Economy* 66: 419–431.

Jovanovic, B. 1987. Micro Shocks and Aggregate Risk. *Quarterly Journal of Economics* 102(2) (May).

Levitt, S. 1997. "The Exaggerated Role of the Changing Age Structure in Explaining Aggregate Crime Changes." Mimeo. University of Chicago.

Manski, C. 1993. "Identification of Endogenous Social Effects: The Reflection Problem." *Review of Economic Studies* 60: 531–542.

Mulligan, C. 1995. "Pecuniary and Nonpecuniary Incentives to Work in the U.S. During World War II." Population Research Center Discussion Paper Series #95-3. University of Chicago.

O'Regan, K., and J. Quigley. 1996. "Spatial Effects upon Employment Outcomes: The Case of New Jersey Teenagers." *New England Economic Review* (May/June): 41–57.

Pesandorfer, W. 1996. "Design Innovation and Fashion Cycles." *American Economic Review* 85(4): 771–792.

Rasmusen, E. 1996. "Stigma and Self-Fulfilling Expectations of Criminality." *Journal of Law and Economics* 39(2): 519–543.

Rauch, J. 1994. "Productivity Gains from Geographic Concentration of Human Capital: Evidence from the Cities. *Journal of Urban Economics* 34: 380–400.

Sah, R. 1991. "Social Osmosis and the Patterns of Crime." *Journal of Political Economy* 99: 1272–1295.

Schelling, T. 1978. *Micromotives and Macrobehavior*. New York: Norton.

Topa, G. 1997. "Social Interactions, Local Spillovers and Unemployment." Mimeo. NYU Economics Department.

Young, P. 1993. "The Evolution of Conventions." *Econometrica* 61: 57–84.

———. 1997. "Social Coordination and Social Change." Mimeo. Johns Hopkins University.

5 The Dynamics of Conformity

H. Peyton Young

Every member of society is to act as an individual only, in entire independence of all other persons.

—Frank Knight, *Risk, Uncertainty, and Profit*

5.1 Introduction

When Catherine de Medici married the future Henry II of France in 1533, she brought with her from Florence several dozen table forks, which at that time were a complete novelty in France and indeed much of Europe. The prevailing custom at table was to pick up the food with one's fingers, or to spear it with a sharp-pointed knife (Giblin 1987). Although eating with a fork was at first viewed by members of court to be an absurd affectation, Catherine persisted, and gradually it became the accepted thing to do, both among the nobility and the bourgeoisie. From France the new custom spread to other countries. Thomas Coryate, who traveled widely in France and Italy in the early seventeenth century, claimed that he was the first person in London to eat with a fork (Coryate 1611). By the end of the next century it had become standard practice. While using a fork may be a superior technology compared to the older custom, the case is not all that clear. What does seem clear is that the fashion spread by a gradual process of diffusion in which people emulated the behavior of others.

Table etiquette may be of relatively little consequence, but it is a representative example of a large class of situations in which Knight's "independence" assumption fails to hold. Decisions about what to wear, what car to buy, what movie to see, and where to live, for example, are affected not only by the price of these goods; their desirability depends on the choices of others. Certain pathological behaviors may also have a substantial social component. There is evidence, for example, that dropping out of school, committing certain types of crimes, and using drugs are influenced by peer groups (see e.g., Case and Katz 1991; Crane 1991; Evans, Oates, and Schwab 1992; Glaeser, Sacerdote, and Scheinkman 1996; Akerlof 1997; Glaeser and Scheinkman, chap. 4).

This chapter discusses the dynamics of processes in which the adoption of a behavior becomes more likely the more that one's neighbors or peers adopt it. Broadly speaking, we may interpret this type of positive reinforcement as a *conformity effect*, though the specific motivations for conforming differ from one case to another, as we shall discuss below. Such processes exhibit quite complex behavior in the aggregate, due in part to the fact that they typically have a great many equilibria. They are also examples of systems in which optimization at the individual level can lead to seriously suboptimal outcomes at the social level—the invisible hand is perverse. The mathematical methods for studying such processes are borrrowed from statistical mechanics, in particular, the theory of Ising models (Liggett 1985; Blume 1993; see also Brock and Durlauf 1995, 1999). Using the concept of a stochastic potential function, one can identify the equilibria of the system that are most likely to emerge from arbitrary initial conditions. In the first part of the chapter we employ these techniques to analyze a conformist model of the type described above in which people change their behaviors to comport with the choices of their neighbors. Then we examine the "dual" situation in which people do not change their behaviors, but choose neighbors who are (at least in part) people like themselves (a Schelling type of model). Although these processes are quite different, they exhibit rather similar aggregate properties. In particular, we show that spatially homogeneous patterns—which in the Schelling model means segregated patterns—are much more likely to emerge than heterogeneous patterns over the long run.[1]

5.2 A Dynamic Model of Conformity

Consider a society in which each person can adopt one of two alternative behaviors: eat with a fork or one's fingers, wear a dress or a suit, stay in school or drop out, use drugs or abstain. In each of these cases we assume that each individual obtains positive reinforcement from conforming with his neighbors. The underlying motivations for conforming vary depending on circumstance. To some extent people simply want to be like other people: to wear clothes that are in fashion, to go to popular entertainments, to adhere to standards of etiquette. This is *pure* or *imitative* conformity. In other cases, conforming facilitates some form of coordination. People use words with their conventional meanings not because they want to be like others, but because they want to be understood. They drive on the same side of the road not because it is fashionable, but because they want to avoid collisions, and so forth. This is *instrumental* conformity. Third, people may adopt a behavior they observe around them because of the demonstration effect—usage by peers conveys information about its desirability, as in the use of new medications, contraceptive devices, farming methods, and various other types of new technologies. This is *informational* conformity.

In this chapter we shall not attempt to disentangle these different motivations for conforming, which in any event vary from one context to the next. Rather, we shall examine the consequences of conformity as it diffuses through the social network. Sometimes it takes only a single individual (a Catherine de Medici) to tip society from one norm to another (though the tipping process in this case took several centuries). This is most likely to occur when the individual is prominent and highly visible. However, prominence and visibility are neither necessary nor sufficient conditions to cause a tipping event: for every Catherine there are undoubtedly many prominent people who tried to institute new norms and failed. And, in addition to the Catherines, there are people whose actions made a difference not because they were prominent, but because they happened to be at the right place at the right time. Consider Rosa Parks, whose refusal to give up her seat in a bus to a white man ignited the Montgomery Bus Boycott and led to the desegregation of public transportation in the South. Although she was known in local civil rights circles, Rosa Parks was not a highly visible person. Furthermore, other blacks before her had refused to give up their seats and nothing came of it (Glennon 1991). Instead her action appears to have came at a fortuitous moment that triggered a society-wide change in expectations.

In this chapter I analyze a simple model of how such norm shifts occur, building on pioneering work by Blume (1993).[2] The idea is not to explain precisely how the use of the fork diffused, or how the norm about bus seating was undone. Instead, our aim is to show how conformist behavior engenders a dynamical process whose behavior depends on the *structure* of the social network. The model assumes a fixed population of agents who are located at the vertices of a graph. If two agents are located at vertices joined by an edge, they are *neighbors*. A simple example of such a structure is the two-dimensional lattice shown in figure 5.1.

The idea is that, over time, people adapt their behavior to the behavior of their neighbors. For simplicity we assume there are exactly two possible behaviors, *A* or *B*: use a fork or one's fingers, have a child or not, and so forth. We shall assume that these behaviors generate positive externalities, that is, the payoff from adopting either *A* or *B* increases with the proportion of one's neighbors who adopt the same behavior. (We do not commit ourselves to the precise reason for the externality; alternative reasons were discussed earlier.) It will be convenient to assume that the payoff from each behavior increases linearly in the number of one's neighbors who have adopted it, as shown in figure 5.2.

In the left panel of the figure, the payoffs to *A* and *B* are symmetric. In other words, it is unimportant whether society is coordinated on *A* or *B*, so long as coordination has been achieved. For example, it makes no social difference whether people customarily shake hands with the right or the left hand, but it does matter that they know which hand to extend. The same holds for driving on the left or right side of the road, or setting the table with the fork on the left and the knife on the right.

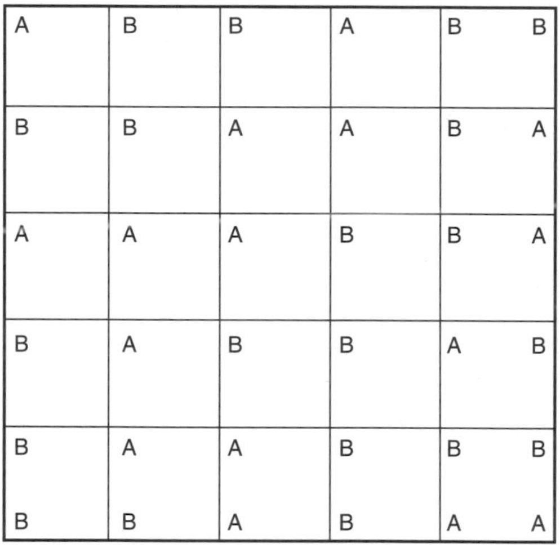

A	B	B	A	B	B
B	B	A	A	B	A
A	A	A	B	B	A
B	A	B	B	A	B
B	A	A	B	B	B
B	B	A	B	A	A

Figure 5.1
A two-dimensional lattice of social interactions.

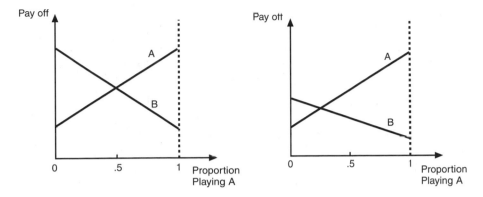

Figure 5.2
Left: symmetric payoffs. Right: asymmetric payoffs.

In other cases one behavior may have inherently higher welfare than another, and the norm does matter (as in the right panel of figure 5.2). For example, A might represent the norm of finishing high school, while B is the norm of dropping out. From the individual's standpoint, the utility from conforming to the suboptimal norm (B) is higher than not conforming; nevertheless, everyone would be better off if the norm were A.

Define the *state* of the system to be a choice of A or B by each agent in the graph. A state is an *equilibrium* if no agent would prefer to switch actions given the actions of his neighbors. One obvious equilibrium is for everyone to choose A or for everyone to choose B. Such a state is called a *social norm*. The two possible norms, all-A and all-B, are equilibria no matter what the details of the social interaction structure are. In addition, equilibrium states will often exist in which some parts of the population are coordinated on A while others are coordinated on B. These are called *local norms*. Their structure depends on the payoffs as well as the specific geometry of the social network.

Consider, for example, a two-dimensional lattice (such as that shown in figure 5.1), and suppose that the payoffs are as follows:

	A	B
A	3, 3	0, 0
B	0, 0	2, 2

(1)

Define an enclave to be a rectangle of agents who are coordinated on the same action (A or B). Consider a state in which every two A-

enclaves are at least three edges apart, as shown in figure 5.3. Then no B-player is adjacent to more than one A-player, and no A-player is adjacent to more than two B-players. Furthermore, no B-player has more than one-third of her interactions with A-players, and no A-player has more than one-half of her interactions with B-players. Hence the state is an equilibrium. By contrast, a B-enclave surrounded by A-players is not an equilibrium, because an agent at a corner of such an enclave must be adjacent to two A-players and two B-players, so this person would prefer to play A. The only B-enclaves that are in equilibrium are *strips* that run from one end of the lattice to the other, as shown in figure 5.4.[3]

As this example illustrates, equilibria are often homogeneous locally but exhibit considerable variation globally. Furthermore there are typically a huge number of distinct equilibria. If society begins in an out-of-equilibrium state, will it converge to one of these equilibria, and, if so, are some of them more likely to emerge than others?

To answer this question, consider the following adjustment process. Each person reconsiders her behavior at random times governed by a Poisson process. These processes are assumed to be independent and identically distributed among individuals. The notion is that individuals are subject to inertia and do not continually reevaluate their deci-

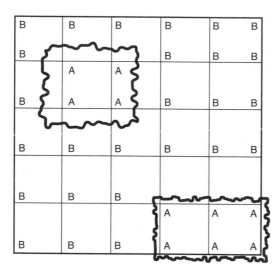

Figure 5.3
Equilibrium state consisting of two A-enclaves.

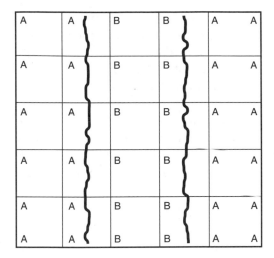

A	A	B	B	A	A
A	A	B	B	A	A
A	A	B	B	A	A
A	A	B	B	A	A
A	A	B	B	A	A
A	A	B	B	A	A

Figure 5.4
Equilibrium state consisting of two A-strips and one B-strip.

sions. When a given individual does reevaluate, she surveys the current choices of her neighbors and chooses a best reply, that is, an action that maximizes her expected payoff given that she will play the game against one of her neighbors drawn at random in the current period. (If A and B are tied as best replies, we shall assume that the agent does not change her behavior.)

We claim that, from any initial state, every sequence of strict best replies leads eventually to an equilibrium state; in other words, best reply cycles cannot occur. For each state x, let $A(x)$ be the number of edges such that the agents at both ends choose A, and let $B(x)$ be the number of edges such that the agents at both ends choose B. The function $\rho(x) = 3A(x) + 2B(x)$ is a *potential function* for the process in the following sense: whenever an agent changes behavior, the change in her payoff equals the change in potential. (The verification is left to the reader.) Since, under our current assumption, agents only change behavior if their payoff from doing so strictly increases, the potential at each stage must stay the same or increase. If the process is not currrently in an equilibrium state, there exists some agent who is not playing a best reply to her neighbors. With positive probability this agent will be the next one to reevaluate, in which case the potential will strictly increase. Moreover in no case will it decrease. It follows that the process cannot cycle; hence with probability 1 it eventually enters an equilibrium state and stays there. Indeed this result holds for any symmetric 2×2 coordination game, as we shall see in a moment.

This result shows how a kind of "spontaneous social order" can arise from the decentralized, purely self-interested decisions of many individuals. Note, however, that it need not maximize social welfare: for example, the process might converge to the state where everyone is playing the inferior action B. Note also that the evolution of the process is unpredictable, because the path followed depends on the order in which people happen to reevaluate their choices. Such a process is nonergodic in the sense that the likelihood of winding up in different equilibrium states depends on the initial state as well as on chance events that occur early on in the history of the process.

While this model is a reasonable first cut at representing the dynamics of conformity, it omits a crucial feature of the real world, namely, the essential unpredictability or heterogeneity of individual behavior. The fact is that people sometimes make idiosyncratic choices for unexplained reasons, that is, for reasons that lie outside of our model. Someone who is surrounded by B-players may nevertheless choose A; similarly someone might opt for B even though it is fashionable to play A. (Indeed, this is how we can interpret Catherine de Medici's action: she persisted in the habit of eating with a fork despite criticism from members of her own court.) To incorporate these *idiosyncratic* aspects of behavior, we shall treat each agent's choice of action as a random variable. In particular, we shall assume that each agent usually chooses a best reply given what her neighbors are doing, but that occasionally she chooses a nonbest reply. This results in a stochastic dynamical process, which (somewhat paradoxically) is easier to analyze than the earlier one. This is because its long-run average behavior is independent of the initial conditions, that is, the process is *ergodic*.

5.3 The Model with Idiosyncratic Shocks

Fix a finite graph Γ, and let x^t denote the *state* of the system at time t, where $x_i^t \in \{A, B\}$ is the choice of action by agent i ($1 \le i \le n$). Let N_i denote the set of agent i's neighbors in the graph. The expected payoff to an agent from choosing a given action is the sum of the payoffs from playing this action once against each of her neighbors in the following game:

$$
\begin{array}{ccc}
 & A & B \\
A & a,a & c,d \\
B & d,c & b,b \quad a>d,\,b>c.
\end{array}
\tag{2}
$$

Thus, if agent i reevaluates at time t, her expected payoffs from choosing A or B, conditional on everyone else continuing with their previous choices are as follows:

$$
\begin{aligned}
u_i(A|x_{-i}) &= a|\{j \in N_i : x_j^t = A\}| + c|\{j \in N_i : x_j^t = B\}| \\
u_i(B|x_{-i}) &= d|\{j \in N_i : x_j^t = A\}| + b|\{j \in N_i : x_j^t = B\}|.
\end{aligned}
\tag{3}
$$

A standard model of discrete choice is to assume that the log probability of choosing either action is a linear function of its expected payoff (McFadden 1974; Blume 1993, 1995; Brock and Durlauf 1995, 1999). That is, for some real number $\beta > 0$,

$$
\begin{aligned}
\Pr\{i \text{ chooses } A \text{ in state } x\} &= e^{\beta u_i(A|x_{-i})} \big/ \big[e^{\beta u_i(A|x_{-i})} + e^{\beta u_i(B|x_{-i})} \big]. \\
\Pr\{i \text{ chooses } B \text{ in state } x\} &= e^{\beta u_i(B|x_{-i})} \big/ \big[e^{\beta u_i(A|x_{-i})} + e^{\beta u_i(B|x_{-i})} \big].
\end{aligned}
\tag{4}
$$

The larger β is, the higher is the probability that i chooses the action with highest expected payoff. This is known as a *log-linear response model with response parameter β*, or simply a *β-response model*.[4]

Beginning in an arbitrary initial state x^0, let $\mu^t(x)$ denote the probability that the system is in state x at time t. It can be shown that, as t becomes large, $\mu^t(x)$ approaches a limit $\mu(x)$ that is independent of the initial state. This is known as the *long-run probability* of state x, and μ is the *stationary distribution* of the stochastic process. The stationary distribution can be computed explicitly from a suitably defined potential function. Namely, for each state x, let $A(x)$ denote the *number* of edges such that the agents at both ends of the edge choose action A in state x. Similarly, let $B(x)$ denote the number of edges such that the agents at both ends choose action B. The *potential* of state x is defined to be

$$
\rho(x) = (a-d)A(x) + (b-c)B(x).
\tag{5}
$$

This same potential function can be used to show that the process converges with probability 1 to an equilibrium state when agents always choose a best reply to their neighbors (see the discussion in section 5.2). When agents' choices are perturbed as in (4), the process does not come to rest in any particular state. However, the long-run probability of being in each state x takes the following form, known as a *Gibbs distribution* (Liggett 1985):

$$\mu(x) = e^{\rho(x)} \Big/ \sum_{y \in \Xi} e^{\rho(y)} . \tag{6}$$

From this we can estimate the relative likelihood of various equilibrium and disequilibrium states. To illustrate, consider the case where the off-diagonal payoffs are zero ($c = d = 0$) and $a > b$ so that A Pareto dominates B. Potential is maximized by the state in which everyone plays A. Denote this state by **A**. The larger β is, the more likely it is that the process is in state **A** at any given large time t. Such a state is said to be *stochastically stable* (Foster and Young 1990; Young 1993). Compared to **A**, the relative likelihood of the all-B state, **B**, is $\mu(\mathbf{B})/\mu(\mathbf{A}) = e^{\beta(b-a)E}$, where E is the total number of edges in the graph. Thus the larger the payoff difference between A and B, the less likely is the all-B state relative to the all-A state.

Suppose instead that A and B are equally desirable, that is, $a = b$ (and $c = d = 0$ as before). Let $L(x) = E - A(x) - B(x)$ denote the total number of edges such that one end is coordinated on A and the other on B. We may interpret $L(x)$ as the length of the boundary between the A-regions and the B-regions. We may then write the potential function as $\rho(x) = a(E - L(x))$. *Thus, when A and B are equally desirable a priori, the log probability of each state is a linear decreasing function of the length of the boundary between the A and B regions.*

The preceding analysis shows that evolutionary forces tend to favor states with maximum potential. Notice, however, that maximizing potential is not necessarily the same thing as maximizing social welfare. In a symmetric game with payoff matrix (2), action A Pareto-dominates B if $a > b$, whereas it risk-dominates B if $a - d > b - c$. Formula (5) shows that potential is maximized when everyone chooses the risk-dominant action. Consider the following example, known as the Stag Hunt game (Rousseau 1762):

	A	B	
A	10,10	0,7	(8)
B	7,0	7,7	

Action A requires teamwork, that is, it has high payoff only if the other side also chooses it. Action B does not require teamwork; its payoff is the same whether the other side chooses it or not. Teamwork is the optimal strategy, but it is also the riskiest if one doubts that the other side will do the right thing. In the model above, the all-B state has higher probability than the all-A state, even though A Pareto-dominates B.

5.4 Social Inertia

The preceding asymptotic analysis shows what kinds of norms are most likely to be observed over the long run. But how long is the long run? If it takes eons to reach the stochastically stable states predicted by theory, then the theory may not tell us much about real-world phenomena. In this section we examine the *inertia* of the process, that is, the expected waiting time until the stochastically stable state (or something close to it) first becomes established, starting from an arbitrary initial state. As we shall see, the waiting time depends crucially on the *geometry* of social interaction, that is, on who interacts with whom. When people interact mainly with small groups of neighbors, the inertia can be dramatically lower than when everyone interacts with everyone else. Ellison (1993) was the first to demonstrate this point in a model where people interact with their neighbors on a circle. Here we shall extend the analysis to more general interaction structures.

Consider a symmetric two-person game with two actions A and B, and suppose that A is the risk-dominant action. (Action A may or may not be Pareto optimal as well.) Let Γ be a graph that defines who interacts with whom. For a given graph Γ and response parameter β, let $W(\Gamma, \beta, \delta)$ be the expected waiting time until the first time that at least $1 - \delta$ of the population is playing A, given that the process started in state **B**. The parameter δ is the *degree of precision* with which the process approximates state **A**. Since there is a positive probability that any given individual will choose B even when all of his neighbors choose A, the probability is very small that the process will actually be in state **A** at any given time when the number of individuals is large. Thus we need to choose δ (for a given level of β) so that with high probability the process stays within δ of state **A** once the process comes within δ of **A**.

We claim that, for certain natural kinds of interaction structures (of which lattices are a special case), the expected waiting time $W(\Gamma, \beta, \delta)$ is bounded *independently of the size of* Γ. Surprisingly, this result does not hinge on the connectivity of the interaction structure, but on the extent to which people interact in small, close-knit groups. In general, to define this concept precisely, fix a subset S of vertices. For each vertex $i \in S$, let $d(\{i\}, S)$ be the number of edges that link i with a member of S. Similarly, for each subset S' of S, let $d(S', S)$ denote the number of edges such that one end is in S' and the other is in S. This is the *internal degree of S' in S*. The *degree d_i* of vertex i is the total number of edges incident with i. The vertex is *isolated* if $d_i = 0$. Let Γ be a graph with no isolated vertices. A nonempty subset S of vertices is *r-close-knit* for some real number $0 \le r \le 1/2$, if for every nonempty subset S' of S,

$$d(S', S) \ge r \sum_{i \in S'} d_i. \tag{9}$$

In other words, the internal degree of S' in S must be at least r times the total degree of S', for each subset S' of S (including $S' = S$). Note that, for every vertex $i \in S$, at least r of i's interactions must be with other members of S. Such a set is said to be *r-cohesive* (Morris 1997). But r-cohesiveness does not imply r-close-knittedness. Suppose, for example, that each member of S has *exactly* r of its interactions with other members of S. Then the internal degree of S with itself is $(r/2)\Sigma_{i \in S} d_i$. Thus (9) holds for $r/2$ instead of r, that is, r-cohesiveness only implies $r/2$-close-knittedness.

Why is condition (9) required to hold for all subsets S' of S, instead of just individuals? The answer is that, even if each individual in S is impervious to conversion by outsiders, there could nevertheless exist a subgroup of S that is convertible, because collectively this subgroup has too many interactions with outsiders compared to interactions with insiders. Condition (9) states that S *and all of its subgroups* are sufficiently impervious to outside influences.

Given a positive integer k, we say that the graph Γ is *(r, k)-close-knit* if every person belongs to some group of size at most k that is at least r-close-knit. A family F of graphs is *close-knit* if for every $0 < r < 1/2$ there exists an integer k (possibly depending on r) such that every graph in the class is (r, k)-close-knit.

As an example, consider the class of all polygons. In a polygon, the degree of every vertex is two. Each subset S of k consecutive vertices contains $k - 1$ edges, so $d(S, S) = ((k - 1)/2k) \Sigma_{i \in S} d_i$. It is easy to check that in fact $d(S', S) \ge ((k - 1)/2k) \Sigma_{i \in S'} d_i$ for every nonempty subset S' of S, hence every subset of k-consecutive vertices is $(1/2 - 1/2k)$-close-knit. Since every vertex is contained in such a set, the class of polygons is close-knit. For a square lattice embedded on the surface of a torus, it can be verified that every subsquare of side h is $(1/2 - 1/2h, h^2)$-close-knit. It follows that the family of square lattices is close-knit. The following result is proved in Young (1998, Theorem 6.2).

THEOREM   Let G be a symmetric 2×2 coordination game with a strictly risk-dominant equilibrium, and let $\mathcal{F}$ be a close-knit family of graphs. Given any precision $\delta > 0$, there exists a number β_δ such that for each fixed $\beta \geq \beta_\delta$, the waiting time $W(\Gamma, \beta, \delta)$ is bounded independently of the number of vertices in Γ.

   The intuition behind this result can be explained as follows. Given a symmetric 2×2 game G with payoff matrix (2), let A be strictly risk-dominant, that is, $a - d > b - c$. Choose r such that $(b - c)/(a - d + b - c) < r < 1/2$ and let k be such that all members of $\mathcal{F}$ are (r, k)-close-knit. Fix a specific graph $\Gamma \in \mathcal{F}$. By construction, each individual is contained in an r-close-knit group S of size k or less. The probability that such an individual chooses a non-best reply in a unit interval of time is bounded below by a positive number that depends on β, k, r, and the payoff matrix, but does not depend on the particular graph Γ. Since these parameters are fixed, the expected waiting time is bounded until the first time that all k members of S play A simultaneously. Once this happens, the close-knittedness of S assures that at every subsequent time, everyone in S plays action A with high probability irrespective of what the players outside of S are doing (assuming that β is sufficiently large). Since every individual is in such a group S, and the process is running simultaneously for all individuals, the waiting time is bounded until the first time that a high *proportion* of the individuals in the graph are playing A.

   Note that this argument does not depend on the idea that actions spread by diffusion (which they may indeed do). For example, if one person switches to action A, it becomes more likely that nearby individuals will also adopt action A, which makes it more likely that *their* neighbors will adopt action A, and so forth. Clearly such a process further speeds up the waiting time, but it also requires a certain degree of connectivity in the interaction structure. The result assumes nothing about connectivity, however. For example, it applies equally well to graphs that consist of many distinct connected components, each of size k. The driving force behind the result is local reinforcement: if people interact mainly within a small group, any switch by the group to the risk-dominant equilibrium takes a long time to undo, and before that happens most of the other groups will have switched to the risk-dominant equilibrium too.

5.5 Sorting and Segregation

A different kind of social order arises when people change those with whom they associate, instead of changing how they behave given their associates. In other words, they *choose* their neighbors instead of *conforming* to their neighbors. This is called a *sorting process* (Schelling 1971, 1978). Here we shall consider a variant of Schelling's model that can be analyzed using the concept of a potential function, and thus parallels the conformity model discussed above. Imagine a population that consists of two types of individuals, the As and the Bs. These might represent different races, different ethnicities, or different religious affiliations, for example. The choice variable is not whether to *be* an A or a B, but whether to *associate* with the As, the Bs, or some mixture of the two, given one's identity as an A or a B. Opportunities for association are given by a graph Γ consisting of vertices linked by edges. Each individual lives at a vertex, and his neighbors are the people who live at adjacent vertices. Each person has a preference for the composition of the neighborhood she lives in, that is, for the proportion of As and Bs who are her neighbors. We adopt the assumption, which seems reasonably consistent with empirical evidence, that most people like to live in neighborhoods that contain *some people* of their own type, though they do not necessarily prefer to reside in areas that contain *only* people of their own type. We shall also assume that everyone has the same utility for the proportion of neighbors who are like themselves; it is not difficult to extend the analysis to populations with heterogeneous preferences.

The general idea is much the same as in Schelling's setup. People move because they prefer the neighborhood they are moving into compared with the neighborhood they are moving from. These decisions impose externalities on one's neighbors, because a move will typically alter the composition of the neighborhood that one moves into, as well as the composition of the neighborhood that one leaves behind. To keep the analysis simple, let us assume that agents are located around a circle, and assume that there are an even number of agents of each type, as shown in figure 5.6. (A similar analysis can be carried out for other geometric arrangements, e.g., for agents located on a two-dimensional lattice.) A *state* of the system is an assignment of A or B to

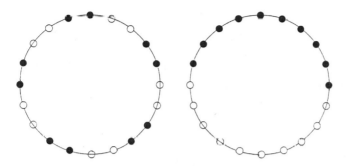

Figure 5.5
Two residential patterns: one integrated, the other segregated.

each location. A state is *completely segregated* if all *A*s form one contiguous group and all *B*s form another contiguous group. It is *completely integrated* if each person lives next to exactly one other person of his own type and one of the opposite type. Obviously there are many intermediate patterns that are partly integrated and partly segregated. One of the purposes of the model is to analyze how stable the various patterns are.

We shall say that a person is *discontent* if both immediate neighbors are unlike herself, she is *moderately content* if both neighbors are like herself, and she is *content* if one is like herself and one is different. Two individuals can *gain from trade* if, by trading places, and carrying out appropriate side payments, both can be made better off. Such a trade is *advantageous* (strictly Pareto improving), and all other trades are *disadvantageous*. We shall suppose that all trades involve moving costs, so that there is no incentive to trade unless the overall level of contentment can be raised.

Clearly, advantageous trades must involve partners who are of opposite types. An examination of the various cases shows that there are only two kinds of advantageous trades. In the first, both partners are discontent before the trade (i.e., they are isolated), and afterward both are moderately content because they now live in homogeneous neighborhoods with those of their own type. (This equires no side payments.) The second kind of advantageous trade involves one partner who is discontent and another who is content; after the trade the former is content and the latter is moderately content. In this case we suppose that the former can compensate the latter to move, so that both are strictly better off after the trade than they were before.

We claim that, if there are at least two people of each type, then in equi-librium no one is discontent. To see this, suppose to the contrary that an A is surrounded by two Bs: ... BAB. ... Moving clockwise around the circle, let B^* be the last B-type in the string of Bs who follows this A, and let A^* be the person who follows B^*:

... BAB ... BB^*A^* ...

Since there are at least two agents of each type, we can be sure that A^* differs from the original A. But then A could trade places with B^*, and be content instead of discontent; further A can compensate B^* to make up for the slight loss of contentment that B^* would suffer, thus making both better off than before. Thus we see that the equilibrium configurations consist of those arrangements in which everyone lives next to at least one person of his own type. No one is isolated.

What happens when the process begins in an out-of-equilibrium situation? Consider the following adaptive dynamic. In each discrete time period, two people are drawn at random and they have a con-versation about their respective neighborhoods. If they find that they can gain from trading places, they do so. The reader may verify that, from any initial state, there always exists some sequence of Pareto improving trades that leads to an equilibrium. Since the number of states is finite, such a sequence will eventually be realized with prob-ability 1, and thus the process will eventually find its way to some equi-librium. As in the conformity model, this equilibrium may or may not be desirable from the standpoint of social welfare. Furthermore, the particular equilibrium reached depends on the order in which people happened to find trading partners: the equilibration process is path dependent.

As in the model of conformity, we shall now incorporate the idea that people sometimes make idiosyncratic choices, that is, they trade places for unexplained reasons. (This is not a feature of Schelling's model.) Consider two individuals who are thinking about making a trade. If it is advantageous, that is, involves utility gains for both sides, we shall assume that it occurs with probability close to one. If the trade is dis-advantageous, we shall assume that it occurs with a small probability that decreases exponentially the larger the utility losses are. An exam-ination of the various cases shows that disadvantageous trades are of three types. In the first, both partners are equally content before and after the trade. Such a trade is not frictionless, however, because it involves moving costs. We shall suppose that such a trade occurs with probability ε^α where ε, $\alpha > 0$. The second type of trade involves one person who is content before and is discontent after, in other words, a person who moved from a mixed neighborhood to one in which he is isolated. His partner (who is of the opposite type) must therefore have been moderately content before the trade and content afterward. We assume that the latter's gain is not sufficient to compensate the former's loss; hence the trade induces a net loss in utility from the new locations plus moving costs. Thus it occurs with a lower probability than the preceding type of trade, say with probabilit ε^β, where $\alpha < \beta$. The third type of disadvantageous trade involves two individuals who were moderately content before and are discontent after, that is, they were in homogeneous neighborhoods to begin with, and after moving both are isolated. This is the most disadvantageous type of trade and we assume that it is least probable, that is, it occurs with probability ε^γ, where $\alpha < \beta < \gamma$.

We shall explore the dynamics of such a process by varying the parameter ε, which measures the degree of "noise" in the system. When ε is large, the idiosyncratic aspect of individual choice overwhelms the gravitational pull toward equilibrium states, and the residential patterns will be in constant flux. The smaller ε is, the more likely the process is to be in (or close to) an equilibrium state. Indeed more is true: *when ε is sufficiently small, the probability is close to one of being in a completely segregated state.*[5] Put differently, when idiosyncratic variations are relatively rare, the most likely form of spontaneous order is one in which all As live on one side of the circle, and all Bs on the other. The segregated states are the only stochastically stable ones.[6]

Note that nobody intended such a state of affairs. Indeed, under our assumptions, everyone would prefer to live in a perfectly integrated society in which As alternate with Bs (assuming there are an equal number of As and Bs). Segregated patterns emerge endogenously due to the cumulative impact of many individual decisions, each of which is locally optimal but not globally so. But the process does not "lock in" to a socially inefficient equilibrium and simply stay there—it keeps evolving due to the idiosyncratic nature of individual choices, whose effect is to keep the process constantly in motion. The net effect is that the residential pattern of As and Bs keeps shifting around: sometimes As will live in the North, sometimes in the South; segregated neighborhoods will eventually become integrated, later they will become segregated again, and so forth. This is not unlike the process we see in the real world.

5.6   Three Qualitative Properties of Social Dynamics

The dynamic models discussed above illustrate how complex social structure can emerge from the cumulative impact of many uncoordinated decisions by individuals. The models are somewhat stylized and are not meant to explain how any one residential neighborhood developed or how a particular social norm came into being. Each such instance will be the product of particular historical circumstances that lie outside the purview of the model. Nevertheless, models of this type can identify certain qualitative patterns that may hold when we average over many particular instances. To describe these patterns, think of society as being divided into many subsocieties or "villages" that do not interact with one another. When the same evolutionary process runs independently and in parallel in each of the villages, we can expect to observe the following three phenomena.

Local conformity, global diversity. Within each village, at any given time, behaviors are likely to be close to some equilibrium, though idiosyncratic, unconventional behaviors will be present to some degree. Different villages may operate under different equilibria due to historical chance. In other words, there is diversity in outcomes at any given time due to path dependency effects.

Tipping. Within each village, there will tend to be long periods of stasis in which a given equilibrium remains in place, punctuated by occasional episodes in which the village tips from one equilibrium to another in response to stochastic shocks. Thus there is temporal diversity in a given place as well as spatial diversity at a given time.

Long-run stability. Some equilibria are inherently more stable than others, and, once established, they tend to persist for longer periods of time. The relative stability of different equilibria will tend to be reflected in the frequency with which they occur among the various villages at a given point in time (and also within each village over a long period of time). Stability depends on the payoff structure of the individual interactions, and it is not true in general that outcomes having maximum stability are those that maximize social welfare.

5.7   Coordinated Action and the Role of Institutions

In this chapter we have shown how aggregate patterns of behavior at the societal level can emerge spontaneously from many decentralized decisions at the individual level. Of course, it would be absurd to claim that this is the only way in which such patterns arise. In the case of sorting by race, groups of individuals may take concerted action to block entry by members of the other group, either through physical force, the threat of physical force, or the erection of legal barriers. We have sidestepped such complications in order to analyze the sorting that results when people care only about the composition of the neighborhoods where they live, there is no coercion, and no legal barriers to the choice of neighborhood. What the model tells us is that segregated patterns are likely to arise even without coercive action, and even when individuals prefer to live in mixed neighborhoods than in homogeneous ones.

Similarly, we do not claim that norms of behavior spread *only* by spontaneous diffusion at the individual level. They are often transmitted on a larger scale by institutions whose purpose it is to inculcate norms, such as families, schools, and religious institutions. Nevertheless we must not lose sight of the fact that these institutions are often themselves the product of social evolution. While it is true that a family may transmit norms of behavior from parents to children, these norms are influenced by the norms being taught in other families. Methods of instruction, and certainly subjects of instruction, are adopted by schools after taking into account what other schools are doing. Thus, while the transmission of norms may be coordinated at one level (the family or school), these coordinating institutions are often responding to the choices of other institutions. In this case institutions are the agents of norm diffusion, and conformity among institutional behaviors is the relevant form of spontaneous order.

Notes

1. For related work on norm formation see Ullman-Margalit (1977), Sugden (1986), and Bicchieri, Jeffrey, and Skyrms (1997).

2. For related work on local interaction models see Anderlini and Ianni (1996), Goyal (1996), Goyal and Janssen (1997), and Bala and Goyal (1998).

3. In addition there is an equilibrium in which everyone on the boundary of the square plays B, and everyone in the interior plays A.

4. This model satisfies certain independence properties that make it appealing a priori and easy to estimate empirically. Variants have been used to explain learning behavior in experimental situations. See for example Roth and Erev (1995).

5. This result is proved in Young 1998 (chap. 3, sec. 5).

6. Schelling (1971) derived a somewhat similar result in a different kind of model.

7. We have established this result only for the circle model in which the number of agents of each type is fixed, but we conjecture that it also holds for two-dimensional structures and for situations where the population is growing through migration.

References

Akerlof, George A. 1997. "Social Distance and Social Decisions." *Econometrica* 65: 1005–1027.

Anderlini, Luca, and Antonella Ianni. 1996. "Path Dependence and Learning from Neighbors." *Games and Economic Behavior* 13: 141–178.

Bala, Venkatesh, and Sanjeev Goyal. 1998. "Learning from Neighbors." *Review of Economic Studies* 65: 595–621.

Bicchieri, Christina, Richard Jeffrey, and Brian Skyrms, eds. 1997. *The Dynamics of Norms.* New York: Cambridge University Press.

Blume, Larry. 1993. "The Statistical Mechanics of Strategic Interaction." *Games and Economic Behavior* 4: 387–424.

———. 1995. "The Statistical Mechanics of Best-Response Strategy Revision." *Games and Economic Behavior* 11: 111–145.

Brock, William A., and Steven N. Durlauf. 1995. "Discrete Choice with Social Interactions. I: Theory." Cambridge, Mass. NBER Working Paper 5291.

———. 1999. "Interactions-Based Models." In *Handbook of Econometrics,* vol. V, ed. James Heckman and Edward Leamer. Amsterdam: North-Holland.

Case, Anne. C., and Lawrence F. Katz. 1991. "The Company You Keep: The Effects of Family and Neighborhood on Disadvantaged Youths." Cambridge, Mass. NBER Working Paper No. 3705.

Coryate, Thomas. 1611. *Coryats Crudities 1611.* London: Scolar Press, 1978.

Crane, Jonathan. 1991. "The Epidemic Theory of Ghettos and Neighborhood Effects on Dropping Out and Teenage Childbearing." *American Journal of Sociology* 96: 1226–1259.

Ellison, Glenn. 1993. "Learning, Social Interaction, and Coordination." *Econometrica* 61: 1047–1071.

Evans, William C., Wallace E. Oates, and Robert M. Schwab. 1992. "Measuring Peer Group Effects: A Study of Teenage Behavior." *Journal of Political Economy* 100: 966–991.

Foster, Dean P., and H. Peyton Young, "Stochastic Evolutionary Game Dynamics." *Theoretical Population Biology* 38: 219–232.

Giblin, James Cross. 1987. *From Hand To Mouth.* New York: Thomas Crowell.

Glaeser, Edward L., Bruce Sacerdote, and Jose A. Scheinkman. 1996. "Crime and Social Interactions." *Quarterly Journal of Economics* 11: 507–548.

Glennon, Robert J. 1991. "The Role of Law in the Civil Rights Movement: The Montgomery Bus Boycott, 1955–1957." *Law and History Review* 9: 59–112.

Goyal, Sanjeev. 1996. "Interaction Structure and Social Change." *Journal of Institutional and Theoretical Economics* 152: 472–495.

Goyal, Sanjeev, and Maarten Janssen. 1997. "Non-Exclusive Conventions and Social Coordination." *Journal of Economic Theory* 77: 34–57.

Liggett, Thomas. 1985. *Interacting Particle Systems*. New York: Springer-Verlag.

McFadden, Daniel. 1974. "Conditional Logit Analysis of Qualitative Choice Behavior." In *Frontiers in Econometrics*, ed. Paul Zarembka. New York: Academic Press.

Morris, Stephen. 1997. "Contagion." Mimeo. Department of Economics, University of Pennsylvania.

Roth, Alvin E., and Ido Erev. 1995. "Learning in Extensive-Form Games: Experimental Data and Simple Dynamic Models in the Intermediate Term." *Games and Economic Behavior* 8: 164–212.

Rousseau, Jean-Jacques. [1762. 196H]. *Du contrat social, ou, principes du droit politique*. In *J.-J. Rousseau, Oeuvres Completes*, vol. 3. Dijon: Editions Gallimard.

Schelling, Thomas C. 1971. "Dynamic Models of Segregation." *Journal of Mathematical Sociology* 1: 143–186.

———. 1978. *Micromotives and Macrobehavior*. New York: Norton.

Sugden, Robert. 1986. *The Evolution of Rights, Cooperation, and Welfare*. New York: Basil-Blackwell.

———. 1978. *Micromotives and Macrobehavior*. New York: Norton.

Ullman-Margalit, Edna. 1977. *The Emergince of Norms*. Oxford: Oxford University Press.

Young, H. Peyton. 1993. "The Evolution of Conventions." *Econometrica* 61: 57–94.

———. 1998. *Individual Strategy and Social Structure: An Evolutionary Theory of Institutions*. Princeton: Princeton University Press.

6

Individual Interactions, Group Conflicts, and the Evolution of Preferences

Samuel Bowles

Political writers have established it as a maxim, that, in contriving any system of government . . . every man ought to be supposed to be a knave and to have no other end, in all his actions, than his private interest.

—David Hume, *Essays: Moral, Political, and Literary*

Lawgivers make the citizen good by inculcating habits in them, and this is the aim of every lawgiver; if he does not succeed in doing that, his legislation is a failure. It is in this that a good constitution differs from a bad one.

—Aristotle, *Nichomachean Ethics*

6.1 Introduction

Economists have followed Hume, and before him Hobbes, rather than Aristotle, in positing a given and self-regarding individual as the appropriate behavioral foundation for considerations of governance and policy. The implicit premise that preferences are selfish and that policies and constitutions do not affect preferences has much to recommend it: the premise provides a common if minimal analytical framework applicable to a wide range of issues of public concern, it expresses a prudent antipathy toward paternalistic attempts at social engineering of the psyche, it modestly acknowledges how little we know about the effects of economic structure and policy on preferences, and it erects a barrier to both ad hoc explanation and the utopian thinking of those who invoke the mutability of human dispositions in order to sidestep difficult questions of scarcity and social choice.

Realism, however, cannot be counted among the virtues of the exogenous preferences premise: the available evidence, while far from conclusive, suggests that economic policies and institutions affect preferences.[1] The primary effects appear to operate though situational construal (or framing), the effect of forms of reward on motivation, the influence of the structure of social interactions on evolution of norms, and the way institutions shape task-related learning as well as indirect effects on the process of cultural transmission itself.

Nor does the assumption that human motivations are entirely self-regarding find convincing empirical support: experiments by social psychologists and economists, ethnographic and historical studies of collective sacrifice toward common objectives, and simple introspection point to the importance of other-regarding preferences.[2] Moreover preferences appear to be defined over processes as well as outcome per se, with individuals making different choices depending on how a given opportunity set was determined.

Economists and to a lesser extent other social scientists have resisted addressing the complexity and endogeneity of human motivations, not because we think the behavioral simplicity of *homo economicus* is an adequate representation, but rather because we lack both adequate conceptual tools and empirical information on the process of preference formation. It thus may be useful to consider a formal model of the process of preference formation, one that admits the possibility that other-regarding and process-regarding preferences, as well as self-regarding and outcome-oriented motivations, might evolve.

Among the desiderata for such a models is recognition of the highly structured (rather than random) ways that humans interact both within and between groups. Just as the norms and tastes motivating individual behavior proliferate in a group when individuals copy successful neighbors, so too do distributive norms, linguistic conventions, religious faiths, and other cultural traits diffuse or disappear through the emulation of the characteristics of successful groups by members of less successful groups, often as a result of military, economic, and other forms of competition. While both individual and group interactions thus influence the updating of preferences, they have been treated quite differently by students of cultural evolution. Evolutionary game theory and the biologically inspired theory of cultural evolution have provided agent-based models of individual updating within populations. But for the most part, group-level effects have played a distinctly lesser role in formal modeling. By contrast, group effects have been the primary focus of empirical studies by historians and anthropologists whose insights on such questions as the encroachment of market societies on indigenous cultures derive from a structuralist approach that eschews the reductionism of agent-based modeling. Moreover many, perhaps most, formal evolutionary models abstract from two additional aspects of human social structure relevant to the process of individual updating: a tendency toward conformism in the adoption of behavioral traits and the fact that human groups are highly segregated, often deliberately so, such that individual interactions are hardly ever random with respect to preferences of the individual.

In this chapter, I provide a unified framework for studying the effects of economic (and other) institutions on the evolution of preferences, taking account of conformist updating, social segregation, and the simultaneous operation of selection processes at the individual and group level. I begin by clarifying what I mean by preferences and explaining how evolutionary processes may be conveniently partitioned into group-level and individual selection effects. I then indicate, by way of concrete examples from the historical, anthropological, and political science literatures, the kinds of real-world phenomena that an adequate model of preference evolution should be able to address. I then develop a model of individual updating incorporating the effects of both social segmentation and conformism. Next I embed this model in the process of intergroup competition. In the penultimate section, I use the resulting model to discuss the effects of social institutions (and by implication economic policies) on the evolution of preferences.

6.2   Group and Individual Effects in Preference Evolution

Preferences are reasons for behavior, that is, attributes of individuals (other than beliefs and capacities) that account for the actions they take in a given situation. To explain why a person chose a point in a budget set, for example, one might make reference to her craving for the chosen goods, or to a religious prohibition against the excluded goods. Conceived this way, preferences go considerably beyond tastes, as an adequate account of individual actions would have to include values or what Amartya Sen (1977) terms "commitments" and John Harsanyi (1982) calls "moral preferences" (as distinct from personal preferences.) Also included are the manner in which the individual construes the situation in which the choice is to be made (Ross and Nisbett 1991), the way that the decision situation is framed (Tversky and Kahneman 1986), cultural beliefs (Greif 1994), compulsions, addictions, habits, and, more broadly, psychological dispositions. Preferences may be strongly cognitively mediated—my enjoying ice cream may depend critically on my belief that ice cream does not make me fat—or they may be visceral reactions—like disgust or fear—evoking strong emotions but having only the most minimal cognitive aspects (Zajonc 1980; Laibson forthcoming; Loewenstein 1996; Rozin and Nemeroff 1990). The term "preferences" for these heterogeneous reasons for behavior is perhaps too narrow, and runs the risk of falsely suggesting that a single model of action is sufficient; P. H. Nowell-Smith's (1954) "pro and con attitudes" or "reasons for choosing" are more descriptive, but unwieldy.[3]

How might group- and individual-level processes influencing the evolution of these "pro and con attitudes" be modeled?

As has been long recognized (Price 1970; Crow and Kimura 1970), in populations composed of groups characterized by a markedly higher level of interaction among members than with outsiders, evolutionary processes may be decomposed into between-group and within-group selection effects. Where the degree of successful replication of a trait depends on the composition the group and where group differences in composition exist, group selection contributes to the pace and direction of evolutionary change. The classic problem of group selection arises when between-group effects favor the proliferation of a group-beneficial trait such as altruism that is disfavored by individual selection within groups.

Few students of human populations doubt that institutions, nations, firms, bands, and other social aggregates are subject to selective pressures operating at the group rather than individual level (Darwin 1873; Alchian 1950; Hayek 1990; Parsons 1964; Tilly 1990). But at least until recently, most biologists who have modeled evolutionary processes under the joint influence of group and individual selection have concluded that the former cannot offset the effects of the latter except where special circumstances heighten and sustain differences between groups relative to within-group differences.[4] Thus group selection models are widely judged to have failed in their defining task, namely, to explain the evolutionary success of altruism and other individually costly forms of group-beneficial sociality. As a result, while the explanation of group-beneficial behaviors has focused on inclusive, kin-based fitness mechanisms, the impressive levels of non-kin-based sociality in the case of humans has remained for the most part unexplained.[5]

But as Boyd and Richerson (1985, 1990), Sober and Wilson (1998), Wilson and Dugatkin (1997), Wilson and Sober (1994), Boehm (1996,

1997), and others have pointed out, group selection may be of considerably greater importance among humans, given the substantial role of cultural inheritance in the replication of human traits, the advanced level of human cognitive capacities, and, as a result of these, the distinctive nature of human groups. Conformist cultural transmission based on frequency-dependent learning rules favoring more prevalent traits (Boyd and Richerson 1985; Cavalli-Sforza and Feldman 1973) will sustain between-group variances and thus may make group selection viable when a purely payoff-based learning rule would not. Boehm notes that egalitarian social processes may also enhance the relative influence of group selection mechanisms; examples include practices such as monogamy or food sharing that reduce the phenotypic variance of traits within a group as well as other practices like consensus decision making that additionally increase between group differences. Wilson and Dugatkin (1997), extending earlier work on assortative (nonrandom) interactions by Hamilton (1975), Grafen (1979, 1984), and others, point out that humans are well equipped to recognize and discriminate among those with whom they interact, the resulting social segmentation sustaining high levels of between-group differences in trait frequencies.[6]

Given that conformist cultural transmission, egalitarian social processes, and social segmentation may enhance the role of group selection, it would appear, first, that group beneficial but individually costly traits might be favored in human evolution, and this may help account for the high levels of sociality of humans. Among these group-beneficial traits are forms of costly punishment of those who transgress social norms and, of course, altruism. A second inference is that through their influence on the group selection process, economic institutions, ingroup-outgroup relationships, social stratification, residence patterns, and other aspects of social structure may influence the evolution of norms, tastes, habits, and other fundamental bases of human behavior (Bowles 1998).

Consider a single trait, which may be absent or present in each individual in large population whose members each belong to one of a large number of groups. Let $p_{ij} = 1$ indicate that individual i in group j has the trait, with $p_{ij} = 0$ otherwise. Using a discrete time nonoverlapping generations framework, let p and p' represent the fraction of the population with the trait during a given period and a subsequent time period, respectively, and $\Delta p \equiv p' - p$. Without specifying the nature of the trait replication and updating process, suppose in any period each

individual present in the previous period is represented by some
number of exact replicas (if the individual had the trait, the replicas do
as well); those favored by the selection process yield more replicas than
those disfavored. Define the selection coefficient w_{ij} as the number of
replicas of individual i in group j, and let w_{ij} depend (additively) on i's
own trait and the frequency of the trait in the group (p_j, $\in [0,1]$) according to

$$w_{ij} = \beta_o + p_j \beta_{wp\sim.p} + p_{ij}\beta_{wp.p\sim} \tag{1}$$

where $\beta_{wp\sim.p}$ and $\beta_{wp.p\sim}$ are the partial regression coefficients of w_{ij} on the
frequency of the trait in the group and the presence of the trait in the
individual, respectively, and β_o is baseline replication, a constant uncor-
related with the trait. Define $\beta_{w\sim p\sim} \equiv \beta_{wp\sim.p} + \beta_{wp.p\sim}$ as the regression of the
group average number of replicas on the frequency of the trait in the
group (the difference in the number of replicas between a group composed entirely of those with the trait and a group entirely without is
$\beta_{w\sim p\sim}$.) Then following Price (1970) we can write

$$\underline{w}\Delta p = \text{var}(p_j)\beta_{w\sim p\sim} + E\{\text{var}(p_{ij})\}\beta_{wp.p\sim} \tag{2}$$

where $\underline{w}$ is the population average selection coefficient and the expectation operator $E\{\ \}$ indicates a weighted summation over groups
(the weights being group size). (See also Grafen 1985, Rogers 1990, and
Frank 1995.) The first term captures the group selection effect, while
the second represents the effect of individual selection within groups[7]
(A simple derivation of this decomposition is in the appendix.)
It follows that (abstracting from degenerate cases such as zero variances) an interior frequency of the trait will be stationary where these
two terms are of opposite sign and equal magnitude (assuming that
the regression coefficients and (weighted) variances making up these
terms are themselves stationary.) For concreteness, consider an altruistic behavior that costs the individual c and confers a benefit of b on
a randomly paired (single) member of the group, so a member in a
group composed entirely of altruists produces $b - c$ more replicas than
does a member of a group with no altruists. As we assume $b - c > 0$,
altruism is group beneficial. Using the definitions above, $\beta_{wp.p\sim} = -c$,
$\beta_{wp\sim.p} = b$ and $\beta_{w\sim p\sim} = b - c$. Then, because $\underline{w} > 0$, equation (2) with a little
rearranging shows that the frequency of the altruistic trait is stationary
if

$$c/b = \text{var}(p_j)/[E\{\text{var}(p_{ij})\} + \text{var}(p_j)], \tag{3}$$

where the right-hand term, the ratio of between-group to total variance of the trait, is identical to the degree of genetic relatedness in kin selection models (Crow and Kimura 1970). It measures the difference between the probabilities that an altruist and a nonaltruist, respectively, will interact with an altruist: when the variance among group means is zero, the probability that both will meet an altruist is identical, namely p. Equations (2) and (3) make it clear that the force of group selection will depend on the magnitude of the group benefit relative to the individual cost (b and c in the example) and the degree to which groups differ in their mean frequency of the trait, relative to the degree of within-group variance of the trait. The reason why food sharing, consensus decision making, and the other within-group homogenizing practices of human societies mentioned above is important for group selection is clear: where groups are homogeneous, no individual selection can take place (the second term in equation 2 vanishes). The importance of between-group differentiation is equally apparent: where group means are identical, group selection is precluded (the first term in equation 2 vanishes).

To adapt this approach to the peculiarities of human cultural evolution, I abstract from differential biological reproduction of the bearers of traits and assume that every member of the population is infinitely lived; behavioral traits, however, are differentially replicated through a process of learning from others. Reflecting the often strategic nature of human social interactions, the benefits and costs of particular behaviors and the cultural transmission process accounting for the replication of traits will depend on the distribution of traits in the population. The population is structured in two respects. First, individuals are members of groups, and interactions within groups (individual strategic interactions and learning) differ from those between groups (group "contests" and cultural assimilation). For this reason, the model exhibits two distinct processes of selection. Groups (like individuals in biological models) may go extinct and may reproduce, under conditions to be specified, yielding inexact replicas. Second, groups are segmented internally, so that while within-group interactions are governed by the same rules for all members, pairings of members may be nonrandom with respect to type.

6.3 Group Selection in Human Populations: An Example

Consider a concrete case: the emergence and spread of an entirely new organizational entity—the national state—and the norms supporting it in Europe, and their eventual diffusion throughout the world during the past half a millennium.[8] I introduce this case not to explain the rise of the national state and the diffusion of the norms associated with it (a far more complex task than can be attempted here), but to make clear what kinds of reasoning a group selection argument requires and what kinds of facts it might explain.[9] Charles Tilly (1990) poses the following problem:

The system of states that now prevails almost everywhere on earth took shape in Europe after 990 AD, then began extending its control far outside the continent five centuries later. It eventually absorbed, eclipsed, or extinguished all its rivals including the systems of states that then centered on China, India, Persia and Turkey.

Empires, city states, federations of cites, networks of landlords, churches, religious orders, leagues of pirates, warrior bands and many other forms of governance prevailed in some parts of Europe at various times over the last thousand years. Most of them qualified as states of one kind or another . . . But only slowly did the national state become the predominant form. Hence the double question: *What accounts for the great variation over time and space in the kinds of states that have prevailed in Europe since 990, and why did European states eventually converge on different variants of the national state?* (Pp. 4–5)

The success of the national state in Europe over a short historical span was dazzling. Again, Tilly (1990):

In AD 1200 the Italian Peninsula alone boasted two or three hundred distinct city states. Around 1490 . . . South Germany alone included 69 free cities in addition to its multiple bishoprics, duchies, and principalities . . . Europe's 80 million people divided into something like 500 states, would be states, statelets, and statelike organizations. By 1990 . . . depending on the rules for counting, the whole of Europe divided into a mere 25 to 28 states. (P. 43)

Figures 6.1 and 6.2 provide glimpses of the situation around 1500. Over the same period, and in part as a result of its success in Europe, replicas of the European national state flourished throughout the world, extinguishing competing forms of organization.

What explains this competitive success? The simple answer is that when national states warred with other forms of governance, they tended to win. According to Tilly (1990):

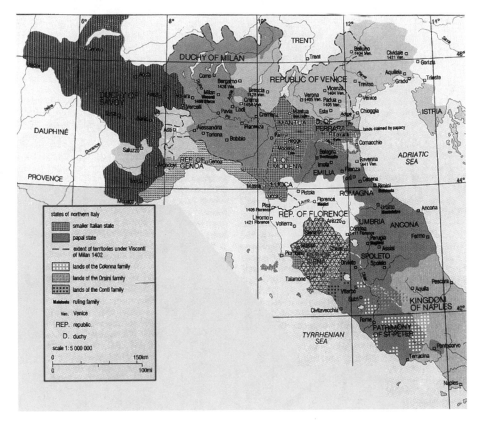

Figure 6.1
Political entities in fifteenth-century Italy. A great many of the smaller sovereign entities
(e.g., San Gimignano) are not shown; note also the many once autonomous entities (e.g.,
Verona, Bergamo, Padua, Vicenza, all absorbed by Venice early in the century). From
Matthew (1983, 212). Reproduced by kind permission of Andromeda Oxford Limited,
<www.andromeda.com>, copyright 1983.

Within limits set by the demands and rewards of other states, extraction and
struggle over the means of war created the central organizational structures of
states. . . . Only late in the millennium did national states exercise clear supe-
riority over city states, empires, and other common European forms of state.
. . . The increasing scale of war and the knitting together of the European state
system through commercial, military and diplomatic interaction eventually
gave the war-making advantage to those states that could field standing
armies; states having access to a combination of large rural population, capi-
talists, and relatively commercialized economies won out. They set the terms
of war, and their form of state became the predominant one in Europe. Eventually European states converged on that form: the national state. (P. 15)

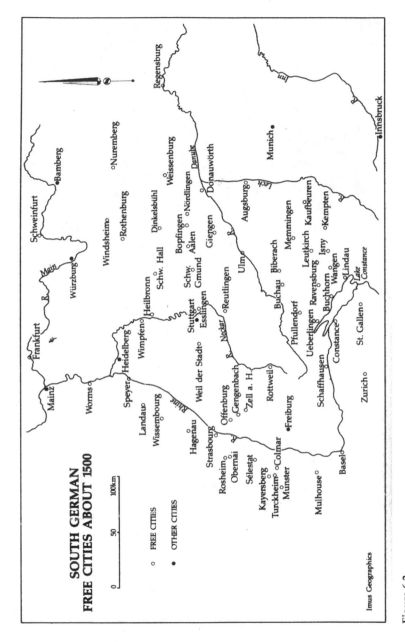

Figure 6.2
Autonomous South German cities. From Brady (1985, xvi).

Successfully making war required both resources and legitimacy:

No monarch could make war without securing the acquiescence of nearly all of his subject population, and the active cooperation of at least a crucial few. (Tilly 1990, 75).

Mobilizing resources to support a standing army required permanent and widespread taxation:

Before 1400 . . . taxes existed in Europe's more commercialized states, but rulers everywhere acquired most of their revenues from tribute, rent, dues, and fees. Individual sovereigns borrowed money, but usually in their own names and against real collateral. (P. 74)

. . . the mass of the subject population resisted direct seizure of men, food, weapons, transport and other means of war much more vigorously and effectively than they fought against paying for them. . . . . European states generally moved toward a system of collecting taxes in money, paying for coercive means with the money thus collected, and using some of the coercive means to further the collection of taxes. (P. 84)

Not all states succeeded in financing war through permanent monetized taxation:

Such a system only worked well under two very demanding conditions: a relatively monetized economy and the ready availability of credit. . . . The relative presence or absence of commercial cities within a state's territories therefore affected the ease of mobilization for war. (Pp. 84–86)

Market environments favored state formation in a less obvious way: by inducing tax compliance:

Participants in markets already do a significant share of the requisite surveillance thorough the recording of prices and transfers. Properly socialized citizens, furthermore, come to attach moral value to the payment of taxes; they monitor themselves and each other, blaming tax evaders as free riders. (P. 89)

Significantly for my interpretation of state formation as a diffusion process, European statemaking exhibited a distinct concentric spatial pattern, with large but thinly controlled states on the periphery (Muscovy and the Ottoman Empire, for example), a grouping of city states and federations near the center (the Italian city states, the Swiss cantons), and the eventually triumphant more centralized states such as France and Brandenburg, intermediate between the two. Successful national states assimilated the populations they absorbed, and over the period they promoted and eventually required a common pattern of childhood socialization through schooling.[10]

Under the auspices of the national state, European populations grew rapidly—multiplying fifteen fold in Britain in the four centuries after 1500 having grown hardly at all over the previous four centuries, and eclipsing population growth elsewhere in the world (except, perhaps, for China during the eightieth century). The diffusion of the national state globally was thus promoted not only by competitive pressures on the states of the European periphery but also by the substantial emigration of European bearers of the cultural traits and military capacities that had favored state building in Europe.

A group selection account of the diffusion of the norms associated with the national state is the following. The national state evolved because it won wars with competing organizations, and the ability to win wars depended on its peculiar ability to mobilize soldiers and other military resources. This ability depended on the extent of commerce and credit, tax compliance, and the willingness to serve rulers in war. These, in turn, were fostered by the diffusion of norms guiding individual behaviors that, while not (at least initially) individually advantageous, contributed to group success in war on this reasoning. Candidates for such norms include voluntary tax compliance, willingness to risk danger in war for a ruler or nation, and respect for property rights. The norm of monogamy may have played a similar, if less obvious role in securing popular cooperation with the projects of the elite.[11] Each of these norms contributes directly or indirectly to the state's war-making capacity, but requires the bearer of the norm to forego possible gains and endure losses (including reduced reproductive success).

Of course national states eventually may have created legal and cultural environments in which those adhering to the norms that enhanced state war-making capacities suffered little or no material loss by comparison to those rejecting these norms.[12] But the emergence and early diffusion of the national state may have relied critically on group-advantageous but individually costly norms.

6.4 Cultural Learning, Segmentation, and Individual Selection

An adequate model of cultural group selection must evidently include a plausible account of the process by which individuals acquire and abandon norms, and how this is influenced by both the structure of groups and the nature of intergroup competition. Who is exposed to which cultural traits under what conditions (as a student, child, consumer, worshiper, neighbor, or citizen, for example) and other details of the cultural learning process—often treated as a black box—may make a big difference in the direction and pace of evolutionary change (Cavalli-Sforza and Feldman 1973). Since nonrandom pairing of individuals in groups and conformism in learning play important parts in the model to follow (and since both are absent in most evolutionary game-theoretic treatments), I will first explain why these aspects of the social architecture of the learning process may be important, before developing the model.

In human populations individuals are nonrandomly paired to meet both cultural models and others with whom they interact such that the probability of meeting a particular type is conditioned on one's own type and differs significantly from the population frequency of the traits in question. One might, for example, be disproportionately likely to interact with individuals who had had the same teacher (or the same "parent"), for example, and this would result in nonrandom pairing in the playing of games. Or the population might be segmented: its members living in culturally homogeneous communities and interacting disproportionately frequently with their co-residents. A "community" could be a village or neighborhood but it might also be a class or ethnic group, or any culturally homogeneous group within which interaction is more likely than in the population at large. Segmentation might also take place in a multigood economy through strictures governing which types of goods or services one may appropriately exchange with members of one's community as opposed to outsiders. Segmentation does not presume recognition of type, since individuals need not choose the basis on which they are paired.

I formalize the *degree of segmentation* in a way equivalent to W. D. Hamilton's (1971, 1975) degree of (genetic) relatedness (r) giving the conditional probability that the bearer of a norm (gene) is paired with the bearer of the same norm as a function of the frequency distribution of the norm in the population. Thus if p is the population frequency of x types, μ_{xy} is the probability of being paired with a y-type conditional on being an x-type (with the obvious extensions of this notation to other pairings), then

$$\mu_{xx} = \delta + (1-\delta)p; \ \mu_{xy} = (1-\delta)(1-p); \ \mu_{yx} = (1-\delta)p; \ \mu_{yy} = \delta + (1-\delta)(1-p)$$

$$(4)$$

and $\delta \in [0,1]$ is the "degree of segmentation."

Concerning the process of cultural transmission per se, I model three influences: differential payoffs, conformism, and the assimilation by winners of contests of the cultures of groups of losers. Norms (like accents) may be acquired unwittingly (as part of a process of childhood socialization, for example), and once acquired they may dictate actions that do not maximize individual benefits. It is nonetheless plausible that individual benefits play an important role in the process of adopting norms. The theory (and empirical study) of cognitive dissonance provides some reasons to expect norms associated with high payoffs to be differentially adopted; one of the ways of coping with dissonance is to modify one's values to be consistent with the perceived imperatives of achieving other ends.[13] Other interpretations are possible. Successful individuals may obtain positions—as governmental leaders, media figures, and teachers, for example—in which they have privileged access to the population as cultural models and thus may be copied for reasons associated with their location in the social structure rather than success per se.

While the influence of differential payoffs on the adoption of norms has direct analogies in the fitness-based natural selection of genetically transmitted traits, the second influence, conformism, does not. Following Boyd and Richerson (1985), by conformist transmission I mean that the likelihood that an individual will adopt a particular norm varies with prevalence of that norm in the population (independently of the possibly frequency-dependent nature of payoffs). The importance of the population frequency of a norm could arise if individuals simply sought to adopt what they consider to be the most common norm. But like the influence of relative payoffs, conformism could arise because social institutions privilege the most common norm in the transmission process. This would be the case if the pool of available cultural models was disproportionately composed of those with the most common norm as occurs in most contemporary school systems.

There are five reasons for thinking that conformist learning of norms may be important. First, social pressures for uniformity are among the most convincingly documented human propensities.[14] Second, evidence exists that the adoption of norms responds not only to individual circumstances (e.g., one's livelihood in farming compared to herding) of the individual, but also to group circumstances per se (e.g., the dominant form of livelihood in one's community.)[15] Third, the cultural transmission processes that govern the adoption of norms and other forms of behavioral learning have themselves evolved, presumably under the influence of natural selection, cultural group selection, and other evolutionary pressures. A plausible model must posit a transmission process that is capable of reproducing itself. Conformist learning passes this test, since there are compelling theoretical reasons to believe that under quite general conditions where learning is costly, conformist transmission of traits will be adaptive and hence might have evolved under the influence of either genetic or cultural inheritance (Feldman, Aoki, and Kumm 1996; Boyd and Richerson 1985; Henrich and Boyd 1998). Fourth, the ethnographically well documented long-term persistence of payoff-reducing norms in many societies (Edgerton 1992; Durham 1991; Nisbett and Cohen 1996) is parsimoniously explained by conformist cultural transmission. Finally, a number of historical and anthropological studies suggest the long-term stability of some norms followed by their precipitous unraveling, as well as the rapid emergence and then enduring stability of new norms: for example, the thousand-year-long duration of foot binding in China and its virtual disappearance in a matter of decades (Mackie 1996), the collapse of socialist values in the German Democratic Republic (Lohmann 1994) and the long-term coexistence of otherwise similar "violent" and "anti-violent" villages in Oaxaca, and the rapid transformation of one of the former (Paddock 1975, 1990).[16] For reasons that will become apparent, these episodes would are readily explained by models in which both conformist transmission of norms and important stochastic influences are important.

For these reasons conformism in learning, and segmentation in both economic and cultural interactions, will be built into the model that follows.

To capture both the payoff-based and conformist influences on the evolution of norms, consider a particular group (j) in which individuals may have one of two norms, x and y, with population frequencies p_j and $1 - p_j$ with $p_j \in [0,1]$. (Because we will be considering just one group in this section, I will drop the group subscripts until we consider many groups in the next section.) Members of the population are paired according to the degree of segmentation δ, to interact in a single-period symmetrical two-person game, payoffs of which are denoted $\pi(\eta,\eta^-)$, the payoff to the strategy dictated by the norm η against a partner playing according to the other norm. (I use "norm" to refer to the strategy dictated by the norm where appropriate.) For any population frequency of the x norm, the expected payoffs are as follows (using equation (4) to take account of nonrandom pairing):

$$b_x(p; \delta) = \mu_{xx}\pi(x, x) + \mu_{xy}\pi(x, y)$$
$$= \{\delta + (1 - \delta)p\}\pi(x, x) + (1 - \delta)(1 - p)\pi(x, y)$$
$$b_y(p; \delta) = \mu_{yx}\pi(y, x) + \mu_{yy}\pi(y, y) \tag{5}$$
$$= (1 - \delta)p\pi(y, x) + \{\delta + (1 - \delta)(1 - p)\}\pi(y, y)$$

Suppose the *frequency of individual updating* is such that at the beginning of each period some fraction of the population, $\omega \in (0,1)$ may update its norm upon exposure to a cultural model (a "teacher" perhaps) drawn from the population according to the degree of segmentation δ. For example, adults may retain their norms throughout life, while children (who constitute ω percent of the population in each period) conditionally inherit the norms of their (sole) parent, but are susceptible to social influences in retaining or replacing the norm. (Or the "parent" and the "teacher" in the above example may simply be two parents, with δ then indicating the degree of assortative mating for the cultural trait under consideration.)

Suppose the updating process is as follows. If the "teacher" and the "parent" have the same norm, it is retained by the individual. But if they have different norms, then the individual retains or replaces the norm inherited from the parent on the basis of a weighting of two pieces of information: the frequency of the norm in the population during the previous period (determined by costlessly sampling the population), and the payoffs enjoyed by a randomly selected bearer of each norm over the period of time since they acquired their norms (also costlessly knowable to the individual). Since it will make no difference, we may suppose for concreteness that the individual in this situation simply compares the benefits enjoyed by the "parent" and the "teacher."

Define the *degree of conformism*, $\alpha \in [0,1)$, as the importance of the conformist aspect of the learning process relative to the payoff-based influences on updating, with $1 - \alpha$ the relative importance of payoffs, and let k be the population frequency of the norm for which conformist learning exerts no effect (possibly one-half), while for $p > k$ the prevalence of the norm in the population favors the norm in the updating process, independently of the (also frequency dependent) expected payoffs to the norms.[17] We define the *replication propensity* of norm η among those updating their norms as r_η where

$$r_x = \tfrac{1}{2}[\alpha(p-k)+(1-\alpha)(b_x-b_y)] \tag{6}$$
$$r_y = \tfrac{1}{2}[\alpha(k-p)+(1-\alpha)(b_y-b_x)].$$

With probability $\beta(r_y - r_x)$ an x type (offspring of an x parent) will change to a y type if their teacher is a y type and $r_x < r_y$; conversely, if $r_x \geq r_y$ the individual does not switch. The *adoption coefficient* β is a positive constant reflecting the greater effect on switching of relatively large differences in replication propensities.[18] The $(1 - \omega)$ fraction of the population not subject to this updating process do not switch.

Thus writing $\rho_{y>x}$ as the probability that r_y exceeds r_x and conversely, we can write the population frequency with norm x in time $t + 1$ or p' as

$$p' = p - \omega p(1-p)(1-\delta)\rho_{y>x}\beta(r_y-r_x)+\omega p(1-p)(1-\delta)p_{x\geq y}\beta(r_x-r_y). \tag{7}$$

This expression may be read as follows: of the base year population of x types (p), in any period a fraction $(1 - \omega)$ are not eligible for updating and hence will not change type. The remainder ω will be eligible for updating, of these $(1 - p)(1 - \delta)$ will be paired with y-type teachers, and with probability $\rho_{y>x}\beta(r_y - r_x)$ the information they acquire about payoffs and population frequencies will lead them to switch to becoming a y type (they make no replicas, the y type with whom they were paired makes two). Offsetting the xs lost in this manner, some of the offspring of y-type parents will encounter x-type teachers and by an analogous process will convert to x types. Noting that $\rho_{y>x} + \rho_{x\geq y} = 1$, and rearranging, we can rewrite equation (7) as the familiar replicator dynamic equation with social-learning-based replication propensities playing the role of fitness or payoffs:

$$\Delta p = p' - p = \omega p(1-p)(1-\delta)\beta(r_x-r_y) = \omega p(1-\delta)\beta(r_x-r), \tag{8}$$

where r is the group average replication propensity.[19] From (8) it is clear that $\Delta p = 0$ if $r_x - r_y = 0$, which requires

$$\alpha(p-k)/(1-\alpha) = b_y(p) - b_x(p), \tag{9}$$

or if p is either 0 or 1 (because when $p = 1$, $r_x = r$) or in the degenerate case that $\delta = 1$ (nobody ever meets a different type.) Equation (8) shows that segmentation dampens the response to disequilibria and implies that in a fully segmented society (one for which all pairings were with one's own type, or $\delta = 1$) all distributions of norms are stationary. When equation (9) is satisfied, the effects of conformist transmission (the lefthand side of equation (9)) offset the effects of differential payoffs (the right-hand side). Thus, in the presence of conformist transmission, and for $p \in (0,1)$, the equilibrium payoffs to the norm disfavored by conformism will always exceed the payoffs of the more prevalent norm.

For $p \in (0,1)$ Δp takes the sign of $r_x - r_y$. Given the one-dimensionality of this dynamical system, an equilibrium is asymptotically stable if the derivative of equation (8) with respect to p is negative, requiring that

$$\alpha < (1-\alpha)(1-\delta)(db_y/dp - db_x/dp) \tag{10}$$

or

$$\alpha/(1-\alpha)(1-\delta) < \pi(y, x) - \pi(y, y) - \pi(x, x) + \pi(x, y), \tag{10'}$$

which is satisfied if the conformist advantage conferred on x by a small increase in p, namely α, is more than offset by the payoff advantage conferred on y by the same increase in p (the right-hand side of equation (10).) We illustrate the equilibrium frequencies of norms in figure 6.3, where p^* represents the solution to equation (9) satisfying equation (10) and is hence a stable equilibrium distribution of norms.

From equations (9) and (10), we see that conformism has two effects. First, equation (9) shows that strategies that yield low payoffs may persist: for example, x is an evolutionarily stable strategy (ESS) as long as the expected payoffs for a small number of y-players introduced into

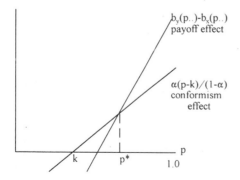

Figure 6.3
Cultural equilibrium. Stationarity of p requires that the conformism based advantages of the prevalent trait (x) be offset by payoff based advantages of y.

a homogeneously x-playing population exceed the x-players' payoffs by less than $\alpha(1 - k)/(1 - \alpha)$, obviously a condition less stringent than the conventional ESS. Second, sufficiently high levels of conformism will violate equation (10), making p^* an unstable equilibrium and thus making it the boundary between the basin of attraction of the equilibria at $p = 0$ and $p = 1$. In the absence of conformism and segmentation, stability requires only that the right-hand side of equation (10′) be positive, obviously a weaker condition. Counterintuitively, conformism thus may help explain rapid cultural change, as well as the long-term survival of individually costly norms, whether collectively beneficial or not, as promised in the previous section.

6.5   Contests, Assimilation, and Group Selection

To integrate this process of individual selection with selection at the group level, we now add subscripts identifying the updating process above as taking place in group j, with r_j the replication propensity of trait x, r_{-j} the replication propensity of trait y and r_j the average replication propensity, all in group j, and rewrite equation (8) as

$$\Delta p_j = \omega(1-\delta)p_j(1-p_j)\beta(r_j - r_{-j}). \tag{11}$$

Equation (11) is related to the second term on the right-hand side of (2) as follows: $p_j(1 - p_j)$ is the within group variance of the trait, while $\omega(1 - \delta)\beta(r_j - r_{-j})$ is $\beta_{wp.p-}$ the effect of an individual's having trait on the number of replicas the individual produces, given the frequency of the trait in the group. The terms $\omega(1 - \delta)$ regulate the speed of within-group out-of-equilibrium adjustment. (Nothing would be gained by letting δ, ω, and β vary among groups, so these terms do not bear subscripts.)

Turning now to the group effects represented by the first term in equation (2), assume that the group just modeled is one of a large number groups in a large population, and let q_j represent the fraction of the whole population that is a member of group j. While individuals are infinitely lived in this model, groups are not; they go extinct, their members absorbed into more successful groups, and winning groups subdivide. Here is the process. Groups are randomly paired for a "contest" that may be military, cultural, economic, or some other, this event happening in each period with probability κ for each group. If the group is not selected for a contest, nothing is affected. However, if the group is engaged in a contest and wins, it absorbs the other group and assimilates its population, the new population replicating the frequency of the trait of the winning group. If the group loses, it is absorbed into the winning group.

As the winning group is now enlarged by the absorption of the losing group, we assume that following the assimilation of the new population, the winning group divides, creating two groups, which to keep things simple will be of the equal size. As the bearers of the group-beneficial trait are likely to be numerically and socially dominant in the winning group, they may determine the composition of the subdivided groups so as to segregate bearers of the "other" trait insofar as recognition of traits or characteristics correlated with traits allows this (in the limiting case of no recognition and no segregation, the two groups would be created by a random draw possibly of family units from the enlarged group).

We assume that groups are always of the same size (normalized to 1) except that winning groups are momentarily (prior to subdividing) of size 2 (and losing groups are of size 0). Groups that have prevailed in a contest and absorbed another group are by this device counted twice. Thus if group j is of size 1 this period, then its expected size next period (before any subdivision)(w_j) depends on the probability that a contest has taken place and the probability of victory in such a contest. Suppose the probability of prevailing in a conflict is equal to its group average payoffs (π_j) scaled by $\gamma/2$, which converts group level payoffs into a probability of victory. Then expected group size following a contest is $\gamma\pi_j$ and the expected size of group j is thus 1, 2, or 0 with probabilities $(1 - \kappa)$, $\kappa\pi_j\gamma/2$, and $\kappa(1 - \pi_j\gamma/2)$, respectively or

$$w_j = 1 - \kappa + \kappa\gamma\pi_j = 1 + \kappa(\gamma\pi_j - 1).$$

Thus the effect of variations in p_j on the number of replicas of the members of group j, namely, β_{w-p-}, is just $\kappa\gamma\pi'$ where $\pi' \equiv (d\pi_j/dp_j)$.

To summarize, the sequence of events at the group level is as follows: following all individual updating, groups are selected for contests and paired, the contest occurs, a winner is determined, losing groups are assimilated to winners, and finally the winning group divides, thereby restoring the number and size of groups. Individual updating then occurs and the process continues. The evolution of the population mean p can be represented as follows (the summation is over groups):

$$p = \sum q_j p_j$$
$$p' = \sum q_{j'}(p_j + \Delta p_j)$$
$$\Delta p = \sum q_j [1 + \kappa(\gamma \pi_j - 1) - 1]p_j + \sum \{q_j[1 + \kappa(\gamma \pi_j - 1)]\Delta p_j\} \tag{12}$$
$$\Delta p = \sum q_j(w_j - 1)p_j + \sum q_j w_j \Delta p_j.$$

The first term captures the influence of group selection. Recall that w = 1 and note that $\Sigma q_j(w_j - w)p = 0$ (because $\Sigma q_j w_j = w$), so the first term on the right-hand side of equation (12) is just $\mathrm{cov}(w_j p_j) = \mathrm{var}(p_j)\beta_{w \sim p \sim}$ where $\beta_{w \sim p \sim} = \gamma\kappa\pi'$, namely, the effect of variations in the frequency of the trait in the group on average payoffs and thereby (via the probability of prevailing in contests) on the number of cultural replicas made. The second term captures within-group selection, namely, Δp_j weighted by the expected relative size of the group w_j summed over all groups. Upon substitution of the previously derived expression for Δp_j (11), and a little rearranging, equation (12) becomes

$$\Delta p = \mathrm{var}(p_j)\gamma\kappa\pi' + \sum q_j[\omega(1-\delta)p_j(1-p_j)\beta(r_j - r_{-j})], \tag{12'}$$

which can also be expressed in the more compact form:

$$\Delta p = \mathrm{var}(p_j)\beta_{w \sim p \sim} + \sum q_j \, \mathrm{var}(p_{ij})\beta_{wp.p \sim}. \tag{12''}$$

If the second term is negative (as it will be in the case of an altruistic trait) the frequency of the trait within all surviving groups will fall over time. But this tendency will be counteracted by the continual extinction of groups with disproportionately low frequencies of the trait and their replacement by "new" groups with disproportionately high trait frequencies. The process of updating, from individual material payoffs to the population-level frequency of the trait, is summarized in table 6.1.

Equation (12″) gives us the change in p over a single period, taking the initial distribution of p_j across groups as given. The equation lacks what Lewontin (1974) termed "dynamic sufficiency" however, because while it provides an account of the population frequency of the trait in the next period, it does not provide the information necessary (the relevant variances) to repeat the analysis for the next-plus-one period. Providing a completely recursive version of equation (12) is a challenging task that I have not attempted. Thus the equation per

Table 6.1
From Individual Payoffs to Population Frequencies

Variable	Description
$\pi(x,y)$	payoff to playing x, against a y-player
$b_x(p,\delta,\pi(\ ))$	expected payoffs to playing x in a population p of which are x players and δ is the degree of segmentation
$r_j(p,b(\ ),\alpha)$	replication propensity (of trait x) in group j, given, $b(\ )$ and degree of conformism, α
$\Delta p_j(p_j,\omega,\beta(r_j - r_{-j}))$	change in the frequency of x players in group j, given p_j the updating frequency ω, and the adoption coefficient β
$\Delta p(\kappa,\gamma,\Delta p_j,p_j)$	change in the population frequency of x players given the frequency of group contests κ, the effect of group mean payoffs on the outcome of contests γ, and Δp_j, p_j, $\forall j\ 1 \ldots n$.

se does not address a crucial question: how is between- and within-group variance sustained in this population?

In the case of human populations, however, it is not difficult to provide an informal answer to the question, one whose plausibility is strongly supported by simulations. Because winner groups subdivide in ways that do not produce exact copies of the winner group (in the limit by a random draw), the variance in group means may increase, decrease, or remain constant over time, with increases more likely the more frequent are intergroup contests, the greater the role of segmentation or other nonrandom processes in generating group divisions, and the smaller the group size (the latter due to the larger relative size of sampling error in the subdivision process). Taking hunter-gatherer bands of twenty-five to fifty individuals as a common grouping in human history and noting that family units tend to have similar cultural traits and to remain together in group subdivision, the effective sample size could be very small (around seven, using the data in Kelly 1995), and the contribution of subdivision by random draws of families could generate substantial contributions to between-group variances. Simulations of the above model (with groups averaging 10 individuals and random subdivision of groups successful in contests) confirm that between-group variances are sufficiently large and persistent to sustain high frequencies of a group-beneficial but individually costly trait, as long as intergroup contests are sufficiently frequent (Bowles and Hopfensitz 2000). Thus while the evolution of within- and between-group variances is not formally modeled here, there is no reason to believe that the between-group variances would vanish, bringing the group selection process to a halt.

6.6   The Effects of Social Structure on the Evolution of Preferences

We are now able to explore the effect of social structure on the multi-level selection process modeled above. It will be helpful to rearrange equation (12′) as follows:

$$\Delta p = \kappa \operatorname{var}(p_j)\gamma\pi' + \omega(1-\delta)\left\{\sum q_j[\operatorname{var}(p_{ij})]\beta(r_j - r_{-j})\right\}, \tag{13}$$

which setting $\Delta p = 0$ gives the stationarity condition

$$\kappa \operatorname{var}(p_j)\gamma\pi' = -\omega(1-\delta)\left\{\sum q_j[\operatorname{var}(p_{ij})]\beta(r_j - r_{-j})\right\}, \tag{14}$$

requiring that the between-group selection effects (the left side) be equal to the within-group effects. To see what equation (13) entails, consider the altruism example based on equations (1) and (3). Let the benefits and costs of altruism be denominated in material goods, and suppose that material goods confer advantages both in the individual trait updating process and in intergroup contests, and that the cultural transmission process does not exhibit conformism so that material payoffs alone govern individual trait replication. The effect of group-beneficial altruism on differential replication at the group level is just $\kappa\gamma(b-c)$ (because $\pi' = b - c$). Taking account of segmentation, the effect of the individual cost of altruism on differential replication at the individual level is $\omega(1 - \delta)\beta(c - b\delta)$, from which it can be seen that if the degree of segmentation exceeds c/b, altruism will not be selected against within the group, thereby assuring that it will proliferate in its entire population.

Consider the more challenging case when $\delta < c/b$. Substituting these expressions into equation (14), the stationarity of the frequency of altruism requires

$$(b-c)/(c-\delta b) = \left\{\sum q_j[\operatorname{var}(p_{ij})]/\operatorname{var}(p_j)\right\}[\omega(1-\delta)/\kappa](\beta/\gamma), \tag{15}$$

which says that *the ratio of group benefit to individual cost* must be equal to the product of the three terms on the right-hand side of equation

(15), each of which is the ratio of a within-group to a between-group process. These are

1. $\Sigma q_j[\text{var}(p_{ij})]/\text{var}(p_j)$, the relative *size of the within group relative to the between group variance* of the trait,

2. $[\omega(1 - \delta)/\kappa]$, the relative *speed of the updating process* represented by the relative frequency with which individuals (compared to groups) have an updating opportunity; and

3. (β/γ), the relative *effect of payoffs on success* in individual cultural replication compared to the effects of material benefits in winning group contests.

Each of these terms will be affected by the economic policies, institutions and other structures governing within- and between-group interactions. Consider the effects of conformism, segmentation, and egalitarianism introduced at the outset.

The following summarizes the effect of conformism on the relative within- and between-group variances: for groups characterized by the above payoff and transmission structures and $p_j \in (0,1)$, conformist cultural transmission reduces the ratio of within-group to between-group variances of the trait, $\Sigma q_j[\text{var}(p_{ij})]/\text{var}(p_j)$, and thus favors the evolution of group beneficial but individually costly traits. Indeed it is not difficult to demonstrate in this model that there exists a sufficiently high level of conformism, $\alpha < 1$, such that within-group variance vanishes, leaving selection to operate only at the group level. The intuition behind this unsurprising result is clear from equation (10): sufficient conformism must violate the stability condition for an interior equilibrium.

The manner in which segmentation promotes the replication of an individually costly but socially beneficial trait within a group is well known and has been mentioned above. There is another effect, however, this one applying to group selection processes per se. As is obvious from equation (14), segmentation retards the within-group updating process because in more segmented societies for every frequency of the trait in the population (other than 0 and 1), individuals are less likely to be paired with an individual with a different trait: as δ approaches unity, within-group updating ceases, and hence group selection is the only selection process at work ($\delta = 1$ is clearly degenerate, as such a population is just two internally homogeneous groups).

Egalitarianism among group members—food sharing, monogamy and progressive taxation, for example—dampens the effect of payoffs on trait replication, effectively reducing within-group differences in replication propensities and thus retarding the processes of within group selection. For example, a (costlessly administered) tax on game payoffs paid by the higher payoff individuals and distributed as a lump sum to all members of the population attenuates the individual cost to those bearing the group-beneficial trait, and is thus similar to the effects of monogamy described at the outset. Because there is no analogous effect operating at the group level, egalitarianism (as defined here) enhances group selection pressures.

Rewriting equation (14) to take account of conformist transmission, with τ the linear tax rate,

$$\kappa \operatorname{var}(p_j)\gamma(b-c) = -\omega(1-\delta)\sum q_j[\operatorname{var}(p_{ij})]\beta[\alpha(p-k)+(1-\alpha)(1-\tau)(b\delta-c)], \tag{14'}$$

it can also be seen that conformism has a dampening effect on individual-level selection, similar to the effect of egalitarianism, and operating independently of its effect on the ratio of within- to between-group variances.

Other effects of social structure both at the population and group level can also be discerned from equation (14). Some insight concerning the comparative rates of updating opportunities (ω/κ) might be gained by looking at the number of wars per generation (assuming that updating takes place on a generational basis and wars are a major form of contest), for example. This interpretation may have bearing on the state formation case with which I began. In the two centuries following 1500, for example, there were sixty-three major wars (defined as involving over 1,000 battle deaths a year, counting only the great powers), with wars occurring so frequently that only ten years were without one (Tilly 1990, 72). Another example: changes in military and communications technology may alter π', the effect of between-group differences in payoffs on the outcomes of contests. Finally, the prolongation of childhood and adolescence experienced in most nations over the past four centuries may enlarge the window for individual updating (ω) of traits thus accelerating individual-level selection.

6.7 Conclusion

Two conclusions follow. First, because the structure of social interactions, both within and between groups, affects the pace and direction of cultural evolution, economic institutions and policies that influence the residential patterns, ingroup-outgroup relationships, and other aspects of these structures will affect preferences, casting doubt on the economists' canonical premise that preferences are exogenous. Second, selection processes operating in human populations are likely to support group-level effects, allowing the diffusion of individually costly but group-beneficial behaviors. This is particularly the case for traits governed by cultural rather than genetic transmission. Thus, other-regarding and process-related preferences may be evolutionarily successful, and the presumption in favor of an entirely selfish *homo economicus* would appear to have little basis in evolutionary reasoning.

One wonders, then, if economists have been unwise in following Hume's advice that "every man ought to be supposed to be a knave and to have no other end, in all his actions, than his private interest" ([1754] 1898). Constitutional designs and policy interventions that abstract from the endogeneity of preferences and ignore the presence—in our variegated repertoire of motivations—of unselfish and process-regarding preferences, may evoke preferences that exacerbate the underlying constitutional or policy problem, and may fail to draw upon or foster those motivations that might assist in a solution. The effectiveness of policies and their political viability may thus depend on the preferences they induce or evoke.

Albert Hirschman (1985) points out that economists typically assume otherwise and for this reason propose

to deal with unethical or antisocial behavior by raising the cost of that behavior rather than proclaiming standards and imposing prohibitions and sanctions. The reason is probably that they think of citizens as consumers with unchanging or arbitrarily changing tastes in matters civic as well as commodity-related behavior. . . . A principal purpose of publically proclaimed laws and regulations is to stigmatize antisocial behavior and thereby to influence citizens' values and behavioral codes. (P. 10)

A more adequate approach to the problem of preferences along the lines suggested by Hirschman (as well as Sunstein 1993) might find broad application in policy areas such as tax compliance, criminal justice, educational policy, environmental protection, labor relations and work organization, and informal contractual enforcement. For example, there is considerable evidence that attempts to induce higher levels of work effort, compliance to norms, or environmental conservation by mobilizing self-interested motives through the use of fines and sanctions may undermine reciprocity and other motives (Fehr and Gaechter 2000; Bewley 1995; Gneezy and Rustichini 2000; Cardenas, Stranlund, and Willis 2000). Thus, what counts as an improvement of an incentive structure in a world of exogenous selfish preferences may be counter productive where at least some preferences are other-regarding and endogenous. Similarly, ill designed policies to redistribute income to the poor may fail if they foster perceptions of the poor as undeserving or otherwise undermine generous motives for redistribution (Bowles and Gintis, 1998–1999, 2000).

Appendix: Individual and Group Selection Effects

Drawing on Price (1970, 1972), Wilson (1977), Grafen (1985), Frank (1995), and Rogers (1990), this appendix presents a derivation of the Price equation for the case of group and individual selection of a dichotomous trait. The selection coefficient (number of replicas in the next period) of individual i in group j depends on one's own trait (p_{ij} $\in$ {0,1} and the frequency of the trait in the group (p_j, $\in$ [0,1]) according to

$$w_{ij} = \beta_o + p_j\beta_{wp-.p} + p_{ij}\beta_{wp.p-}. \tag{A1}$$

Let $q_j \equiv Q_j/Q$, where Q_j is the number of individuals in group j, and Q is the total number of individuals summed over all groups. The frequency of the trait in the population may be expressed as the summation of group averages weighted by relative group size

$$p \equiv \sum q_j p_j, \tag{A2}$$

and using a prime to indicate the next period

$$p' \equiv \sum q'_j p'_j, \tag{A3}$$

with

$$q'_j \equiv q_j(w_j/w), \tag{A4}$$

where w_j is the average number of replicas produced by members of group j, and w is average number of replicas over the entire population. So

$$\Delta p \equiv p' - p = \sum q_j(w_j/w)(p_j + \Delta p_j) - \sum q_j p_j$$
$$= \sum q_j[(w_j/w) - 1]p_j + \sum q_j(w_j/w)\Delta p_j \qquad \text{(A5)}$$

or

$$w\Delta p = \sum q_j(w_j - w)p_j + \sum q_j w_j \Delta p_j. \qquad \text{(A6)}$$

Notice that the second expression on the right-hand side is just the weighted average of $w_j \Delta p_j$, defining at the group level exactly what equation (A6) defines for the population as a whole. So, repeating the procedure above but at the group level, we have

$$w\Delta p = \sum_j q_j(w_j - w)p_j + \sum_j q_j[\sum_i (w_{ij} - w_j)p_{ij} + \sum\sum q_j w_{ij}\Delta p_{ij}], \qquad \text{(A7)}$$

where single summation is over groups and double summation is over groups and individuals. But $\Delta p_{ij} = 0$ for all i and j, by the assumption that traits are replicated without error. So equation (A7) becomes

$$w\Delta p = \sum q_j(w_j - w)p_j + \sum_j q_j[\sum_i (w_{ij} - w_j)p_{ij}]$$
$$= \text{cov}(w_j p_j) + \sum q_j[\text{cov}(w_{ij} p_{ij})] \qquad \text{(A8)}$$
$$= \text{var}(p_j)\beta_{w \sim p \sim} + \sum q_j[\text{var}(p_{ij})\beta_{wp.p \sim}],$$

where $\beta_{w \sim p \sim}$, defined in the text is $\beta_{wp.p} + \beta_{wp.p \sim}$.

The interpretation in the text of the ratio of between to total variance of the trait as identical to Hamilton's r is motivated as follows. We know from equation (4) that δ, the degree of relatedness (or of segmentation, as defined in the text), is simply the difference in the probability of interacting with someone with the trait conditional on having or not having the trait oneself, or δ. From Price (1970), we know that

$$w\Delta p = \text{cov}(w, p) = \text{var}(p)\beta_{wp}$$

or, using equation (A1),

$$w\Delta p = \text{var}(p)[\beta_{wp.p \sim} + \beta_{wp \sim.p} \, dp_j/dp_{ij}]$$

with the stationarity condition for interior values of p thus requiring that

$$-\beta_{wp.p\sim}/\beta_{wp\sim.p} = dp_j/dp_{ij}.$$

Recalling that p_{ij} takes the value of one for those with the trait and zero otherwise, dp_j/dp_{ij} tells us the difference in the conditional probability of meeting someone with the trait, conditional on having the trait oneself, or not. In the altruism case, the stationarity condition (analogous to Hamilton's rule) is just

$$c/b = dp_j/dp_{ij},$$

which is identical to equation (3) in the text, the right-hand side of which is now seen to be just the difference in the frequency of interactors expected by those with the trait and those without it, namely δ, defined in equation (4) as the degree of segmentation, or in population-genetic models, the degree of relatedness.

Notes

Thanks to Katie Baird Robert Boyd, Gerald Cohen, Marcus Feldman, Steven Frank, Astrid Hopfensitz, Charles Tilly, David Sloan Wilson, Elisabeth Wood, Peyton Young, and workshop participants at the Santa Fe Institute and the Massachusetts Institute of Technology for helpful comments, to the University of Siena for hospitality, to Bridget Longridge for research assistance, and to the MacArthur Foundation for financial support.

1. See Bowles (1998) for a survey. Indeed Hume, immediately following the passage just quoted, muses that it is "strange that a maxim should be true in politics which is false in fact." While in academic settings most economists still adhere to the exogenous preferences canon and its *"de gustibus non est disputandum"* implication (Stigler and Becker 1977), many appear aware of its limitations when it comes to evaluating institutions and policies. Thus Becker (1995) refers to "the effects of a free-market system on self reliance, initiative, and other virtues" and, referring to government transfers to the poor, claims that "the present system corrupts the values transmitted to children."

2. See Caporeal et al. (1989), Andreoni, Brown, and Vesterlund (1997), Fehr and Gaechter (2000), Ostrom (1998), Wilson and Sober (1998), Bowles (forthcoming) and Bowles and Gintis (1998) for surveys.

3. In order to account for an individual's actions, preferences need not coincide with the reasons given by the particular individual, of course. Nor do preferences alone generally give a sufficient account of behaviors: my consumption of aspirin is accounted for by my aversion to pain plus my belief that aspirin will relieve the pain and that this little white object is indeed an aspirin, and so on.

4. Williams (1966), Crow and Kimura (1970), Boorman and Levitt (1973), Maynard Smith (1976). The negative assessment of the likely empirical importance of group selection stems primarily from the presumed more rapid rate of selection within as opposed to

between groups and the generation of differences in group means solely by drift or random assortment (Crow and Kimura point to "the much larger variance within a group than between group means, the larger numbers that minimize the "noise" from random events, and the slower effective "generation length" for intergroup selection" (1970, 242.). But subsequent work suggests that impediments to group selection may be less general than the critics contend (Uyenoyama 1979; Uyenoyama and Feldman 1980; Harpending and Rogers 1987).

5. These do not exhaust the explanations offered, of course. Simon (1990), Eibl-Eibesfeldt (1982), and others have proposed a mechanism whereby costly but group-beneficial behaviors free-ride on the individually beneficial behaviors ("docility," or "indoctrinability," for example) with which they are pleiotropically paired.

6. Other animals practice similar kinds of discrimination and segmentation; in some social insects, an odor distinctive to a colony (acquired through food exchanges) allows individuals to distinguish colony members from unrelated outsiders, and there are other examples, including rodents and some mammals (Hamilton 1971). However, human cognitive capacities allow for discrimination on a scale unmatched by other animals.

7. The covariance between group means and individual fitness will not be zero even if no group effects exist (the individual's fitness contributes to the mean); I assume groups are large enough to allow the interpretation of the regression coefficient as a group effect.

8. Unlike its competitors—empires, city states, and urban federations—national states in Tilly's usage "unite substantial military, extractive, administrative, and sometimes even distributive and productive organizations in a relatively coordinated central structure" (1990, 21). In addition to Tilly (1990), I draw here on Gellner (1983), Bright and Harding (1980), Tilly (1975), Mack Smith (1959), Anderson (1974), Wallerstein (1974), and Gintis and Bowles (1980).

9. Soltis, Boyd, and Richerson (1995) applied a group-selection model to data on group differences and extinction rates in New Guinea. Other well-documented empirical cases where a group selection argument may readily be applied are the conquest and assimilation of the Dinka by the Nuer (Boyd 1997; Kelly 1985) and the practice of llama sharing among needy nonkin in the Peruvian highlands (Flannery, Marcus, and Reynolds (1989), Weinstein Shugart, and Brandt (1983).

10. Weber (1976) describes the assimilation of distinct populations by the French national state. Gellner (1983) develops the connection between the rise of commerce, the national state, and the rise of what he terms "exo-education," that is, childhood socialization by specialists who are not members of one's family or group of close associates.

11. Herlihy and Klapische-Zuber (1985) write: "The great social achievement of the early Middle Ages was the imposition of the same rules of sexual and domestic conduct on both rich and poor" (157). See also MacDonald (1995). While reducing the advantages of the successful and powerful, the norm of monogamy may have been instrumental, as Alexander (1979) and others suggest in allowing the powerful to recruit others to their projects, including war. Referring to an earlier period, Herlihy (1991) writes:

Under conditions of acute [intergroup] competition, it was necessary to maintain the moral commitment and physical energies of the citizens . . . [A] crucial means . . . was to offer all citizens access to marriage. . . . But only a system of monogamy could assure that all male citizens would have a reasonable chance of attracting a wife. (14–15).

12. MacDonald stresses the socially imposed nature of monogamy, which if entirely successful would eliminate within-group variance in the number of sexual partners, and reduce the evolution of monogamy to a between-group selection process.

13. Adopting cultural variants that contribute to economic success in a particular game invokes but one of the standard dissonance-reducing strategies. Leon Festinger (1957), the originator of cognitive dissonance theory, describes its basic premise: "the human organism tries to establish internal harmony, consistency or congruity among his opinions, attitudes, knowledge, and values. . . . There is a drive toward consonance among cognitions" (260). Kohn (1969) found statistically robust effects of the personality demands of parents' occupational roles on parental child-rearing values, parents seemingly seeking to develop in their children the values that would contribute to success in their own work situation.

14. Boyd and Richerson (1985, 223ff) and Ross and Nisbett (1991, 30ff) provide surveys. See also Asch (1956) and Sherif (1937). Newcomb and his collaborators' studies of learned political orientations suggest a powerful effect of conformism that endured decades after the originating environments (Newcomb et al. 1967).

15. Edgerton (1971) found that herders value independence more highly than do farmers, but that farmers in predominantly herding societies value independence more than farmers in predominantly farming communities. In India fertility is strongly related to district average levels of women's education but surprisingly weakly related to individual women's educational levels. For similar evidence on contraceptive use in Bangladesh, see Munshi and Myaux (1998).

16. See also Kuran (1995).

17. The conformist effect need not be linear in p, of course, but nothing would be gained by a more general formulation.

18. Differential responsiveness to given differences in r imply different values of $\beta \in (0, (\Delta r^{max})^{-1}]$, where Δr^{max} is the absolute value of the maximum difference in the replication propensities (the upper bound on β restricts the probability of switching to not exceed unity.).

19. For $\delta = 0$, equation (8) is an exact analogy to Price's (1970) expression for the change in gene frequency as a function of the population variance of the trait ($p(1 - p)$) multiplied by the contribution of the trait to individual fitness ($\beta(r_x - r_y)$).

References

Alchian, Armen A. 1950. "Uncertainty, Evolution, and Economic Theory." *J. Polit. Econ.* 58: 211–221.

Alexander, R. D. 1979. *Darwinism and Human Affairs*. Seattle: University of Washington Press.

Anderson, Perry. 1974. *Lineages of the Absolutist State*. London: Verso.

Andreoni, James, Paul Brown, and Lise Vesterlund. 1997. "Fairness, Selfishness and Selfish Fairness: Experiments on Games with Unequal Equilibrium Payoffs." Unpublished paper. November.

Aristotle. 1962. *Nicomachean Ethics*. Indianapolis: Bobbs-Merrill.

Asch, Solomon E. 1956. "Studies of Independence and Conformity: A Minority of One Against a Unanimous Majority." *Psychological Monographs* 70(9): 1–70.

Becker, Gary S. 1995. "The Best Reason to Get People off the Dole." *Business Week* (May 1): 26.

Bewley, Truman F. 1995. "A Depressed Labor Market as Explained by Participants." *American Economic Review* 85(2): 250–254.

Boehm, Christopher. 1996. "Emergency Decisions, Cultural-Selection Mechanics, and Group Selection." *Current Anthropology* 37(5): 763–793.

———. 1997. "Impact of the Human Egalitarian Syndrome on Darwinian Selection Mechanics." *The American Naturalist* 150 Suppl.: S100–S121.

Boorman, S., and P. R. Levitt. 1973. "Group Selection on the Boundary of a Stable Population." *Theor. Pop. Biol.* 4: 85–128.

Bowles, Samuel. 1998. "Endogenous Preferences: The Cultural Consequences of Markets and other Economic Institutions." *Journal of Economic Literature* 36 (March): 75–111.

———. 2000. "Reciprocity, Self Interest and the Welfare State." *Nordic Journal of Political Economy* 26(1) (January).

———. Forthcoming. *Economic Institutions and Behavior: An Evolutionary Approach to Microeconomics.* Princeton: Princeton University, Press.

Bowles, Samuel, and Herbert Gintis. 1998. "The Evolution of Strong Reciprocity." Sante Fe Institute Working Paper. July.

———. 1998–1999. "Is Equality Passe? The Evolution of Reciprocity and the Future of Egalitarian Politics." *Boston Review* 23(6) (Winter): 4–35.

Bowles Samuel, and Astrid Hopfensitz. 2000. "The Coevolution of Institutions and Preferences." Santa Fe Institue Discussion Paper, October.

Boyd, Robert. 1997. "Evolutionary Models of Equilibrium Selection." International School of Economic Research. Siena, Italy.

Boyd, Robert, and Peter J. Richerson. 1985. *Culture and the Evolutionary Process.* Chicago and London: University of Chicago Press.

———. 1990. "Group Selection among Alternative Evolutionarily Stable Strategies." *Journal of Theoretical Biology* 145: 331–342.

Brady, Thomas. 1985. *Turning Swiss: Cities and Empire, 1450–1550.* Cambridge, Cambridge University Press.

Bright, Charles, and Susan Harding, eds. 1980. *Statemaking and Social Movements.* Ann Arbor: University of Michigan Press.

Caporeal, Linnda, et. al. 1989. "Selfishness Examined: Cooperation in the Absence of Egoistic Incentives." *Behavioral and Brian Sciences* 12: 683–697.

Cardenas, Juan Camilo, John K. Stranlund, and Cleve E. Willis. 2000. "Local Environmental Control and Institutional Crowding-out." *World Development* 28(10) (October).

Cavalli-Sforza, L., and Marcus W. Feldman. 1973. "Models for Cultural Inheritance: Group Mean and Within Group Variation." *Theoretical Population Biology* 4(42): 42–55.

Crow, James F., and Motoo Kimura. 1970. *An Introduction to Population Genetic Theory.* New York: Harper & Row.

Darwin, Charles. 1873. *The Descent of Man.* New York: D. Appleton and Company.

Durham, William H. 1991. *Coevolution: Genes, Culture, and Human Diversity.* Stanford: Stanford University Press.

Edgerton, Robert B. 1971. *The Individual in Cultural Adaptation.* Berkeley: University of California Press.

————. 1992. *Sick Societies: Challenging the Myth of Primitive Harmony.* New York: The Free Press.

Eibl-Eibesfeldt, Irenaus. 1982. "Warfare, Man's Indoctrinability and Group Selection." *Journal of Comparative Ethnology* 60(3) (November): 177–198.

Fehr, Ernst, and Simon Gaechter. 2000. "Fairness and Retaliation: The Economics of Reciprocity." Forthcoming in *Journal of Economic Perspectives* (August).

Feldman, Marcus W., Kenichi Aoki, and Jochen Kumm. 1996. "Individual Versus Social Learning: Evolutionary Analysis in a Fluctuating Environment." Working paper no. 96-05-030. Santa Fe Institute. March 14.

Festinger, Leon. 1957. *A Theory of Cognitive Dissonance.* Stanford: Stanford University Press.

Flannery, Kent, Joyce Marcus, and Robert Reynolds. 1989. *The Flocks of the Wamani: A Study of Llama Herders on the Puntas of Ayacucho, Peru.* San Diego: Academic Press.

Frank, Steven A. 1995. "George Price's Contributions to Evolutionary Genetics." *Journal of Theoretical Biology* 175: 373–388.

Gellner, Ernest. 1983. *Nations and Nationalism.* Ithaca: Cornell University Press.

Gintis, Herbert, and Samuel Bowles. 1980. "State and Class in Europe and Feudalism." In *Statemaking and Social Movements,* ed. C. Bright and S. Harding. Ann Arbor: University of Michigan Press.

Gneezy, Uri, and Aldo Rustichini. 2000. "A Fine Is a Price," *Journal of Legal Studies* 29, pt. 1: 1–17.

Grafen, Alan. 1979. "The Hawk-Dove Game Played Between Relatives." *Animal Behavior* 27(3): 905–907.

————. 1984. "Natural Selection, Kin Selection and Group Selection." In *Behavioral Ecology: An Evolutionary Approach,* ed. J. R. Krebs and N. B. Davies, 62–84. Sunderland, MA: Sinauer Associates Inc.

————. 1985. "A Geometric View of Relatedness." In *Oxford Surveys in Evolutionary Biology,* Vol. 2, ed. R. Dawkins and M. Ridley, 28–89. Oxford: Oxford University Press.

Greif, Avner. 1994. "Cultural Beliefs and the Organization of Society: A Historical and Theoretical Reflection on Collectivist and Individualist Societies." *Journal of Political Economy* 102(3): 912–950.

Hamilton, William D. 1971. "Selection of Selfish and Altruistic Behavior." In *Man and Beast: Comparative Social Behavior,* ed. J. F. Eisenberg and W. S. Dillon. Washington, DC: Smithsonian Press.

————. 1975. "Innate Social Aptitudes of Man: an Approach from Evolutionary Genetics." In Robin Fox, ed., *Biosocial Anthropology*, ed. R. Fox, 133–155. New York: John Wiley and Sons.

Harpending, Henry, and Alan Rogers, 1987. "On Wright's Mechanism for Intergroup Selection." *Journal of Theoretical Biology* 127: 51–61.

Harsanyi, John. 1982. "Morality and the Theory of Rational Behavior." In *Utilitarianism and Beyond*, Amartya Sen and Bernard Williams, 39–62. Cambridge: Cambridge University Press.

Hayek, F. A. 1990. *The Fatal Conceit: The Errors of Socialism*, Vol. I, The Collected Works of F. A. Hayek, ed. W. W. Bartley III. Chicago: University of Chicago Press.

Henrich, Joe, and Boyd, Robert. 1998. "The Evolution of Conformist Transmission and the Emergence of Between-Group Differences." *Evolution and Human Behavior* 19: 215–241.

Herlihy, D., and C. Klapische-Zuber. 1985. *Tuscans and Their Families*. New Haven, CT: Yale University Press.

Herlihy, David. 1991. "Biology and History: Suggestions for a Dialogue." Brown University.

Hirschman, Albert O. 1985. "Against Parsimony." *Economic Philosophy* 1: 7–21.

Hume, David. [1754] 1898. *Essays: Moral, Political, and Literary*. London: Longmans, Green and Co.

Kelly, Raymond C. 1985. *The Nuer Conquest: The Structure and Development of an Expansionist System*. Ann Arbor: University of Michigan Press.

Kelly, Robert. 1995. *The Foraging Spectrum: Diversity in Hunter-Gatherer Lifeways*. Washington, DC: Smithsonian Institution Press.

Kohn, Melvin L. 1969. *Class and Conformity: A Study in Values*. Homewood: Dorsey Press.

Kuran, Timur. 1985. *Private Truths, Public Lies*. Cambridge and London: Harvard University Press.

Laibson, David. Forthcoming. "A Cue-Theory of Consumption." *Quarterly Journal of Economics*.

Lewontin, R. C. 1974. *The Genetic Basis of Evolutionary Change*. New York: Columbia University Press.

Loewenstein, George. 1996. "Out of Control: Visceral Influences on Behavior." *Organizational Behavior and Human Decision Processes* 65: 272–292.

Lohmann, Susanne. 1994. "Dynamics of Informational Cascades: The Monday Demonstrations in Leipzig." *World Politics* 47(1) (October): 42–101.

MacDonald, Kevin. 1995. "The Establishment and Maintenance of Socially Imposed Monogamy in Western Europe." *Politics and the Life Sciences* 14(1): 3–23.

Mack Smith, Denis. 1959. *Italy: A Modern History*, Ann Arbor: University of Michigan Press.

Mackie, Gerry. 1996. "Ending Foot Binding and Infibulation: A Convention Account." *American Sociological Review* 61(6): 999–1017.

Matthew, Donald. 1983. *Atlas of Medieval Europe*. New York: Facts on File.

Maynard Smith, John. 1976. "Group Selection." *Quarterly Review of Biology* 51: 277–283.

Munshi, Kaivan, and Jacques Myaux. 1998. "Social Effects in the Demographic Transition: Evidence from Matlab, Bangladesh." Unpublished paper. Boston University and the International Centre for Diarrhoeal Disease Research, Bangledesh, June.

Newcomb, Theodore, M., et al. 1967. *Persistence and Change: Bennington College and Its Students After Twenty-Five Years*. New York: John Wiley & Sons, Inc.

Nisbett, Richard E., and Dov. Cohen. 1996. *Culture of Honor: The Psychology of Violence in the South*. Boulder: Westview Press, Inc.

Nowell-Smith, Patrick H. 1954. *Ethics*. London: Penguin.

Ostrom, Elinor. 1998. "A Behavioral Approach to the Rational Choice Theory of Collective Action." *American Political Science Review* 92(1) (March): 1–16.

Paddock, John. 1975. "Studies on Anti-Violent and 'Normal' Communities." *Aggressive Behavior* 1: 217–233.

———. 1990. "Blood Ties: Life and Violence in Rural Mexico, by James B. Greenberg," *Aggressive Behavior* 16: 399–401.

Parsons, Talcott. 1964. "Evolutionary Universals in Society." *American Sociological Review* 29(3) (June): 339–357.

Price, George R. 1970. "Selection and Covariance." *Nature* 227(5257) (Aug. 1): 520–521.

———. 1972. "Extension of Covariance Selection Mathematics." *Annals of Human Genetics* 35: 485–490.

Rogers, Alan R. 1990. "Group Selection by Selective Emigration: The Effects of Migration and Kin Structure." *The American Naturalist* 135(3): 398–413.

Ross, Lee, and Richard Nisbett. 1991. *The Person and the Situation*. Philadelphia: Temple University Press.

Rozin, Paul, and Carol Nemeroff. 1990. "The Laws of Sympathetic Magic: A Psychological Analysis of Similarity and Contagion." In *Cultural Psychology: Essays on Comparative Human Development*, ed. James W. Stigler, Richard A. Shweder, and Gilbert Herdt, 205–232. Cambridge: Cambridge University Press.

Sen, Amartya K. 1977. "Rational Fools: A Critique of the Behavioral Foundations of Economic Theory." *Philosophy and Public Affairs* 6 (Summer): 317–344.

Sherif, Muzafer. 1937. "An Experimental Approach to the Study of Attitudes." *Sociometry* 1 (July–Oct.): 90–98.

Simon, Herbert A. 1990. "A Mechanism for Social Selection and Successful Altruism." *Science* 250 (Dec. 21): 1665–1668.

Sober, Elliot, and David Sloan Wilson. 1998. *Unto Others: The Evolution and Psychology of Unselfish Behavior*. Cambridge, MA: Harvard University Press.

Soltis, Joseph, Robert Boyd, and Peter Richerson. 1995. "Can Group-Functional Behaviors Evolve by Cultural Group Selection: An Empirical Test." *Current Anthropology* 36(3) (June): 473–483.

Stigler, George J., and Gary S. Becker. 1977. "De Gustibus Non Est Disputandum." *Amer. Econ. Rev.* 67(2) (Mar.): 76–90.

Sunstein, Cass R. 1993. "Endogenous Preferences, Environmental Law." *The Journal of Legal Studies* 22 (June): 217–254.

Tilly, Charles. 1975. *The Formation of National States in Western Europe*. Princeton: Princeton University Press.

———. 1990. *Coercion, Capital, and European States, AD 990–1990*. Cambridge, MA: Basil Blackwell.

Tversky, A., and D. Kahneman. 1986. "Rational Choice and the Framing of Decisions." *Journal of Business* 59: 251–281.

Uyenoyama, M., and M. W. Feldman. 1980. "Theories of Kin and Group Selection: A Population Genetics Approach." *Theoretical Population Biology* 17: 380–414.

Uyenoyama, Marcy K. 1979. "Evolution of Altruism under Group Selection in Large and Small Populations in Fluctuating Environments." *Theoretical Population Biology* 15: 58–85.

Wallerstein, Immanuel. 1974. *The Modern World-System: Capitalist Agriculture and the Origins of the European World-Economy in the Sixteenth Century*. New York: Academic Press.

Weber, Eugen von. 1976. *Peasants into Frenchmen: The Modernization of Rural France, 1870–1914*. Stanford: Stanford University Press.

Weinstein, D. A., H. H. Shugart, and C. C. Brandt. 1983. "Energy Flow and the Persistence of a Human Population: A Simulation Analysis." *Human Ecology* 11(2): 201–223.

Williams, George C. 1966. *Adaption and Natural Selection: A Critique of Some Current Evolutionary Thought*. Princeton, NJ: Princeton University Press.

Wilson, David Sloan. 1977. "Structured Demes and the Evolution of Group-Advantagenous Traits." *The American Naturalist* 111: 157–185.

Wilson, David Sloan, and Lee A. Dugatkin. 1997. "Group Selection and Assortative Interactions." *The American Naturalist* 149(2): 336–351.

Wilson, David Sloan, and Elliott Sober. 1994. "Reintroducing Group Selection to the Human behavioral Sciences." *Behavior and Brain Sciences* 17: 585–654.

Zajonc, R. B. 1980. "Feeling and Thinking: Preferences Need No Inferences." *American Psychologist* 35(2) (Feb.): 151–175.

7 The Emergence of Classes in a Multi-Agent Bargaining Model

Robert L. Axtell,
Joshua M. Epstein, and
H. Peyton Young

7.1 Introduction

Norms are self-enforcing patterns of behavior: it is in everyone's interest to conform given the expectation that others are going to conform. Many spheres of social interaction are governed by norms: dress codes, table manners, rules of deference, forms of communication, reciprocity in exchange, and so forth. In this chapter we are interested in norms that govern the distribution of property. In particular, we are concerned with the contrast between *discriminatory norms*, which allocate different shares of the pie according to gender, race, ethnicity, age, and so forth, and *equity norms*, which do not so discriminate. An example of a discriminatory norm is the practice of passing on inherited property to the eldest son (primogeniture). Another is the custom, once common in the southern United States, that blacks should sit in the back of the bus. A third is the notion that certain categories of people (e.g., women, blacks) should receive lower compensation than others doing the same job, and in other cases that they not be given the job at all. These kinds of discriminatory norms can lead to significant differences in economic class, that is, long-lived differences in property rights based on characteristics that are viewed as socially salient.[1]

In this chapter we study the question of how such classes can emerge and persist, given a norm-free, classless world initially. The framework combines concepts from evolutionary game theory on the one hand and agent-based computational modeling on the other. The essential idea is to show how norms can emerge spontaneously at the social level from the decentralized interactions of many individuals that cumulate over time into a set of social expectations. Due to the self-reinforcing nature of the process, these expectations tend to perpetuate themselves for long periods of time, even though they may have arisen from purely random events and have no a priori justification. We show that social expectations gravitate to one of three conditions: (i) an equity norm in which property is shared equally among claimants, and there are no "class" distinctions; (ii) a discriminatory norm in which the claimants get different amounts based on observable characteristics that have become socially salient (but are fundamentally irrelevant); and (iii) fractious states in which norms of distribution have failed to coalesce, resulting in constant disputes and missed opportunities. In both the first and second cases, society functions efficiently in the sense that no property is wasted. There is no equity-efficiency tradeoff, just a difference in the way property rights are distributed. The third case, by contrast, is highly inefficient and may involve substantial inequality as well.

The long-run probability of being in these three different regimes can be computed using techniques from stochastic dynamical systems theory (Freidlin and Wentzell 1984; Foster and Young 1990; Young 1993a, 1998; Kandori, Mailath, and Rob 1993). But these methods are less helpful in characterizing the short- and intermediate-run behavior of these processes. Here agent-based computational techniques can play a central role, by identifying regimes that are long-lived on intermediate time scales, though not necessarily stable over very long time scales (Epstein and Axtell 1996; Axtell and Epstein 1999).

Overview of the Model

Our model of class formation is based on Young's evolutionary model of bargaining (Young 1993b). The model is bottom-up in the sense that norms emerge spontaneously from the decentralized interactions of self-interested agents.[2] In each time period two randomly chosen agents interact, bargaining over shares of available property. Their behavior, and their expectations about others' behavior, evolve endogenously based on prior experiences. These expectations may be conditioned on certain visible characteristics or "tags" that serve to differentiate people. These tags have no *inherent* social or economic significance—they are merely distinguishing features, such as dark or light skin, or brown or blue eyes. Over time, however, they can acquire social significance due to path dependency effects. It might happen, for example, that blue-eyed people get a larger share of the pie than brown-eyed people due to a series of chance coincidences. The existence of these precedents causes the expectation to develop that blue-eyed people generally get more than brown-eyed people, and a *discriminatory norm* or class system emerges. Alternatively, an *equity norm* can develop in which the tags have no significance, and both sides get equal shares.

It can be shown that, asymptotically, the equity norm is more stable than any discriminatory norm. In other words, starting from arbitrary initial conditions, society is more likely to be at or near an equal sharing regime than an unequal or discriminatory one if we wait long enough. Nevertheless, metastable regimes can emerge that are discriminatory and inequitable, yet persist for substantial periods of time. These inequitable regimes correspond, roughly speaking, to situations where a discriminatory intergroup norm divides society into upper and lower classes, while a different, intragroup norm causes dissension within one (or both) of the classes. Based on many realizations of the agent-based computational model, we estimate the time it takes to exit from these discriminatory regimes as a function of the number of agents, the length of agents' memory, and the level of background noise. In this case, the waiting time increases *exponentially in memory length and the number of agents*, and can be immense even for relatively modest values of the parameters. The contrast between asymptotic and nonequilibrium results illustrates how analytical and computational methods complement one another in studying a given social dynamic.

7.2   Bargaining

We begin by modeling a bargaining process between individual agents. Consider two players, A and B, each of whom demands some portion of a "pie," which we take as a metaphor for a piece of available property. The exact nature of the property need not concern us here. For simplicity, however, we shall suppose that the property is divisible, and that both parties have an equal claim to it a priori.[3] A posteriori differences in claim will emerge endogenously from the process itself.

To specify the process, we must first delineate how agents solve the one-shot bargaining problem. A standard way of modeling this situation is the *Nash demand game*: each party gets his demand if the *sum* of the two demands is not more than 100 percent of the pie; otherwise each gets nothing. For instance, if employers and employees demand more than 100 percent of total revenues, negotiations break down.

To simplify the analysis, we shall suppose that each agent can make just three possible demands: low (30 percent of the pie), medium (50

Table 7.1
The Nash demand game

	H	M	L
H	0,0	0,0	**70,30**
M	0,0	**50,50**	50,30
L	**30,70**	30,50	30,30

percent), and high (70 percent).[4] For example, if row demands H and column plays M, their demands sum to 120 and each gets nothing. The payoffs (in percentage share) from all combinations of demands are shown in table 7.1.

This yields a coordination game in which there are exactly three pure-strategy Nash equilibria, shown in bold: (L, H), (M, M), and (H, L). While various theories have been advanced that identify a particular equilibrium as being most plausible a priori (e.g., Harsanyi and Selten 1988), we do not find these equilibrium selection theories to be especially compelling. Instead of assuming equilibrium, we wish to explore the process by which equilibrium emerges (if indeed it does) at the aggregate level, from the repeated, decentralized interactions of individuals.

7.3   The Model with One Agent Type

We begin by studying this question for a population of agents who are indistinguishable from one another, but who have different experiences (life histories) that condition their beliefs. Then we consider a population consisting of two distinct types of agents, who are differentiated by a visible "tag" (dark or light skin, brown or blue eyes) that has no intrinsic economic significance, but on which agents may condition their behavior. In the latter case, long-lived discriminatory norms can develop purely by historical chance, while this does not happen in the case of homogeneous agents. But in both situations, fractious regimes can emerge in which society fails to develop any coherent norm for long periods of time.

Let the population consist of N agents. Each time period consists of $[N/2]$ "matches." In each match, one pair of agents is drawn at random from the population, and they play the game in table 7.1.[5] Each agent's data about its world—its beliefs—are based on experience from previous plays. In particular, every agent remembers the demands—H, M, or L—played by each of her last m opponents, where m is *memory length*.[6] The concatenation of all agent memories defines the current *state* of the society. Behaviorally, each agent forms an expectation about her opponent's demands. She assumes that the probability of the current opponent demanding L, M, or H is equal to the relative frequency with which her previous opponents made these demands in the last m interactions. But with some relatively small probability, ε, she selects her demand randomly. Her behavior is thus a kind of "noisy best reply" to her past experience:

• With probability $1 - \varepsilon$ an agent makes a demand that maximizes her expected payoff given her expectations about the opponent's behavior. If several demands maximize expected payoff, they are chosen with equal probability.

• With probability ε the agent does not optimize but chooses one of the three demands, H, M, or L, at random.

These rules for matching, belief formation, and behavior define a particular *social dynamic* as a function of the population size N, memory length m, and error rate ε. Notice that it is a Markov process, because there is a well-defined probability of moving from any given state s to any other state s' in the next period.

In this model, agents' beliefs evolve according to their particular experiences. Thus, at any given time, the beliefs can be highly heterogeneous because agents will have had different histories of interactions with others. Importantly, moreover, these beliefs may be inconsistent with the actual state of the world. A given agent's experiences may not be representative of behavior in the whole population. For example, one agent, say A, might by chance have been matched against opponents who demanded H in each of the last m periods. Thus A will believe that the next opponent is likely to demand H, so she is very likely to demand L (which is a best reply to H). But another agent, say B, may have been matched against opponents who always demanded M; for this agent it makes sense to demand M. The reality, however, could be that most people in the population actually plan to demand L, in which case the beliefs of both A and B are at variance with the facts. Moreover, if A is matched against B in the next round, they will make the demands (L, M) with high probability, which is not an equilibrium of the one-shot bargaining game.

A *social norm* is a self-perpetuating state in which players' memories, and hence their best replies, are unchanging. In other words, it is a rest point or equilibrium of the dynamical system when the error term $\varepsilon = 0$. Consider, for example, the state in which everyone's experience is that opponents always demand M. Then everyone believes that her next opponent will play M. Given these beliefs, M is a best response. Assuming there are no errors ($\varepsilon = 0$), both sides demand M in the next period. Thus, agents' beliefs about opponents turn out to be correct, and this situation perpetuates itself from one period to the next. This is the *equity norm* in which everyone *expects* the other to demand one-half, and as a result everyone *does in fact* demand one-half. Note that this social norm involves no tradeoff between equity and efficiency: the solution is equitable because both sides get equal shares of each pie, and it is efficient because there is no rearrangement of shares that makes all agents better off. It can be verified that, when there are no observable differences among agents, the equity norm is the unique equilibrium of the Nash demand game and is the unique rest point of the unperturbed social dynamic.

7.3.1 Simplex Representation of Agent States

We represent the state of the agent population on a simplex with three differently shaded regions, as shown in figure 7.1. At each time, every

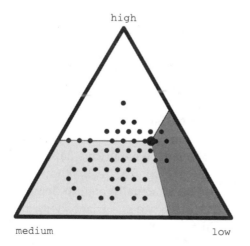

Figure 7.1
Memory simplex for one agent type.

agent occupies a position on the simplex that is determined by the content of her memory. For example, an agent who has encountered only agents playing L is located at the lower-right vertex of the simplex (labeled "low"). The shading within the simplex represents the best reply strategy *given* the agent's memory. That is, since each agent best replies to her memories, an agent's location on the simplex can be though of as representing her *expectation* about her opponents' play. In the white region, L is the best reply since memory configurations here are dominated by H. In the dark gray zone, the opposite occurs— memories are dominated by Hs—so L is the best reply. Agents in the light gray zone have memories for opponents playing M, so it is best for them to play M as well.

Starting from different initial states, we can examine various real-izations of the process.[7] Suppose, for example, that $N = 100$, $m = 10$, and $\varepsilon = 0.1$, and the initial state is random about the point of indifference between the three strategies. After eighty periods the process can evolve to the situation shown in figure 7.2.[8] In this new state, all agents have encountered frequent demands of M in the past, and thus they expect their opponents to play M in the next period. Given this expec-tation, M is the best response. Hence most agents play M next period, which reinforces the expectation of M. However, by a process we do not model, agents occasionally deviate from best reply and play either H or L. This may occur due to random errors, conscious

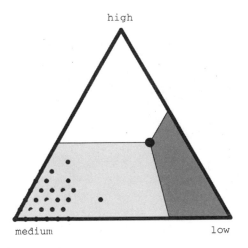

Figure 7.2
Convergence to the equity norm.

experimentation, simple imitation, or for any number of other reasons. This is analogous to mutation in biological models and serves to create variety in the population.[9]

If the process is allowed to continue from the state shown in figure 7.2, the probability is high that most agents will remain in the light gray region for quite a long period of time. This is because the equity norm has a large basin of attraction, and even substantial deviations caused by random "mutations" in individual behavior may not be enough to tip society into a fundamentally different regime. Nevertheless such tipping events will eventually occur, and they can lead to regimes that have a fundamentally different character.

Such inequitable regimes may also emerge right away when we start from a different initial state. Figure 7.3 illustrates this for one realization of the process, showing the state after 150 periods.

In this *fractious* state, people at each instant are either aggressive or passive; they have not learned to compromise. If, in one's experience, a sufficient proportion of one's opponents are aggressive (demand H), then it is better to submit (play L) than to offer to share equally, and conversely. (It can be checked, in fact, that M is *never* a best response for someone who has never experienced an opponent who played M.) This fractious state persists in excess of 10^9 time periods, though it is neither equitable nor efficient. There is frequent miscoordination in which the players either demand too much (both play H) or demand

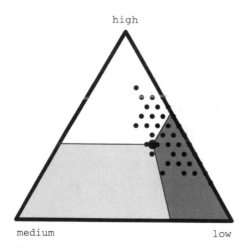

Figure 7.3
Emergence of a fractious state.

too little (both play L) and end up leaving part of the pie on the table. In the state shown in figure 7.3, the average share of pie per person in each period is only about one-quarter, or about half the expected share under the equity norm. But while this is an inefficient state, it does not exhibit classes, because agents frequently migrate between zones, sometimes demanding H and sometimes demanding L.

7.3.2 Transitions between Regimes

Using asymptotic methods, it can be shown that when m and N are sufficiently large, the probability of being in the equity region is substantially higher than being in the fractious region if one waits long enough and the error rate ε is small. In the terminology of evolutionary game theory, the equity norm is *stochastically stable* (Foster and Young 1990). The intuitive reason is that it takes much longer to undo the equity norm once it is established than to undo the fractious regime once it is in place. However, the *inertia* of the system—the waiting time to reach the stochastically stable regime—can be very large indeed. Suppose that we start the agent society off in the fractious regime with $N = 10$, $\varepsilon = 0.10$, and compute the expected number of periods to transit to a neighborhood of the equity norm (i.e., to a state where all agents have at least $(1 - \varepsilon)m$ instances of M in their memories). As figure 7.4 shows, the waiting time increases exponentially in memory length. For

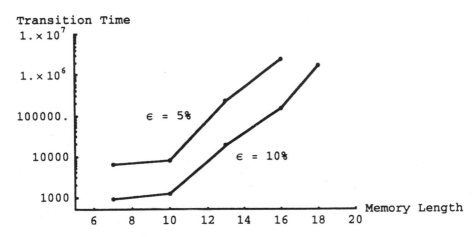

Figure 7.4
Transition time between regimes as a function of memory length, $N = 10$, various ε.

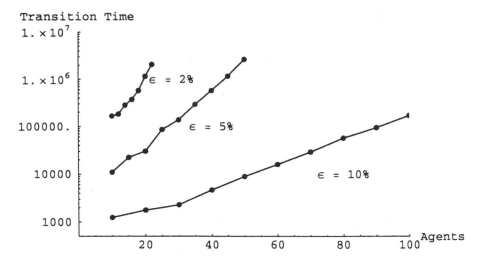

Figure 7.5
Transition time between regimes as a function of population size, $m = 10$, various ε.

example, when $m = 13$ it takes in excess of 10^5 periods on average for the fractious regime to be displaced in favor of the equity norm.

Similarly, the transit time increases exponentially with population size, as shown in figure 7.5.

Hence, although the equity norm is stochastically stable, the agent-based computational model reveals that—depending on the number of agents and the memory length—the waiting time to transit from the fractious regime to the equity norm may be astronomically long.[10]

7.3.3 Broken Ergodicity

In figure 7.4, for $m = 18$, the expected number of time periods the society must wait in order to move from the split regime to the equity norm is $O(10^6)$. In human societies, a million interactions per agent is not realizable. So how are we to interpret such large interaction requirements?

Dynamical systems that are formally ergodic but that possess subregions of the state space that confine the system with high probability over a long time scale are said to display *broken ergodicity*[11] with respect to that time scale.[12] Call $R_{\text{trans}}(m, N, \varepsilon)$, the rate of transition from the split state to the equity norm. For example, from figure 7.4, for $m = 18$, this rate would be approximately 10^{-6}. Now, say that the lifetime of the society is $T \ll 1/R_{trans}(m, N, \varepsilon)$. Then, to a first approximation the probability of regime transition $Pr_{trans}(T, m, N, \varepsilon) = TR_{trans}(m, N, \varepsilon)$. A system has *effective* broken ergodicity if $Pr_{trans}(T, m, N, \varepsilon) < p_0$, where p_0 is some small level of significance, say 0.001. Clearly, the exponential dependence of transition times on memory length and population size implies that our model society displays broken ergodicity.

We can summarize these results as follows. *Occasional random choices create noise in the system, which implies that no state is perfectly absorbing. However, there are two regions of the state space—one equitable, the other fractious—that are very persistent: once the process enters such a region, it tends to stay there for a long period of time. A particular implication is that, while there is only one pure equilibrium of the game (corresponding to the equity norm), it may be difficult for decentralized decision makers to discover this equilibrium from certain initial conditions. Put differently, the computation of the equity norm by a decentralized society of agents is "hard" in the sense that it takes exponential time to achieve it from some states.*[13]

7.4 Two Agent Types: The "Tag" Model

Thus far agents have been indistinguishable from one another. Even though they have different experiences that lead them to act differently, they look the same to others. Let us now suppose that agents carry a distinguishing tag (e.g., light or dark).[14] The tag is completely meaningless in that agents are identical in competence; for example, they have the same amount of memory and follow the same behavioral rule (conditional on experience). However, the presence of the tag allows agents to condition their behavior on the tag of their opponents. To be specific, assume that each agent records in his memory the tag of his opponent and the demand that he made. Faced with a new dark opponent, the agent demands an amount that maximizes the expected payoff against his remembered distribution of dark opponents.[15] Faced with a light opponent, the agent plays a best reply against his remembered distribution of light opponents. All of this happens with high probability, but with some small probability $\varepsilon > 0$ agents make random demands. In this model, the social possibilities are richer than before, since equity or fractiousness can prevail both between and within types.

To fix ideas, assume for the moment that there is no noise in the agents' strategy choice ($\varepsilon = 0$). Define an *intergroup equilibrium* as a state in which each agent in the light group demands x against members in the dark group, each agent in the dark group demands $1 - x$ against each opponent from the light group, and this is true for every previous encounter that each agent remembers. An *intragroup equilibrium* is a state in which everyone demands one-half against members of his own group, and this is true for every previous encounter that each agent remembers.

Using methods from perturbed Markov process theory (Young 1993a), it can be shown that when m and N/m are sufficiently large, then the unique stochastically stable state corresponds to the particular case where $x = 1/2$; that is, equity prevails both between and within groups. When ε is sufficiently small, this state or something close to it will be observed with very high probability in the long run. But, as before, there exist fractious states and inequitable norms that have considerable staying power. Furthermore, the dynamics governing the emergence (and dissolution) of intergroup norms differs from that governing intragroup norms.

To study these dynamics computationally, we shall represent events on two simplexes: the one on the right corresponds to agent memory states when playing agents of the *opposite* type—it depicts the intergroup dynamics—while the one on the left displays agent memories for playing agents of the same type—the intragroup dynamics. Black dots refer to dark agents, gray dots to light ones. In each run, there are a total of one hundred agents, fifty of each type. All agents have memory length twenty and the noise level $\varepsilon = 0.1$. The initial state differs between the runs in order to illustrate the effects of path dependency.

Figure 7.6 illustrates our first case. Starting from random initial conditions, it depicts the state of the system at time $t = 150$.

At this point the process has reached a state where something close to the equity norm prevails both between and within groups. In particular, the process is in the basin of attraction of the equity norm for dark against dark, light against light, and light against dark. Average payoffs in this regime are high, because most agents succeed in dividing the pie rather than fighting over it.

Figure 7.7 tells a different story. Starting from different random initial conditions, it shows the system at $t = 150$. Internally, the darks (black dots) have come close to the equity norm while the lights (gray dots) are still in a fractious state. However, something close to the equity norm prevails *between* the lights and the darks.

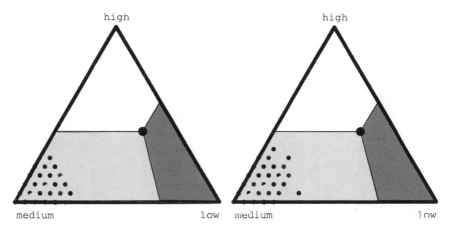

Figure 7.6
Equity between and within types.

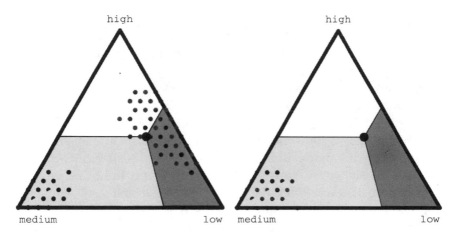

Figure 7.7
Equity between, but not within, types.

7.4.1 Classes

Yet another history unfolds in figure 7.8. In this case the process evolves fairly rapidly (after 225 periods) to a state in which the equity norm holds within each group, whereas a discriminatory norm governs relations between the two groups. When agents meet others of their own type, most of them expect to divide the pie in half. But when a dark agent meets a light agent, the darks act aggressively and the lights act

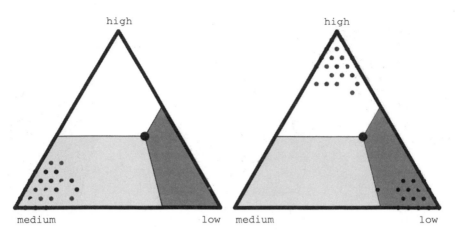

Figure 7.8
Equity within, but not between, types.

passively. The result is that, on average, the payoff to dark agents (70) is over twice as high as it is to light agents (30). In other words, *class distinctions have emerged endogenously*. Once established, such class structures can persist for very long periods of time. The reason is that lights have come to expect that darks will be very demanding, so it is rational to submit to their demands. Similarly, darks have come to expect that lights will submit, so it is rational to take advantage of them.

The final case is to us the most interesting and disturbing. Starting from a different random initial state, society evolves after 260 periods to the state shown in figure 7.9. As evident in the right (inter-type) simplex, the darks dominate the lights. However, from the left simplex, it is clear that the equity norm prevails within the dominant darks while the lights are a fractious society. This, then, is the picture of *a divided underclass oppressed by a unified elite*. This result seems particularly disturbing in that every individual is behaving rationally—playing the best reply strategy—and yet the social outcome is far from optimal. Even though this regime does not correspond to a coordination equilibrium of the bargaining game (unlike fig. 7.8), it may nevertheless persist for long periods of time.

7.4.2 Transition Dynamics

Figures 7.4 and 7.5 above show how the transition time from the fractious configuration to the equity state depends on the population size

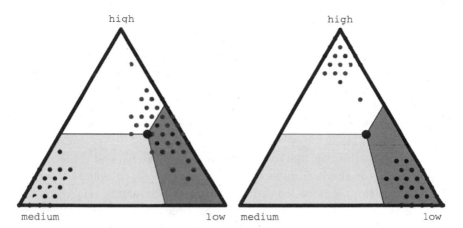

Figure 7.9
Equity above, division below.

and memory length, for various values of ε. A similar analysis is possible for the classlike configurations displayed in figure 7.9. That is, we can start the system off in a configuration with classes and measure how long it takes to transit to the equity norm, as a function of the model parameters. We have not executed such analyses for a simple reason: even for model configurations that should be hospitable to such transitions (e.g., 10 agents of each type, $m = 10$, and $\varepsilon = 0.1$), these events are very rare, and thus difficult to systematically investigate. This is in sharp contrast to earlier results where $O(10^3)$ periods were sufficient on average for such equity transitions to occur. The "basin of attraction" of the classlike configuration is much deeper than the fractious outcome, and the transition times are correspondingly longer. It is an open problem to estimate analytically the expected duration of these transient regimes as a function of the parameters of the process.

7.5   Summary

Although class systems can certainly arise through outright coercion (Wright 1985), we have argued that various kinds of social orders—including segregated, discriminatory, and class systems—can also arise through the decentralized interactions of many agents in which accidents of history become reinforced over time. In these path-dependent dynamics, society may self-organize around distinctions that are quite arbitrary from an a priori standpoint. Above, initially meaningless "tags" acquire socially organizing salience: tag-based classes emerge. Asymptotically, equity norms have an advantage over discriminatory norms. Computational analysis indicates, however, that long-lived regimes may emerge that are very far from equitable and may be highly inefficient as well.

Appendix: State Space of the Multiagent Bargaining Game

This model admits a Markovian formulation. Briefly, call ξ the set of all possible individual memory configurations—each one a string of length m (the memory length) recording the demands (H, M, or L) made by an agent's opponents in the most recent m periods played. In a population of N agents, the state space Z of this process is the set of all possible N-tuples of ξ. The random matching and strategy choice rules then determine a Markov chain with fixed transition probabilities—that is, a $|Z| \times |Z|$ transition matrix, dependent on N, m, and the noise level ε.

The origin of the broken ergodicity displayed by this model for seemingly modest configurations—10 to 100 agents, each of whom has memory length $O(10)$—arises from the enormous dimension of the state space, Z. For memory length m and three strategies, the number of distinct memory configurations is 3^m. Generally, for S strategies there are S^m memory configurations. For N agents, since individual memories are independent, $|Z| = 3^{Nm}$; S^{Nm} generally. Therefore, the $|Z| \times |Z|$ transition matrix will have 3^{2Nm} entries, S^{2Nm} generally. However, because any individual's memory configuration can only be converted into nine others in a single interaction (S^2 others generally), the transition matrix is sparse—there are only 3^{2N} transitions possible for each state, thus only $3^{2N} \times 3^{Nm} = 3^{N(m+2)}$ entries in the transition matrix are nonzero; generally, $S^{N(m+2)}$. Table 7A.1 below gives numerical values for these various quantities as a function of m, for a population of ten agents ($N = 10$).

Even for this relatively small population size, most of these quantities are enormous. As a practical matter, a state-of-the-art workstation is not even capable of holding the $m = 2$ state vector in memory, since this would require some 6 gigabytes of RAM at two bytes per entry, a conceivable although untypically large quantity of memory (ca. 1999). Furthermore, the corresponding (sparse) transition matrix is so large that it could not be stored by conventional means—its entries would therefore have to be computed as needed.

Table 7A.1
Number of memory configurations, dimension of the state space and number of entries in the sparse transition matrix, for $N = 10$, various m

	3^m	3^{Nm}	$3^{N(m+2)}$	$S^{Nm}; S = 5$
$m = 2$	9	$\approx 3 \times 10^9$	$\approx 1 \times 10^{19}$	$\approx 1 \times 10^{14}$
$m = 7$	2187	$\approx 3 \times 10^{33}$	$\approx 9 \times 10^{42}$	$\approx 8 \times 10^{48}$
$m = 10$	59,049	$\approx 5 \times 10^{47}$	$\approx 2 \times 10^{57}$	$\approx 8 \times 10^{69}$
$m - 20$	3,486,784,401	$\sim 3 \times 10^{95}$	$\approx 9 \times 10^{104}$	$\approx 6 \times 10^{139}$

Table 7A.2
Number of memory configurations, dimension of the state space and number of entries in the sparse transition matrix, for $N = 100$, various m

	3^m	3^{Nm}	$3^{N(m+2)}$	$S^{Nm}; S = 5$
$m = 2$	9	$\approx 3 \times 10^{95}$	$\approx 1 \times 10^{190}$	$\approx 1 \times 10^{139}$
$m = 7$	2187	$\approx 3 \times 10^{334}$	$\approx 9 \times 10^{429}$	$\approx 8 \times 10^{489}$
$m = 10$	59,049	$\approx 5 \times 10^{477}$	$\approx 2 \times 10^{572}$	$\approx 8 \times 10^{698}$
$m = 20$	3,486,784,401	$\approx 3 \times 10^{954}$	$\approx 9 \times 10^{1049}$	$\approx 6 \times 10^{1397}$

The situation is vastly worse for a population size of one hundred. Table 7A.2 gives the number of memory configurations, dimension of the state space, and the size of the sparse transition matrix, this time for $N = 100$.

These quantities are unimaginably large. However, it turns out that it is possible to shrink these sizes significantly. This is because the best reply (BR) rule of the type employed here does not use any information on the order in which past opponents' strategies were encountered. That is, for $m = 6$, memory string (H, H, H, L, L, L) is equivalent to (L, L, L, H, H, H) for purposes of BR; in each the frequency of L and H is 0.5. Because the order of an agent's memories is unimportant—at least to this variant of BR—the number of BR-distinct memory configurations is much smaller than S^m. This permits significant reduction in sizes of the state space and transition matrix of the overall Markov process. Let us call Z, where $|Z| = 3^{Nm}$, the naive state space. We explore this smaller (aggregated) state space, Z', presently.[16]

Call n_L, n_M, n_H the number of low, medium, and high memories, respectively, that some particular agent possesses. Because these must sum to m, n_H can be written as $m - n_L - n_M$. Thus, the pair (n_L, n_M) gives all information needed by the agent in order to execute BR. Now, since each $n_{(\cdot)} \in [0, 1, \ldots, m]$, the number of distinct memory states is simply $(m + 1) + m + (m - 1) + \ldots + 1 = (m + 1)(m + 2)/2 = (m^2 + 3m + 2)/2$; for $m = 10$, the total is 66. So, $|Z'| = [(m + 1)(m + 2)]^N/2^N$; for $N = m = 10$ the state space has $66^{10} \approx 1.6 \times 10^{18}$ dimensions, which is smaller than the naive state space from table 7A.1 of 5×10^{47} by approximately 3×10^{29}. A dense transition matrix for a state space of this size is $[(m + 1)(m + 2)]^{2N}/4^N$ in size. But for the problem at hand this is yet sparse—each state can be converted into only nine others—and thus only $3^{2N}[(m + 1)(m + 2)]^N/2^N$ entries need to be stored; for $N = m = 10$, there are some 5×10^{27} nonzero entries, which is a massive reduction from the 3×10^{52} entries of the transition matrix associated with the naive state space.

Unfortunately, the vast reduction in the size of the state space in going from Z to Z' does not make the problem tractable computationally. In particular, consider the case of $S = 3$, $N = m = 10$. In this instance, there are only two recurrent communication classes (see Young 1993a, 68 for definition), one in which all agents are in state (M, M, M, M, M, M, M, M, M, M), the unperturbed equity norm—call it H_1, $|H_1| = 1$—and one in which each agent has some combination of (only) Ls and Hs in memory—call this H_2, and note that there are at most $2^{100} \approx 1.3 \times 10^{30}$ of these states in the naive state space, while in Z', $|H_2| = 11^{10} \approx 2.6 \times 10^{10}$. Since $|Z'| = 66^{10}$, the number of states outside of both H_1 and H_2 is $66^{10} - 11^{10} - 1 \approx 66^{10} \approx 1.6 \times 10^{18}$. Finding the path with least total resistance between H_1 and H_2 is indeed a shortest path problem (Young 1993a, 69), but in 1.6×10^{18} vertices with approximately $9^{10} \approx 3.5 \times 10^9$ times that many edges, namely, 5.5×10^{27} total. Now, shortest path problems can be solved in an amount of time linear in the number of vertices + edges (cf. Bertsekas and Tsitsiklis 1989), but a problem of this magnitude is far beyond the scope of conventional computation.

Notes

For valuable comments the authors thank Sam Bowles, Jeff Carpenter, Steve Durlauf, Nienke Oomes, John Roemer, John Rust, Thomas Schelling, John Steinbruner, Leigh Tesfatsion, Frank Thompson, Erik Olin Wright, and seminar participants at Brookings, Davis, Michigan, the Santa Fe Institute, Stanford, and the University of Massachusetts (Amherst). Steven McCarroll's research assistance was invaluable. Support from the National Science Foundation under grant IRI-9725302 is gratefully acknowledged. Additional support was provided to the Center on Social and Economic Dynamics by the MacArthur Foundation.

1. For other models of classes see Roemer (1982) and Cole, Mailath, and Postlewaite (1998). This chapter differs from these by focusing on the dynamic process by which classes emerge, rather than on the equilibrium conditions that sustain them.

2. We use the term "emergent" as defined in Epstein and Axtell (1996) to mean simply "arising from the local interactions of agents." The term and its history are discussed at length in Epstein (1999).

3. Indivisible forms of property, such as a bus seat, can be made divisible by giving the claimants equal a priori chances at being the occupant.

4. The more general case is considered in Young (1993b).

5. Some agents may be active more than once in a particular period, while others are inactive. On average, agents are active once per period.

6. Some agents may have larger memories than others; that is, m may be a random variable in the agent population.

7. A working version of this model is available on the World Wide Web. It is written in Java and can be found at the following
URL: www.brookings.edu/es/dynamics/papers/classes.

8. There are less than one hundred dots shown in the figures because some agents have the same memory state.

9. Each matched agent chooses randomly with probability $\varepsilon = 0.20$. However, there is a one-third chance that the random choice will in fact be the best reply, hence the probability that an "error" is realized is 0.1333 . . .

10. It is important to note that the expected waiting time depends crucially on the geometry of the interaction structure. In this model we have assumed that agents are paired at random from the whole society. In reality, agents interact in social networks in which there are both local (neighborhood) and global (long-range) interactions. The existence of such neighborhood structures can greatly reduce the dependence of the social learning process on population size (Ellison 1993; Young 1998). Intuitively, the reason is that a local switch in regime—say from fractious to equitable—may be relatively easy because it involves only a small number of agents (the local population size is small). Agent behavior in local interaction models is, however, quite different than in the model described here. Agents repeatedly interact with the same agents in such models, and memory plays no essential role, namely, interactions are not anonymous.

11. The authors thank Kai Nagel and Maya Paczuski for suggesting the relevance of this concept to our results.

12. For a review article on broken ergodicity see Palmer (1989).

13. The view of social systems as distributed computational devices and the associated characterization of various social problems as computationally hard are developed more fully in Epstein (1999) and Epstein and Axtell (1996), see also Shoham and Tennenholtz (1996) and DeCanio and Watkins (1998).

14. For different uses of tags and taglike devices in agent-based models, see Epstein and Axtell (1996), Holland (1996), and Axelrod (1997).

15. In the event that an agent has no memory of blue opponents, it picks a random strategy.

16. For more on aggregating Markov processes, see Howard (1971).

References

Axelrod, R. 1997. "The Dissemination of Culture: A Model with Local Convergence and Global Polarization." *Journal of Conflict Resolution* 41: 203–226.

Axtell, R. L., and J. M. Epstein. 1999. "Coordination in Transient Social Networks: An Agent-Based Computational Model of the Timing of Retirement." In *Behavioral Dimensions of Retirement Economics*, ed. H. Aaron. Washington, DC: Brookings Institution Press.

Bertsekas, D. P., and J. N. Tsitsiklis. 1989. *Parallel and Distributed Computation*. Englewood Cliffs, NJ: Prentice-Hall.

Cole, H. L., G. J. Mailath, and A. Postlewaite. 1998. "Class Systems and the Enforcement of Social Norms." *Journal of Public Economics* 70: 5–35.

DeCanio, S. J., and W. E. Watkins. 1998. "Information Processing and Organizational Structure." *Journal of Economic Behavior and Organization* 36: 275–294.

Ellison, G. 1993. "Learning, Local Interaction, and Coordination." *Econometrica* 61: 1047–1071.

Epstein, J. M. 1999. "Agent-Based Computational Models and Generative Social Science." *Complexity*.

Epstein, J. M., and R. Axtell. 1996. *Growing Artificial Societies: Social Science from the Bottom Up*. Cambridge, MA and Washington, DC: The MIT Press and Brookings Institution Press.

Foster, D. P., and H. P. Young. 1990. "Stochastic Evolutionary Game Dynamics." *Theoretical Population Biology* 38: 219–232.

Freidlin, M., and A. Wentzell. 1984. *Stochastic Dynamical Systems Theory*. New York: Springer Verlag.

Harsanyi, J., and R. Selten. 1988. *A General Theory of Equilibrium Selection in Games*. Cambridge, MA: The MIT Press.

Holland, J. H. 1996. *Hidden Order: How Adaptation Builds Complexity*. Cambridge, MA: Perseus Publishing.

Howard, R. 1971. *Dynamic Probabilistic Systems*. New York: Wiley.

Kandori, M., G. Mailath, and R. Rob. 1993. "Learning, Mutation, and Long-Run Equilibria in Games." *Econometrica* 61: 29–56.

Nash, J. 1950. "The Bargaining Problem." *Econometrica* 21: 128–140.

Palmer, R. 1989. "Broken Ergodicity." In *Lectures in the Sciences of Complexity*, ed. D. Stein. Vol. 1 in the Santa Fe Institute Studies in the Sciences of Complexity. Reading, MA: Addison Wesley Longman.

Roemer, J. E. 1982. *A General Theory of Exploitation and Class*. Cambridge, MA: Harvard University Press.

Shoham, Y., and M. Tennenholtz. 1996. "On Social Laws for Artificial Agent Societies: Off-Line Design." In *Computational Theories of Interaction and Agency*, ed. P. E. Agre and S. J. Rosenschein. MIT Press: Cambridge, MA: The MIT Press.

Wright, E. O. 1985. *Classes*. Verso: London.

Young, H. P. 1993a. "The Evolution of Conventions." *Econometrica* 61 (1): 57–84.

———. 1993b. "An Evolutionary Model of Bargaining." *Journal of Economic Theory* 59 (1): 145–168.

———. 1998. *Individual Strategy and Social Structure*. Princeton, NJ: Princeton University Press.

8   The Breakdown of Social Contracts

Ken Binmore

All animals are equal but some are more equal than others.
—George Orwell, *Animal Farm*

8.1   Introduction

Much has been written on revolution, rebellion, and civil unrest.[1] Historians offer blow-by-blow accounts of the succession of events that led to the fall of this or that government. Sociologists and political theorists collate the circumstances that have precipitated revolutions in an attempt to find correlations that may tell us something about their common causes. Economists construct models that seek to predict when a revolution will occur by measuring the dissonance between the private aspirations of the citizens and realities of their lives under an oppressive regime. But none of these approaches get at the fundamental properties of human nature that make popular insurrections possible for us. Coups in which one elite replaces another are easy enough to understand, since humans would seem to differ little from other primates in their urge to claw their way up a dominance hierarchy. But what of the historically important uprisings fueled by resentment of the unjust or arbitrary use of power?

In this chapter, I try to show how the language of game theory can be used to discuss questions of this type concerning the stability of social contracts. The basic ideas are discussed at greater length in my two-volume work, *Game Theory and the Social Contract* (Binmore 1994, 1998).

8.2   What Is a Social Contract?

Hume (1985b) makes fun of the idea of an original contract as the basis of the legitimacy of the state. As he observes, the claim that we are morally obliged to obey the written and unwritten laws of the society into which we were born because our ancestors surrendered our natural rights at some ancient conclave is a naive fiction. Harsanyi (1987) rejects all social contract theories on similar grounds. As he puts it: "People cannot rationally feel committed to keep any contract unless they have *already accepted* a moral code requiring them to keep contracts. Therefore, morality cannot depend on a social contract because contracts obtain all their binding force from a *prior* commitment to morality." If Harsanyi were right to argue that one cannot be a contractarian without believing that everyone is somehow committed to honor the terms of the social contract, then I would be forced to join Hume in poking fun at social contract theories. But I am not alone in thinking that Harsanyi's characterization of contractarianism is too narrow. Both Gauthier (1979) and Mackie (1980), for example, offer contractarian readings of Hume. Binmore (1994) does the same for Harsanyi (1977). Such readings require that we abandon the quasi-legal sense in which the notion of a social contract has been traditionally understood.

This chapter does not argue that members of society have an a priori obligation or duty to honor the social contract. On the contrary, the only viable candidates for a social contract are those agreements, implicit or explicit, that police *themselves*. Nothing enforces such a self-policing social contract beyond the enlightened self-interest of those who regard themselves as a party to it. Such duties and obligations as are built into the contract are honored, not because members of society are committed in some way to honor them, but because it is *in the interests* of each individual citizen with the power to disrupt the contract not to do so, unless someone else chooses to act against his own best interests by deviating first. The social contract therefore operates *by consent* and so does not need to rely on any actual or hypothetical enforcement mechanism. In game-theoretic terms, it consists simply of an agreement to coordinate on an *equilibrium*.[2]

When it is suggested that a social contract is no more than a set of common understandings among players acting in their own enlightened self interest, it is natural to react by doubting that anything very sturdy can be erected on such a flimsy foundation. Surely a solidly

built structure like the modern state must be firmly based on a rock of
moral certitude, and only anarchy can result if everybody just does
what takes his fancy? As Gauthier (1986, 1) expresses it in denying
Hume (1975, 280): "Were duty no more than interest, morals would be
superfluous."

I believe such objections to be misconceived. First, there are no rock-
like moral certitudes that exist prior to society. To adopt a metaphor
that sees such moral certitudes as foundation stones is therefore to
construct a castle in the air. Society is more usefully seen as a dynamic
organism, and the moral codes that regulate its internal affairs are
the conventional understandings which ensure that its constituent
parts operate smoothly together when it is in good health. Moreover,
the origin of these moral codes is to be looked for in historical theories
of biological, social, and political evolution, and not in the works
of abstract thinkers no matter how intoxicating the wisdom they
distill. Nor is it correct to say that anarchy will necessarily result if
everybody "just" does what he wants. A person would be stupid in
seeking to achieve a certain end if he ignored the fact that what other
people are doing is relevant to the means for achieving that end. Intel-
ligent people will *coordinate* their efforts to achieve their individual
goals without necessarily being compelled or coerced by real or imag-
inary bogeymen.

The extent to which simple implicit agreements to coordinate on an
equilibrium can generate high levels of cooperation among populations of egoists is not something that is easy to appreciate in the
abstract. That *reciprocity* is the secret has been repeatedly discovered,
most recently by the political scientist Axelrod (1984) in the eighties
and the biologist Trivers (1971) in the seventies. However, Hume (1978,
521) had already put his finger on the relevant mechanism three
hundred years before:[3]

I learn to do service to another, without bearing him any real kindness: because
I foresee, that he will return my service, in expectation of another of the same
kind, and in order to maintain the same correspondence of good offices with
me or others. And accordingly, after I have serv'd him and he is in possession
of the advantage arising from my action, he is induc'd to perform his part, as
foreseeing the consequences of his refusal.

In spite of all the eighteenth-century sweetness and light, one should
take special note of what Hume says about foreseeing the consequences
of refusal. The point is that a failure to carry out your side of the

arrangement will result in your being *punished*. The punishment may consist of no more than a refusal by the other party to deal with you in future. Or it may be that the punishment consists of having to endure the disapproval of those whose respect is necessary if you are to maintain your current status level in the community. However, nothing excludes more active forms of punishment. In particular, the punishment might be administered by the judiciary, if the services in question are the subject of a legal contract.

At first sight, this last observation seems to contradict the requirement that the conventional arrangements under study be *self-policing*. The appearance of a contradiction arises because one tends to think of the apparatus of the state as somehow existing independently of the game of life that people play. But the laws that societies make are not part of the rules of this game. One *cannot* break the rules of the game of life, but one certainly can break the laws that man invents. Legal rules are nothing more than particularly well-codified conventions. And policemen, judges, and public executioners do not exist outside society. Those charged with the duty of enforcing the laws that a society formally enacts are themselves only players in the game of life. However high-minded a society's officials may believe themselves to be, the fact is that society would cease to work in the long run if the duties assigned to them were not compatible with their own individual incentives. I am talking now about corruption. And here I don't have so much in mind the conscious form of corruption in which officials take straight bribes for services rendered. I have in mind the long-term and seemingly inevitable process by means of which bureaucracies gradually cease to operate in the interests of those they were designed to serve, and instead end up serving the interests of the bureaucrats themselves.

Game theorists rediscovered Hume's insight that reciprocity is the mainspring of human sociality in the early fifties when characterizing the outcomes that can be supported as equilibria in a repeated game. The result is known as the *folk theorem*, since it was formulated independently by several game theorists in the early fifties (Aumann and Maschler 1995). The theorem tells us that external enforcement is unnecessary to make a collection of Mr. Hydes cooperate like Dr. Jekylls. It is only necessary that the players be sufficiently patient and that they know they are to interact together for the foreseeable future. The rest can be left to their enlightened self-interest. The next section introduces the terminology necessary to operationalize the result for the purposes of this paper.

8.3 Sustaining Equilibria

Moral philosophers are traditionally classified as deontologists or consequentialists. The former argue that morality lies in doing your duty regardless of the consequences. I believe that the moral absolutes of deontologists are actually intuitions acquired by taking note of the rules one follows when honoring whatever social contract is current. In game-theoretic terms, deontologists emphasize the importance of understanding how to operate the strategies that *sustain* an equilibrium. Consequentialists emphasize the importance of the criteria used to *select* a new equilibrium when the circumstances change.

This section briefly reviews the language that game theory uses in discussing how equilibria are sustained. For a naturalist like myself, this is the kind of language into which one needs to translate deontological theories of the Right in order to evaluate the extent to which they succeed in capturing important aspects of our social contract. Axelrod (1984), Binmore (1994, 1998), Schotter (1981), Skyrms (1996), and Sugden (1986) are among those who have written accessible books that popularize the relevant ideas. Schelling (1960), Lewis (1969), and Ulmann-Margalit (1977) say similar things less formally.

The idea of a *Nash equilibrium* is the most fundamental notion of game theory. It is a strategy profile that assigns a strategy to each player that is an optimal reply to the strategies it assigns to the other players. A book that claimed to be an authoritative guide on rational play in games would necessarily have to recommend a Nash equilibrium in each game for which it made a specific recommendation. Otherwise, at least one player would choose not to follow the book's advice if he believed that that the other players were planning to play as advised. Since everyone would figure this out in advance, the book's claim to be authoritative could therefore not be sustained.

The game Chicken in figure 8.1b has two players, Adam and Eve. Adam chooses one of the two rows and Eve chooses one of the two columns. Adam's payoffs lie in the southwest of each cell and Eve's lie in the northwest. A *pure strategy* for a player in a game is a complete description of what the player plans to do whenever he or she might

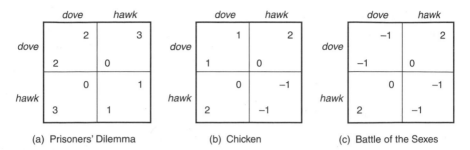

Figure 8.1
Canonical one-shot games.

be called upon to make a decision. In Chicken, a player has to choose only between *dove* and *hawk*. These are therefore his pure strategies. A *mixed strategy* arises when a player randomizes over his pure strategies—perhaps by tossing a coin or rolling dice.

Chicken has three Nash equilibria. Two of these are pure-strategy equilibria. The third is a mixed equilibrium. The Nash equilibria in pure strategies for Chicken are (*dove*, *hawk*) and (*hawk*, *dove*). To see this in the case of (*dove*, *hawk*), notice that *hawk* is the best reply for Eve to Adam's choice of *dove*, while *dove* is simultaneously the best reply for Adam to Eve's choice of *hawk*. Neither player would therefore have a motive to deviate from a book that recommended (*dove*, *hawk*) for Chicken, unless there was reason to suppose that the opponent might also deviate. The mixed strategy for Chicken calls for both players to use each of their two pure strategies with probability $\frac{1}{2}$. If Eve plays this way, *dove* and *hawk* are equally good for Adam. Adam therefore does not care which he uses, and so he might as well play each with probability $\frac{1}{2}$. If he does so, then the same reasons show that Eve might as well play each of *dove* and *hawk* with probability $\frac{1}{2}$. Both Adam and Eve will then be making a best reply to the choice made by the other.

In spite of all the huffing and puffing to the contrary, the only possible outcome of rational play in the Prisoners' Dilemma of figure 8.1a is the unique Nash equilibrium (*hawk*, *hawk*) (Binmore 1994). If the human Game of Life were the one-shot Prisoners' Dilemma, we therefore would not have evolved as social animals. Fortunately, our Game of Life is better modeled as a repeated game.

In the *indefinitely repeated* Prisoners' Dilemma, Adam and Eve play the Prisoners' Dilemma over and over again until some random event intervenes to bring their relationship to an end. The random event is modeled by postulating that each time they finish playing a round of the Prisoners' Dilemma, there is a fixed probability p that they will never play again. Interest then centers on the case when p is very small, so that the players will have good reason to believe that they have a long-term relationship to nourish and preserve.

The strategic considerations in an indefinitely repeated game are totally different from those in a one-shot game, because the introduction of time permits the players to reward and punish their opponents for their behavior in the past.

Figure 2a is based on the the Prisoners' Dilemma of figure 8.1a. It shows the four payoff pairs $(2, 2)$, $(0, 3)$, $(3, 0)$, and $(1, 1)$ that can result if the players restrict themselves to pure strategies in the one-shot version of the game. The broken line encloses the convex hull[4] of these four points. The unique Nash equilibrium outcome for the one-shot Prisoners' Dilemma is located at $(1, 1)$. To facilitate comparison, the equilibrium outcomes for the repeated Prisoners' Dilemma are given on a per-game basis. Thus the points in the shaded region R of figure 8.2a show the long-run *average* payoffs corresponding to all Nash equilibria in the indefinitely repeated Prisoners' Dilemma in the case when the probability p that any repetition is the last becomes vanishingly small.

Notice that R is a *large* set because the indefinitely repeated Prisoners' Dilemma has *many* Nash equilibria. One of these calls for Adam and Eve to use *hawk* at every repetition of the game. Repeating the game does not therefore guarantee that rational players will cooperate.

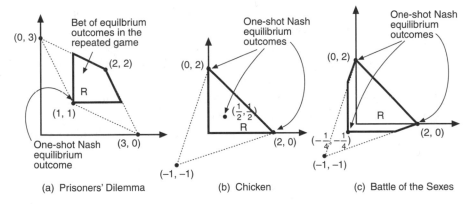

Figure 8.2
Equilibrium outcomes in repeated games.

But neither is the possibility of rational cooperation excluded, since (2, 2) is also a member of the set R of equilibrium outcomes.

It is easy to verify that (2, 2) is a Nash equilibrium outcome for the indefinitely repeated Prisoners' Dilemma. Consider the strategy TIT-FOR-TAT. This calls for a player to begin by using *dove* in the repeated game and then to copy whatever move the opponent made at the previous stage. If Adam and Eve both stick with TIT-FOR-TAT, *dove* will get played all the time. Moreover, it is a Nash equilibrium for both players to stick with TIT-FOR-TAT.

To see this, it is necessary to check that neither can profit from deviating from TIT-FOR-TAT if the other does not. Suppose it is Adam who deviates by playing *hawk* at some stage. Eve does not deviate, and hence she continues by copying Adam. Eve therefore plays *hawk* in later stages until Adam signals his repentance by switching back to *dove*. If p is sufficiently close to 0, Adam's income stream during his period of deviance will be approximately 3, 1, 1, . . . , 0 instead of 2, 2, 2, . . . , 2. It follows that his deviation will have been unprofitable. The TIT-FOR-TAT strategy therefore has a built-in provision for punishing deviations. If both believe that the other is planning to use TIT-FOR-TAT, neither will have a motive for using an alternative strategy. Thus it is a Nash equilbrium for both players to stick with TIT-FOR-TAT.[5]

Figures 2b and 2c show how the preceding discussion for the Prisoners' Dilemma needs to be modified for the games Chicken and Battle of the Sexes given in figure 8.1b and 8.1c. These diagrams show that the fine structure of a game that is to be repeated indefinitely is often largely irrelevant. Once attention has been directed away from the infertile one-shot case, the question ceases to be *whether* rational cooperation is possible. Instead, one is faced with a bewildering variety of different ways in which the players can cooperate rationally, and the problem becomes that of deciding *which* of all the feasible ways of cooperating should be selected.

This observation puts the question of what is the "right" game to serve as a paradigm for the problem of human cooperation on the sidelines. Once it is appreciated that reciprocity is the mechanism that makes things work, it becomes clear that it is the *fact* of repetition that really matters. The structure of the game that is repeated is only of secondary importance.

8.4   Selecting Equilibria

Deontological theories of the Right focus on the rules that must be followed to sustain an equilibrium. Consequentialist theories of the Good focus on the mechanisms that have evolved along with the human species to move a society from one social contract to another when the circumstances change. I believe that we are unique among social species in having available two separate and distinct equilibrium selection devices at our disposal. The first is to turn the choice of an equilibrium over to a leader. This solution to the equilibrium selection problem creates a society organized along the same lines as the dominance hierarchies of chimpanzees or baboons. The second mechanism is to use *fairness* as a coordinating device in the manner still practiced by the hunter-gatherer societies that continue to occupy marginal habitats around the world.

This chapter suggests that the fundamental cause of popular uprisings lies in the tension that exists between these two rival devices for selecting among equilibria in our Game of Life. Maryanski and Turner (1992) go further when they suggest that mankind is doomed to live a life of frustration inside the "social cage" created when we found a way around our genetic disposition to coordinate using fairness norms and began instead to recognize the authority of leaders. My own view is more optimistic, since the institutions of democracy provide a means of reconciling the two equilibrium selection devices. On the other hand, the social contracts of societies whose leaders are not held in check by constitutional checks and balances are always at risk of collapse if the equilibrium selected by the leadership diverges too far from the equilibrium perceived as fair by the rank and file.

I believe that retelling this old idea in the language of game theory may perhaps make it possible to construct models that quantify the relevant phenomena. To this end, the next two sections seek to tie down what is involved in using leadership or fairness as equilibrium selection devices.

8.5   Leadership and Authority

As explained in the next section, modern foraging societies have no bosses. Moreover, their social contracts are equipped with mechanisms that are designed to inhibit the emergence of bosses. My guess is that these social mechanisms exist because such subsistence societies cannot

afford to take the risk of allowing a reformer to persuade them to experiment with their traditional survival techhniques. But the immediate
point is that the existence of such leaderless societies implies that
humans do not need bosses to live in societies. So why do we have
them? What is the source of their authority?

One popular argument holds that leaders are necessary because, like
Uncle Joe Stalin, they know what is good for us better than we know
ourselves. But whether or not leaders know what they are doing better
than their followers, they can be very useful to a society as a coordinating device for solving the equilibrium selection problem in games
for which the traditional methods are too slow or uncertain. In a sailing
ship in a storm or in a nation at war, one cannot afford to wait for due
process to generate a compromise acceptable to all. Henry Ford told us
that history is bunk, but at least it teaches us that the way to get a
society moving together in a crisis is to delegate authority to a single
leader.

The mention of authority may make it seem that one cannot discuss
leadership without stepping outside the class of phenomena that can
be explained by the folk theorem. But the authority of a leader does
not need to be founded in some theory of the divine right of kings, or
in a Hobbesian social contract theory in which citizens surrender their
rights to self-determination in return for security, or in some meta-
physical argument purporting to prove it rational to subordinate one's
own desires to the general will as perceived by the head of state. As
Hume (1985) puts it:

Nothing appears more surprising to those who consider human affairs with a
philosophical eye, than the ease with which the many are governed by the few,
and the implicit submission with which men resign their own sentiments and
passions to those of their rulers. When we inquire by what means this wonder
is effected, we shall find that, as Force is always on the side of the governed,
the governors have nothing to support them but opinion. It is therefore on
opinion only that government is founded, and this maxim extends to the most
despotic and most military governments as well as to the most free and most
popular.

In short, the authority of popes, presidents, kings, judges, policemen,
and the like is just a matter of convention and habit. Adam obeys the
king because such is the custom—and the custom survives because
the king will order Eve to punish Adam if he fails to obey. But why
does Eve obey the order to punish Adam? In brief, who guards the
guardians?

Kant (1949, 417) absurdly thought that to answer this question is necessarily to initiate an infinite regress, but the proof of the folk theorem is explicit in *closing* the chains of responsibility. Eve obeys because she fears that the king will otherwise order Ichabod to punish her. Ichabod obeys because he fears that the king will otherwise order Adam to punish him. The game theory answer to *quis custodiet ipsos custodes?* is therefore that we must all guard each other by acting as official or unofficial policemen in keeping tabs on our neighbors. In the particularly simple case of a society with only two persons, Adam and Eve tread the strait and narrow path of rectitude because both fear incurring the wrath of the other.

To take a crude example, if Adam is the leader in the one-shot Battle of the Sexes of figure 1c, he could play fair by tossing a coin to decide which of the two pure Nash equilibria to nominate. If he nominates (*hawk, dove*) and Eve believes that he will therefore play *hawk*, it is optimal for her to play *dove*. Similarly, if he believes that his nomination of (*hawk, dove*) will induce her to play *dove*, then it is optimal for him to play *hawk*. A similar convergence of expectations applies if he nominates (*dove, hawk*). But experience strongly suggests that the opportunities for Adam to abuse his position of authority by cheating are too tempting to resist. Over time he will learn to bias the coin in his favor, so that the equilibrium (*hawk, dove*) is chosen more often than the equilibrium (*dove, hawk*). Eventually, he or his successors will convince themselves that they have a right to choose the equilibrium (*hawk, dove*) all the time.[6] Justice is therefore always a rare commodity in authoritarian states.

8.6   Fairness

Knauft (1991) argues that the evolution of authority in human societies can be seen in terms of a U-shaped curve, in which dominance-structured prehuman societies give way to anarchic bands of human hunter-gatherers that were then replaced by the authoritarian herding and agricultural societies with which recorded history begins. As Erdal and Whiten (1996) document, the evidence is strong that leadership in modern hunter-gatherer societies lies only in influencing the consensus: "But when a consensus has been reached, no-one has to follow it against their will—there is no enforcement mechanism."

The fact that modern hunter-gatherers operate social mechanisms that prevent potentially authoritarian leaders from getting established does not imply that their societies do not enforce norms. On the contrary, the evidence is that the social contract operated by a hunter-gatherer community is enforced with a rod of iron. No individual exercizes a leadership role, but the relatively small size of a hunter-gatherer band makes it possible for *public opinion* to fulfill the same function. When Adam asks himself whether he should offer some of his meat to Eve, he knows very well that he will be relentlessly mocked and ridiculed by the band as a whole should he fail to share in the customary fashion. Full-scale ostracism would follow if he nevertheless persisted in behaving unfairly.

Reports that modern hunter-gatherer communities share on a quasi-utilitarian basis are consistent with the view that public opinion serves as a substitute for a leader in such societies, but it is hard to share the enthusiasm expressed by some anthropologists for the oppressive social mechanisms by which discipline is maintained. Envy is endemic. For example, among the !Kung of the Kalahari desert, nobody cares to keep a particularly fine tool for too long. It is passed along to someone else as a gift lest the owner be thought to be getting above himself. But such gifts do not come without strings. In due course, a fair return will be expected. In some foraging societies, the close attention to the accountancy of envy in such a social contract makes progress almost impossible. According to Hayek's (1960, 153) definition, the citizens of such a society are free because they are subject to no man's will, but it would be a bad mistake for libertarians to idolize such societies. They would do better as a role model for the socialist utopia that Marx envisaged would emerge after the apparatus of the state had withered away.

My *Game Theory and the Social Contract* I speculates at length on the reasons that fairness evolved as a coordinating device among out hunter-gatherer ancestors (Binmore 1994, 1998). I argue that the foraging bands of prehistory must have operated a much less tightly organized social contract than their modern counterparts. In particular, the freedom enjoyed by subgroups to strike out on their own in a world largely empty of humans makes it unlikely that public opinion could have been an effective weapon for punishing deviates. Food-sharing arrangements must therefore have been self-policing. If one takes this seriously, the same arguments that lead one to predict that a modern foraging society will share on a quasi-utilitarian basis suggest that prehistoric bands must have shared on a quasi-egalitarian basis that can be modeled in terms of the proportional bargaining solution of cooperative game theory. This conclusion matches encouragingly with empirical work from psychology on attitudes to justice.

It now seems to be almost uncontroversial that we are born with the deep structure of language wired into our brains. I think that the same is true of the deep structure of our sense of justice. This would explain the (limited) success that psychologists have enjoyed in predicting that problems of social exchange will be resolved by equalizing the ratio of each person's gain to his worth.[7] As in Wilson (1993), the theory is usually called "modern" equity theory, although it originates with Aristotle[8] (1985), and has been neglected in recent years after being introduced to social psychologists by Homans (1961) and Adams (1963, 1965) more than thirty years ago.

Although modeling the manner in which fairness norms work is of the first importance, the chapter can do no more than register the fact that theories exist that are compatible with what is known of our evolutionary history and that enjoy some empirical support. It is necessary to move on to the question of how the fair social contracts of our foraging ancestors were displaced by the authoritarian social contracts of traditional farming societies.

Cohen (1977) attributes the origins of agriculture to a food crisis in prehistory that arose when human hunter-gatherer bands had expanded until the locally available habitat was no longer able to support their economies. The response to this overpopulation problem was twofold. One adaptation allowed foraging to continue in marginal habitats through the use of tightly organized social contracts in which population size is kept under firm control, as in modern hunter-gatherer societies. The other proved to be the mainstream cultural adaptation: the emergence of agriculture and herding as new modes of production.

The organization necessary both to exploit the increasing returns to scale available in these new modes of production and to prevent the surplus from being appropriated by outsiders made it necessary to abandon the anarchic structure of prehistoric foraging bands. Instead authority began to be vested in leaders. This readoption of the hierarchical organization typical of ape societies did not require a new set of biological adaptations. We did not lose our capacity to submit to leadership when we acquired the new program that permitted our proto-human ancestors the flexibility necessary to sustain the anarchic lifestyle of hunter-gatherers with a whole world into which to expand. Even in the uncompetitive ambience of a modern foraging society, our natural urge to dominate one another is not extinguished by our natural urge to be fair. Otherwise social mechanisms that inhibit dominance behavior would not be necessary.

Anthropologists attribute the social retooling necessary for the transition back to the type of hierarchical social contract needed to maintain a communal farming society to *cultural* evolution. The time available seems too short for a further *biological* adaptation to have been responsible.

It has been argued that the human species paid a heavy price for the opportunity to become farmers. When social evolution erected an authoritarian superstructure on a biological foundation that had evolved to permit our ancestors to live a free-wheeling leaderless existence, a war began between part of our biological nature and our social conditioning. Commentators like Maryanski and Turner (1992) believe that we are still fighting this war. In the language of game theory, their characterization of a modern industrial society as a social cage is expressed by saying that our habituated use of leadership as an equilibrium selection device conflicts with our natural instinct to employ fairness for this purpose.[9]

8.7 Deselecting Equilibria

This section turns to the relative stability of authoritarian and egalitarian social contracts. At first sight, game theory would seem to have nothing to say on this subject, since both types of social contract can be realized as Nash equilibria of our Game of Life. However, the notion of a Nash equilibrium fails to capture the possibility that a whole group of individuals may succeed in orchestrating a simultaneous deviation. One might seek to deal with such an eventuality by introducing one of the various definitions of a "coalition-proof equilibrium" that have been proposed. But such equilibria typically fail to exist. That is to say, any social contract can be overthrown if the right kind of coalition can get its act together. However, it is necessary to bear in mind that a revolutionary coalition is itself a society that needs a social contract of its own if its members are to make their collective power felt. This social contract typically uses our built-in sense of justice as its coordinating focus.

Recall that I follow the anthropological line that sees the emergence of hierarchical human societies as a social adaptation required by the need to turn to farming in order to cope with increasing population pressure. But such authoritarian forms of social organization have to operate within the framework of a biologically determined fairness norm that evolved as a coordinating tool among the leaderless foraging bands of prehistory. A tension therefore exists between the conventional authority of leaders and the instinctive urge to coordinate using fairness criteria.

The instabilities created by our failure to be properly adapted to authoritarian social cages are not detected by the folk theorem, because the folk theorem depends on a notion of equilibrium that only considers deviations by one individual at a time. However, leaders who are too partial in choosing an equilibrium that favors the group that put them in power risk creating a coalition for mutual protection among those they treat unfairly. Such an alienated group will treat the *nomenclatura* as outsiders and coordinate on a rebellious equilibrium of its own, in which the first tenet is never to assist a boss in punishing one's own kind. Alexander Hamilton (Hamilton, Jay, and Madison 1992, 3) explains how demagogues take over the leadership of such alienated groups by temporarily facilitating coordination on the fair equilibrium that serves as its focus. But if such demagogues are propelled into power, history shows that they soon become as corrupt as the tyrants they replace.

The recent revolution in Zaire exhibits all the typical hallmarks of a classical popular uprising. It remains to be seen how long it takes for the new elite to become indistinguishable from their predecessors. But the Western democracies have no grounds for complacency. It is true that we have evolved institutions that can take the sting out of the incipient conflict between the rival coordination mechanisms of fairness and leadership. First, we constrain our leaders by a system of checks and balances that are intended to limit the extent to which leaders can act without some measure of popular support. Second, the constitution provides regular opportunities for switching leaders. But although these measures can have the effect of preventing leaders taking a society to a markedly unfair equilibrium and keeping it there, they achieve this aim only haphazardly. Nor is it clear that matters are improving. American presidents are nowadays far more powerful than they were ever intended to be. In the United Kingdom, Mrs. Thatcher made it clear that British prime ministers have even greater opportunities to ride roughshod over constitutional arrangements that were originally intended to check the power of a monarch who is now a mere figurehead.

8.8   Classifying Political Attitudes

The reflections offered in this chapter on the stability of the social contracts that our all-too-human nature permits also suggest a radical revision of the classical taxonomy of political systems. Rather than seeing
political philosophy in terms of a battle between a utilitarian Left and
a libertarian Right, it seems to me that we need to think in terms of a
battle between social contracts based on the authority of individuals or
elites and those based on fairness norms. I refer to the former as *neofeudal* and the latter as *whiggish*.[11] In adopting this terminology, I do not
mean to suggest that even a whiggish society can dispense with leaders
altogether under modern circumstances. Without entrepreneurs, we
would never find the Pareto-frontier of the set of feasible social contracts. Nor is due process appropriate when quick decisions need to be
made. But a fair society needs to hold its leaders in check—as the
founding fathers of the American Republic knew only too well when
they wrote its constitution.

It seems to me that one needs at least two dimensions to come any-
where near capturing the richness of current political attitudes. Figure
8.3a uses two axes to separate the plane into four regions that I could
untendentiously have labeled unplanned centralization, unplanned
decentralization, planned decentralization, and planned centralization.

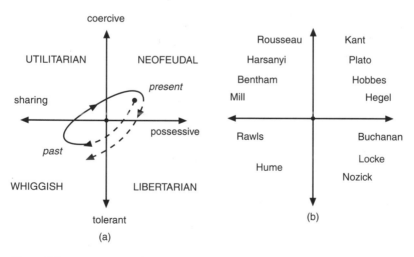

Figure 8.3
Classifying political attitudes.

But the language of economics is so dismally dull that I have translated these terms into neofeudalism, libertarianism, whiggery, and utilitarianism. A journalist would go further down this road and interpret a utilitarian as a bleeding-heart, big-spending liberal and so on, but I prefer to keep my prejudices under slightly firmer control.

In terms of the traditional Left-Right political spectrum, utilitarianism sits out on the socialist Left and libertarianism sits out on the capitalist Right. However, the orthogonal opposition that I think should supercede the sterile and outdated dispute between Left and Right contrasts whiggish societies in which fairness is used to coordinate collective decisions with neofeudal societies that delegate such decisions to individuals or elites. All large organized states of historical times have been neofeudal in character—including those that think of their prime characteristic as being capitalist or socialist. As is obvious from the totalitarian regimes operating before the Second World War in Germany and Japan, and the species of social consensus that has operated so far in both countries since the war, capitalism does not need libertarian political institutions to flourish. Equally, as is shown by the experience of Britain after the Second World War, a country can ruin its economy by turning to socialism without any need to abandon freedom and democracy along the way. One therefore goes astray in seeking to draw conclusions about the relative merits of the political aspects of the social contracts operating on the two sides of the Iron Curtain in the Cold War from the fact that market economies outperform command economies. Insofar as the choice is between the political regimes of living memory, the issue for political philosophers is not how we organize our economies, but whether our children will find more fulfillment in a society in which the same oligarchs rule all the time, or in a society that rotates its oligarchs using a method traditionally regarded as fair.

A classification system that emphasizes the contrast between neofeudalism and whiggery puts corruption at the top of the agenda of problems facing the modern state. Everyone is willing to condemn the straightforward bribery and nepotism that afflict all societies, but we need to worry at least as much about the corruption of our institutions that arises when their officers cease to operate the institutions to further the purpose for which they were created, but instead imperceptibly and unknowingly come to use the power of their office to advance their own personal goals. To what extent are democratic elections fair now that rich men have learned how to get their puppets elected by employing spin doctors to reduce political debate to an exchange of meaning-less advertising slogans? How is justice to be obtained in a law case when the other side has all the money? What poor man seeking his legal rights now expects due process to be respected by the various Jacks-in-office who gnaw at the heart of our public institutions? Our institutions were mostly founded with the most benevolent of inten-tions, but good intentions are not enough to prevent time from unrav-eling the firmest weave if loose ends are left at which it can tug. As the Monty Python catchphrase has it. "Nobody expects the Spanish Inqui-sition." But this is what corruption eventually made of the institution set up to spread the gospel of Jesus Christ.

Utilitarians and libertarians are as dissatisfied as whigs with our current neofeudal institutions, but respond by making the same mistake as Santayana's *Lucifer*, who rebelled against the *feasibility* con-straint in God's decision to create the best of all possible worlds. But there is no point in designing ideal social systems whose workability depends on first changing human nature. Human nature is as it is, and no amount of wishing that it were different will make it so. We there-fore have to resign ourselves to living in a second-best society because first-best societies are not stable. Utopians who seek to establish first-best societies are actually condemning us to live in whatever hell evolution eventually makes of their unstable utopia.

The founding fathers of the American Republic understood this point perfectly well when they built a system of checks and balances into the American Constitution in an attempt to confine neofeudalism to the Old World. But what remains of their construction is now hopelessly unfitted to meet the new forms of neofeudalism that have emerged in modern times. My own country does not even have a written Constitution or a Bill of Rights to obstruct the triumphal advance of neofeudalism. If we do not wish to destabilize our societies by creating a new class of outsiders who can focus their resentment around a call for natural justice, we need to rethink the thoughts of the classical liberals who wrote the American Constitution, as they would rethink them if they were alive today.

In summary, we need to put aside outdated thoughts about where we would like to locate society on a Left-Right spectrum. Choosing between utilitarianism and libertarianism makes as much sense as debating whether griffins make better pets than unicorns. We need to start thinking instead about how to move in the orthogonal direction that leads from neofeudalism to whiggery.

Notes

I am grateful to the Economic and Social Research Council and to the Leverhulme Foundation for funding this work through the Centre for Economic Learning and Social Evolution at University College London.

1. Some typical references are Buchanan (1979), Coleman (1990), Davies (1962), Gurr (1970), Kuran (1989, 1995), Rice (1991), Tullock (1974, 1989), and Zagorin (1973).

2. There is admittedly sometimes a risk of misunderstanding when the term *social contract* is identified with the conventional rules that a society uses to coordinate on an equilibrium. It is incongruous, for example, that the common understanding in France that conversations be conducted in French should be called a "contract." Words other than contract—such as compact, covenant, concordat, custom, or convention—might better convey the intention that nobody is to be imagined to have signed a binding document or be subject to external enforcement. Perhaps the best alternative term would be "social consensus." This does not even carry the connotation that those party to it are necessarily aware of the fact. However, it seems to me that, with all its dusty encumbrances, "social contract" is still the only term that signals the name of the game adequately and that, as Gough (1938, 7) confirms, I am not altogether guilty of stepping outside the historical tradition in retaining its use while simultaneously rejecting a quasi-legal interpretation.

3. Note that he goes beyond simple reciprocity between two individuals. If someone won't scratch my back, a third party may fail to scratch his.

4. The convex hull of a set S is the smallest convex set containing S. In the current context, it represents the set of all pairs of expected payoffs that can result if the players *jointly* randomize over their pure strategies. For example, Adam and Eve can organize the pair of expected payoffs (1, 2) by agreeing to play (*hawk, dove*) with probability $\frac{1}{3}$ and (*dove, hawk*) with probability $\frac{2}{3}$. Adam will then expect $1 = \frac{1}{3} \times 3 + \frac{2}{3} \times 0$ and Eve will expect $2 = \frac{1}{3} \times 0 + \frac{2}{3} \times 3$.

5. The strategy TIT-FOR-TAT has been used to illustrate this point because Axelrod (1984) emphasized this particular strategy in his influential *Evolution of Cooperation*. However, there are many other symmetric Nash equilibria that led to the cooperative outcome (2, 2), some of which are at least as worthy of attention as TIT-FOR-TAT.

6. Economists should note that it is only by accident that (*hawk, dove*) happens to be the so-called Stackelberg equilibrium of the Battle of the Sexes. But Adam is not a leader in the Stackelberg sense—he doesn't publicly make his move *before* Eve, leaving her with a take-it-or-leave-it problem. His initial choice of an equilibrium is merely a signal that commits nobody to anything.

7. See, for example, Adams and Freeman (1976); Austin and Hatfield (1980); Austin and Walster (1974); Baron (1993); Cohen and Greenberg (1982); Furby (1986); Mellers (1982); Mellers and Baron (1993); Messick and Cook (1983); Pritchard (1969); Wagstaff (1994); Wagstaff and Perfect (1992); Wagstaff, Huggins, and Perfect (1996); Walster and Walster (1975); Walster, Berscheid, and Walster (1973); Walster, Walster, and Berscheid (1978). Wagstaff (1997) has a user-friendly book in draft that sets the philosophical scene, and reviews the history and current status of modern equity theory. Selten (1978) provides an account of the theory that is easily accessible to economists.

8. What is just . . . is what is proportional—(Aristotle 1985).

References

Adams, J. 1963. "Towards an Understanding of Inequity." *Journal of Abnormal and Social Psychology* 67: 422–436.

———. 1965. "Inequity in Social Exchange." In *Advances in Experimental Social Science, Vol. II*, ed. L. Berkowitz. New York: Academic Press.

Adams, J., and S. Freedman. 1976. "Equity Theory Revisited: Comments and Annotated Bibiliography." In *Advances in Experminental Social Science, Vol. IX*, ed. L. Berkowitz. New York: Academic Press.

Aristotle. 1985. *Nichomachean Ethics*. Trans. T. Irwin. Indianopolis: Hackett.

Aumann, R., and M. Maschler. 1995. *Repeated Games with Incomplete Information*. Cambridge, MA: MIT Press.

Austin, W., and E. Hatfield. 1980. "Equity Theory, Power and Social Justice." In *Justice and Social Interaction*, ed. G. Mikula. New York: Springer-Verlag.

Austin, W., and E. Walster. 1974. "Reactions to Confirmations and Disconfirmations of Expectancies of Equity and Inequity." *Journal of Personality and Social Psychology* 30: 208–216.

Axelrod, R. 1984. *The Evolution of Cooperation*. New York: Basic Books.

Baron, J. 1993. "Heuristics and Biases in Equity Judgments: A Utilitarian Approach." In *Psychological Perspectives on Justice: Theory and Applications*, ed. B. Mellors and J. Baron. Cambridge: Cambridge University Press.

Binmore, K. 1994. *Playing Fair: Game Theory and the Social Contract I*. Cambridge, MA: MIT Press.

———. 1998. *Just Playing: Game Theory and the Social Contract II*. Cambridge, MA: MIT Press.

Buchanan, A. 1979. "Revolutionary Motivation and Rationality." *Philosophy and Public Affairs* 9: 59–82.

Cohen, M. 1977. *The Food Crisis in Prehistory: Overpopulation and the Origins of Agriculture*. New Haven: Yale University Press.

Cohen, R., and J. Greenberg. 1982. "The Justice Concept in Social Psychology." In *Equity and Justice in Social Behavior*, ed. R. Cohen and J. Greenberg. New York: Academic Press.

Coleman, J. 1990. *Against the State: Studies in Sedition and Rebellion*. London: Penguin Books.

Davies, J. 1962. "Toward a Theory of Revolution." *American Sociological Review* 27: 5–19.

Erdal, D., and A. Whiten. 1996. "Egalitarianism and Machiavellian Intelligence in Human Evolution." In *Modelling the Early Human Mind*, ed. P. Mellars and K. Gibson. Oxford: Oxbow Books.

Furby, L. 1986. "Psychology and Justice." In R. Cohen, ed. *Justice: Views from the Social Sciences*. Cambridge, MA: Harvard University Press.

Gauthier, D. 1979. "David Hume: Contractarian." *Philosophical Review* 88: 3–38.

———. 1986. *Morals by Agreement*. Oxford: Clarendon Press.

Gough, J. W. 1938. *The Social Contract*. Oxford: Clarendon Press.

Gurr, T. 1970. *Why Men Rebel*. Princeton: Princeton University Press.

Hamilton, A., J. Jay, and J. Madison. 1992. *The Federalist*, ed. W. Brock. London: Everyman. (First published 1787–1788.)

Harsanyi, J. 1977. *Rational Behavior and Bargaining Equilibrium in Games and Social Situations*. Cambridge: Cambridge University Press.

———. 1987. "Review of Gauthier's 'Morals by Agreement.'" *Economics and Philosophy* 3: 339–343.

Hayek, F. 1960. *The Constitution of Liberty*. Chicago: University of Chicago Press.

Homans, G. 1961. *Social Behavior: Its Elementary Forms*. New York: Hartcourt, Brace and World, New York.

Hume, D. 1975. *Enquiries Concerning Human Understanding and Concerning the Principles of Morals*, 3d ed., ed. L. A. Selby-Bigge. Rev. P. Nidditch. Oxford: Clarendon Press. (First published 1777.)

———. 1978. *A Treatise of Human Nature*, 2d ed., ed. L. A. Selby-Bigge. Rev. P. Nidditch. Oxford: Clarendon Press. (First published 1739.)

———. 1985a. "Of the First Principles of Government." In *Essays Moral, Political and Literary, Part I*, ed. E. Miller. Indianapolis: Liberty Classics. (First published 1758.)

———. 1985b. Of the original contract. In *Essays Moral, Political and Literary*, ed. E. Miller. Indianapolis: Liberty Classics. (First published 1748.)

Kant, I. 1949. "Theory and Practice." In *The Philosophy of Kant*, ed. C. Friedrich. New York: Random House. (First published 1793.)

Knauft, B. 1991. "Violence and Sociality in Human Evolution." *Current Anthropology* 32: 223–245.

Kuran, T. 1989. "Sparks and Prairie Fires: A Theory of Unanticipated Political Revolution." *Public Choice* 61: 41–71.

———. 1995. *Private Truths, Public Lies: The Social Consequences of Preference Falsification*. Cambridge MA: Harvard University Press.

Lewis, D. 1969. *Conventions: A Philosophical Study*. Cambridge, MA: Harvard University Press.

Mackie, J. 1980. *Hume's Moral Theory*. London: Routledge and Kegan Paul.

Maryanski, A., and J. Turner. 1992. *The Social Cage: Human Nature and the Evolution of Society*. Stanford: Stanford University Press.

Mellers, B. 1982. "Equity Judgment: A Revision of Aristotelian Views." *Journal of Experimental Biology* 111: 242–270.

Mellers, B., and J. Baron. 1993. *Psychological Perspectives on Justice: Theory and Applications*. Cambridge: Cambridge University Press.

Messick, D., and K. Cook. 1983. *Equity Theory: Psychological and Sociological Perspectives.* New York: Praeger.

Pritchard, R. 1969. "Equity Theory; A Review and Critique." *Organizational Behavior and Human Performance* 4: 176–211.

Rice, E. 1991. *Revolution and Counter Revolution.* Oxford: Blackwell.

Schelling, T. 1960. *The Strategy of Conflict.* Cambridge: Harvard University Press.

Schotter, A. 1981. *The Economic Theory of Social Institutions.* Cambridge: Cambridge University Press.

Selten, R. 1978. "The Chain-Store Paradox." *Theory and Decision* 9: 127–159.

Skyrms, B. 1996. *Evolution of the Social Contract.* Cambridge: Cambridge University Press.

Sugden, R. 1986. *The Economics of Rights. Cooperation and Welfare.* Oxford: Basil Blackwell.

Trivers, R. 1971. "The Evolution of Reciprocal Altruism." *Quarterly Review of Biology* 46: 35–56.

Tullock, G. 1974. *The Social Dilemma: The Economics of War and Revolution.* Blacksberg VA: University Publications.

———. 1987. *Autocracy.* Dordrecht: Kluwer.

Ulmann-Margalit, E. 1977. *The Emergence of Norms.* New York: Oxford University Press.

Wagstaff, G. 1994. "Equity, Equality and Need: Three Principles of Justice or One?" *Current Psychology: Research and Reviews* 13: 138–152.

———. 1997. "Making Sense of Justice." Draft book. Psychology Department, University of Liverpool.

Wagstaff, G., and T. Perfect. 1992. "On the Definition of Perfect Equity and the Prediction of Inequity." *British Journal of Social Psychology* 31: 69–77.

Wagstaff, G., J. Huggins, and T. Perfect. 1996. "Equal Ratio Equity, General Linear Equity, and Framing Effects in Judgments of Allocation Divisions." *European Journal of Social Psychology* 26: 29–41.

Walster, E., and G. Walster. 1975. "Equity and Social Justice." *Journal of Social Issues* 31: 21–43.

Walster, E., E. Berscheid, and G. Walster. 1973. "New Directions in Equity Research." *Journal of Personality and Social Psychology* 25: 151–176.

Walster, E., G. Walster, and E. Berscheid. 1978. *Equity: Theory and Research.* London: Allyn and Bacon.

Wilson, J. 1993. *The Moral Sense.* New York: Free Press.

Zagorin, P. 1973. "Theories of Revolution in Contemporary Historiography." *Political Science Quarterly* 88: 23–52.

Index